WAR AND IDEOLOGY

To the specialists and staff of the Cardiothoracic Centre at the Freeman Hospital, Newcastle, without whose care and expertise this book would never have been completed.

WAR AND IDEOLOGY

Eric Carlton

London

First published 1990
by Routledge
11 New Fetter Lane, London EC4P 4EE

© 1990 Eric Carlton
Set in 10/12pt Palatino by
Input Typesetting Ltd, London
and printed in Great Britain by
TJ Press (Padstow) Ltd, Padstow, Cornwall

British Library Cataloguing in Publication Data
Carlton, Eric
War and ideology.
1. War. Sociological perspectives
I. Title
303.6'6
ISBN 0–415–04157–0

CONTENTS

Preface   vii

SECTION I THE PROBLEM OF WAR   1

SECTION II WAR AND IDEOLOGY   18

SECTION III PERCEPTIONS OF 'THE ENEMY'   29

 1 THE EGYPTIANS OF THE NEW KINGDOM: The
   enemy as non-people   34

 2 THE SPARTANS: The enemy as political obstacles   45

 3 THE CARTHAGINIANS: The enemy as economic
   rivals   57

 4 THE ROMANS: The enemy as uncouth barbarians   67

 5 THE EARLY ISRAELITES: The enemy as ritual
   outlaws   81

 6 THE CRUSADER KNIGHTS: The enemy as
   unbelievers   95

 7 THE MONGOLS: The enemy as effete
   degenerates   110

 8 THE AZTECS: The enemy as ritual fodder   119

 9 THE ZULU: The enemy as colonial intruders   132

10 THE ATHENIANS: The enemy as opponents of
   democracy   143

11 THE MAOISTS: The enemy as class antagonists   154

12 EXCURSUS ON RACE, MASSACRE, AND
   GENOCIDE: The enemy as racial inferiors   168

CONTENTS

SECTION IV WAR AND THE PROBLEM OF VALUES   180

  Bibliography   197

  Index   203

PREFACE

The subject of war lends itself to a variety of possible treatments. So much depends upon the required emphasis of the research in question, whether it is to be primarily historical or social and economic, or whether it has to include more abstract philosophical elements. In the past, it has often proved helpful to take a great-battles-of-history approach by tracing chronologically the key conflicts that have occurred in, say, the last two thousand years. This kind of treatment is popular and reasonably uncomplicated but it makes the study of war necessarily selective. It begs the question: by what criteria does one decide what is great as opposed to the not so great, or identify the 'decisive' as distinct from the not so decisive. Alternatively, one could adopt a more analytical patterns-of-conquest approach which attempts a categorization of the nature and methods of military expansionism. This can be extremely useful, but its weakness is that it tends to concentrate almost exclusively on predatory societies, and does not give enough attention to those societies that cannot be neatly pigeon-holed in this all too convenient way.

The present study is a little more oblique. It is concerned with analysis and categorization, but it is also interested in motivation and interpretation. It asks the question: why do men have recourse to war to solve their socio-economic problems? It thus relates war to ideology, and takes as its *sine qua non* the proposition that men act as they think, and think as they believe, and that belief – religious or otherwise – conditions attitudes to the nature and conduct of war. It argues that various constellations of values – often intellectualized as ideologies – not only constitute the rationalizations and justifications for war, but may also provide the actual imperatives for warfare itself.

It is assumed that one of the best ways of doing this is to examine war and ideology in the context of what is believed to constitute the 'enemy'. Perceptions of the adversary, possibly more than anything else, determine the nature as opposed to the fact of warfare. And it is also taken as a basic presupposition that this discussion can be most instructive if it is conducted in a historical and comparative setting. This means that the text has to include extensive substantive material as well as theoretical analysis. It should, therefore, be suitable for students of both history and sociology, as well as those who are specifically engaged in war studies. As such, it is intended to be scholarly without being intimidating.

The work is thus organized in four unequal portions. Section I introduces the discussion on 'The problem of war'; Section II elaborates on this with 'War and ideology', which is, in effect, a sociological treatment of what is – or can be – meant by the term 'ideology'. Section III – 'Perceptions of "the enemy" ' – is divided into an Introduction and twelve case studies covering war in different societies. This is by far the largest part of the book, and is written in a straightforward, descriptive way. It is intended to inform the reader about the military structures of these societies whilst, at the same time, highlighting some of the theoretical points about the nature of war in general and specific appreciations of the enemy in particular. Section IV concludes the study with an examination of 'War and the problem of values'; this rounds off the discussion by drawing together the threads of the prior arguments and reaffirming the relationship between war and ideological belief and commitment.

Section I

THE PROBLEM OF WAR

At the most elementary level, war is a problem simply because most of us would like to know how it can be avoided. But it is a problem in other senses as well. At a theoretical level it raises all sorts of supplementary issues, and it is these which constitute the basis of our initial discussion. Most societies have persistently resorted to violent solutions to their political–economic problems. And this has not always been in moments of desperation. There have been exceptions, but – as we shall see – these have been extremely rare; so rare, in fact, that the phenomenon of seeking *peaceful* solutions to such problems is itself in need of explanation.

Why then do men go to war? Are they basically competitive and self-seeking, with war as an institutionalized outlet for their aggressive instincts? Or is war a cultural invention rather than a biological necessity? Complementarily, why do *societies* go to war? Are the reasons rooted in the human psyche and its personal motivations, or should we be looking rather to historical situations of need and scarcity for an explanation? In these circumstances, the 'answer' to war may be seen in terms of social change, in the outlawing of classes and the more equal distribution of goods.

Underlying all these issues are yet further questions concerning the inevitability of war and the possibility of its elimination as a barbarous extension of political endeavour. But there are no simple answers. All these matters require careful analysis and exemplification, so in the ensuing discussion, the treatment will be both comparative and historical in order to show something of the wide diversity of human conduct in relation to the nature and conduct of war. The object is not necessarily to detail particular campaigns or probe the natures of would-be conquerors and political personalities, but to investigate the ostensible causes of human conflict and the ways in which these are then rationalized and justified. This will entail a preliminary analysis of the theories which are commonly adduced to explain the phenomenon of war and its implications.

1

The general problem can be looked at from a number of perspectives, that of the historian, the political scientist, the economist, and the like, but the behavioural scientist will want to know to what extent war is a function of cultural development. A 1970s Harris poll, for example, found that a 'substantial majority' of Americans agreed with the statement 'Human nature being what it is, there will always be war and conflict' (Robertson 1977: 55). But nobody knows exactly what is meant by 'human nature'. Genetic inheritance obviously sets limits on human potential and provides a framework for possible patterns of behaviour. Within this, however, there is appreciable flexibility, hence the considerable cultural variation which can be seen in relation to war and violence. For instance, it is argued that modern western society is highly competitive and therefore puts an undue emphasis on wealth and success. It is said that this preoccupation with achievement and prestige fosters aggression, and that this is a necessary function of its market orientations, although this does tend to discount very similar values in some complex *pre*-industrial societies (Carlton 1977).

By contrast, there are societies among whom this kind of aggressive behaviour is apparently unknown. These are, without exception, small-scale societies at a relatively low level of technological development such as the Arapesh of New Guinea, the Kung Bushmen of the Kalahari, and the pygmies of the Ituri forest. One account of the Lepchas of Sikkim (Gorer 1938), for instance, insists that they do not understand war – even defensive war. These may be compared with the Dani who have 'pretend wars'. Their simulated violence which amounts to little more than the exchange of abuse reduces injury to a minimum. Such societies are remarkable and are held up as examplars; their very existence is regarded as a challenge to western assumptions about 'human nature'. They have become famous in the 'trade' for their uncharacteristic singularity, and are often cited in the texts as illustrations of a shaming moral simplicity. The implications being that we in the developed nations might also share in these pristine virtues if only we had not allowed ourselves to become corrupted by a whole series of extrinsic factors.

But these societies *are* very unusual. They may represent some kind of lost ideal, but their existence only demonstrates the exceptions that prove the rule. They cannot even be cited as evidence for the theory that increasing war and aggression are really functions of the scale and complexity of society; there are too many known contra-instances, such as the Amazonian Jivaro, for this to be upheld as a general truth. The fact is that most societies throughout history have been well aware of the advantages and disadvantages of aggression to attain their ends, and the vast majority have been prepared to have recourse to violence if it would further or protect their basic interests.

2

It is perhaps worth noting here the useful distinction between the 'military way' and 'militarism' made by Alfred Vagts (1959). This maintains that the military way is marked by 'a . . . concentration of men and materials on winning specific objectives' whereas militarism is a 'vast array of customs, interests, prestige and actions . . . [involving] authority and belief'. In other words, war and military adventure may not be quite the same thing. Societies everywhere indulge in warfare, and some take the resigned and rational view that, if war becomes necessary, it should be prosecuted with the utmost care and efficiency. By contrast, militarism is a way of life. It involves a complex of traditions and values which is integral to particular social systems, such as those of the Assyrians and the Spartans. This has not, therefore, been a common characteristic of historical societies.

We can say, then, that amidst all this cultural variation, the practice of war – with given qualifications – may be regarded as a cultural universal. The forms it takes give the impression of considerable diversity, but these disguise its essential similarity. Very broadly speaking, war derives either from the nature of men, or from the common situations in which they find themselves – or from some subtle combination of the two. The *causes* of war, therefore, can be categorized as either social or psychological in kind; attributable either to traceable structural variables or to personality factors which are recognized but difficult to define. So, fundamentally, the question we are really asking here is whether aggression is a social product or whether it is related to some form of infirmity which is integral to the human condition.

Perhaps the most useful way of tackling this fundamental issue would be to look at some of the theoretical positions which have been – and still are – taken concerning the causes of war:

WAR AS A BIOLOGICAL NECESSITY

Many people take the view that man is a naturally aggressive creature. Writers as different in their philosophical orientations as Augustine and Machiavelli agree that, by nature, men are greedy, selfish, and rapacious. Thomas Hobbes, the political thinker, writing in the seventeenth century, maintained that there is no justice in nature. Men, therefore, become the inevitable victims of war in which there is no security for anyone. In such an unendurable situation, Hobbes argued, any sensible person would be willing to give up his natural liberty to gain peace. Thus government came into being as a source of power to restrain the natural rapacity of human kind (Hobbes 1963).

Similar views about man's 'natural state' have been expressed by both philosophers and psychologists. Kant insisted that peace among men is not a natural state. He saw violence as a permanent feature of

3

all societies, and thought that peace would only obtain when some form of strict discipline was imposed. Similarly, Sigmund Freud, one of the most seminal thinkers in this field, saw aggressiveness as normal. According to Freud, man was naturally at variance with society. His egoistic interests were not in harmony with community interests; the individual instinctively rebelled against social constraint. Freud's 'hydraulic theory' of the human personality assumes that there is a reservoir of pent-up aggression just waiting to be released, and unless it finds some reasonably harmless form of expression, it could eventually lead to mental breakdown. Men need some kind of social catharsis – a release mechanism – to prevent unwelcome psychological repercussions.

If aggression needs, therefore, to be expressed rather than suppressed, how can it be effectively channelled? Would, say, games be a suitable substitute? The psychologist, W. Menninger (in Bylinsky 1976) has argued for sport as an 'outlet for the aggressive drive', and he believes that this would (and does?) result in forms of 'controlled aggression'. But contrary to this, another psychologist, Leonard Berkowitz (in Bylinsky 1976), insists that in sport – particularly contact sport – tensions actually increase, and aggression finds all sorts of harmful and objectionable expressions. It is further argued that this is not confined to the field, but is also communicated to the spectators. Of course, it could be that the reactions are reciprocal. For instance, in soccer, it is possible that the hostility on the terraces simply mirrors the win-at-all-costs mentality of the players. Less plausibly, it may be that the players take their cues from the crowd.

So we see that some research evidence indicates that, rather than expression having the desired cathartic effect, violence actually breeds more violence. Work done by James Prescott on violence to children suggests that children who are seriously maltreated by their parents, tend to maltreat their children in turn – almost as though they accept it as the normal mode of conduct (Bylinsky 1976).

On the question of how violence is generated, the data – as usual – are conflicting. There seems to be some correlation between actual or known violence in one area and replication in another. For example, in cases dating from 1900 studied by Archer and Garner (in Bylinsky 1976) there appears to be some relationship between wartime violence and domestic violence. But *how* this can be explained is not clear. Similarly, there is the long-standing debate as to whether television violence actually generates aggressive attitudes in children, or whether it simply characterizes what children really want. Do some television programmes make children violent, or are they like it anyway? The evidence is not really conclusive either way. Back in the 1950s when the amount of bloodshed on television was not quite so copious, research

4

suggested that parents had little to fear from the media, but more recent reports seem to indicate otherwise. What we can say is that, whether children are naturally aggressive or not, there is some evidence to suggest that the continual depiction of violence *legitimizes* violent acts and attitudes in impressionable viewers. Perhaps it is all fantasy and make-believe, but fantasy may actually increase rather than sublimate possible aggression. Furthermore, there is the question of habituation, which applies to adults as well as to children. *If* the depiction of violence does not actually *make* people violent, does it inure them to violence? Does the continual portrayal of aggression make it more acceptable? We all know how haphazard television scheduling can be, and how – say – a magazine programme of a general kind can switch from a deeply serious subject such as war or terrorism to the mediocrity of the 'Rock and Pop Awards'. One suspects that this could lead to the trivialization of violence as just another aspect of entertainment, and the diffusion of its impact in the mind of the viewer. The effects of such presentations may therefore be quite subtle. It is not that people, and especially children, will necessarily copy the violent acts they see, but rather that their commonality will generate an increasing indifference. The problem is not therefore so much one of reproduction as one of desensitization.

Some ethologists in their studies of animal behaviour have come to their own conclusions about the naturalness of aggression. One of the most influential, Konrad Lorenz, has developed an evolutionary theory of violence and warfare in which he postulates that aggression has a vital biological function in preserving those who are fittest to survive. The theory is basically a very simple one: those who survive are, *ipso facto*, those who are best adapted to the evolutionary process. They have the necessary qualities of strength, courage, and cunning which have enabled them to endure where others have perished (Lorenz 1966).

According to this view, there is a complex but inexorable process of differentiation, selection, and adaptation taking place which takes in not only the natural order but the social order as well. Even in the man-made world, none of us can escape the tyranny of our own biology. This is the way the world is. If it applies to creatures, it certainly also applies to man. It is further argued that not only has this process a kind of amoral inevitability, it also has certain positive advantages. Competition is healthy, and competition is facilitated by the aggressive instinct. Only by the elimination of the weak and unsuitable can any real progress take place.

This position has a rather unsavoury provenance. It can be found in the strained and least defensible arguments of the nineteenth-century social evolutionists such as Herbert Spencer who wrote in the heyday of Victorian social optimism (Schneider 1976). It can also be found in an extreme form in the worst excesses of the Nazis who hurried along the so-called evolutionary process in genocidal terms.

As a theory of human development, it also begs an awful lot of questions. For instance, who decides exactly who are the weak and unsuitable, and by what criteria are these judgements to be made? Does 'nature' make the decisions or is nature aided and abetted by human agency? Are the assumed imperatives of the evolutionary process to be 'implemented' as acts of policy? Yet a further problem concerns the positive virtues of the relevant human 'instincts'. If we concede a natural human tendency towards aggression, we are still left with the question of the other instincts which are also present in conflict situations. What about the positive advantages of co-operation and even flight? It may actually take more courage to retreat from a situation than to be drawn into an unwanted engagement. There may be occasions when flight rather than fright is to everyone's long-term advantage. However, perhaps the most obvious weakness of the biological necessity argument centres on the issues of whether or not war actually does result in the elimination of the weak and undesirable – however these are defined. In traditional society the old, the sick, and the very young certainly suffered in conflict situations, but usually at the *secondary* level. Their fortunes – or misfortunes – were often incidental to the main action: their sufferings from disease, starvation, and pillage were largely by-products of enemy activity. One might cite the fate of the northern European tribes during the Roman invasions under Julius Caesar (58–56 BC) which was so horrifying that even a seasoned campaigner such as the late Field Marshal Montgomery (1972: 61–2) could say that 'no man made war so horrible as Caesar did in Gaul'. But at the primary level, in terms of the armies themselves, the biological argument is surely open to question. In actual engagements between fighting men, it is not the old but the young who die, it is not the sick but the flower of a nation's manhood which is destroyed. And if men were not killed in the battle itself, it was not unknown for them to be massacred afterwards and their women and children sold into slavery – a practice not uncommon among the Greeks in the classical period (Garlan 1975).

Even in modern times, this has hardly changed for the better. Massacres are still a practice, if not actually a policy, in certain conflict situations, and the phenomenon of 'total war' made possible by advanced technology means that no one effectively escapes. When war is unleashed, there is no biological discrimination, everyone suffers – the young and the old, the sick and the healthy together. Nuclear weapons are hardly selective in their devastation.

The argument that aggression is natural is really rooted in the presupposition that it is part of our 'original' or 'primitive' nature. This view – as popularized by Freud – holds that the aggressive instinct was necessary in early man to enable him to cope with the rigours of his primitive existence. But this is something that can be modified as men adapt to new – and presumably better – social conditions. Of course, from time to time, so the argument goes, there will be a reversion to type. Even modern man will betray his primordial past when circumstances permit. After all, in evolutionary terms, he has only just emerged from a state of barbarism, so it is only to be expected that he will occasionally display some of the savagery that facilitated his climb from the abyss. Hence the many manifestations of the aggressive instinct still to be seen in everyday experience.

Again the argument presents problems. If man's nature is being modified by social conditions, why is it that society seems to be as egocentrically oriented as ever? It is all very well to maintain that we can see vestigial elements of man's primitive past in various institutionalized risk-taking activities. But there is a great deal of difference between such things as motor-racing, mountaineering, and parachuting, and the formalized flutters on the pools. Can we really believe that in these pursuits aggression *has* become sublimated in socially innocuous terms? Do they really indicate that aggression is now canalized as ritualized competition, as, say, sport or business enterprise?

What is very much more serious is the question as to why it is that men's aggressive tendencies show disturbingly few real signs of change. Despite all the modern means for sublimating and canalizing aggression, despite the fact that men like to think that they have reached some measure of developmental maturity, the evidence suggests that, if anything, things are getting worse rather than better. Take as just one example, crime – especially violent crime. This is on the increase in most advanced societies, and can be seen especially in the stark crime statistics from the advanced society *par excellence*, the USA. Here we are told (*Time Magazine* 1981) that there is a burglary every ten seconds, a rape every seven minutes, and a murder every twenty-four minutes. In fact, the murder rate in cities such as Dallas exceeds that for the whole of the UK. Violent crime, i.e. murder, rape, aggravated assault, etc., has increased by approximately 50 per cent from 1970 to 1980; in one area of Miami alone rape figures show a dramatic jump from 70 in 1969 to 700 in 1979 with the ages of victims ranging from 2 months to 92 years.

Certain trends in the types of crime are possibly more disturbing than the figures themselves: the rise in the numbers of apparently motiveless murders, in drugs-related crimes, and, of course, in race-related crimes. This last category is particularly interesting because murder is now the leading cause of death among black males between 24 and 34 years of age; the rate is eight times higher than for whites where the leading causes of death in the same age category are car and motor-cycle accidents. But this ethnic factor is not that simple to explain. What can be established is that each racial group is in *more* danger from those within its own fraternity than from those outside; whites have more to fear from other whites, and blacks are in more danger from other blacks than anyone else. Some crime obviously has an *in*direct interracial dimension; there are economic and status factors behind some of the relatively high rates of black crime. But 83 per cent of assaults and 70 per cent of robberies and rapes are *same*-race crimes, so a *direct* inter-racial element is not really substantiated.

Persuasive as crime statistics are that man is not exactly outgrowing his animal past, they tend to pale into insignificance beside the injury rates and mortality figures for recent wars. To argue that natural aggressive instincts are simply necessary in order that men might cope with the everyday exigencies of a primitive existence takes little account of the horrific carnage of wars between civilized societies. The view that aggressive acts will diminish with time looks pretty sick when one looks at the evidence, with 50 millions dead in the First World War alone, and an estimated death rate of 300 millions in the first hour of a full-scale nuclear holocaust.

So we are back to the 'real' nature of man's problem. Is there a natural altruism which only needs the right circumstances for it to be realized? Or are we naturally egocentric, depending on the necessary constraints of society to keep us all under control?

WAR AS AN ECONOMIC EXPEDIENT

The view that war derives from some kind of economic necessity or expediency is extremely persuasive. Even where societies did not actu-ally go to war for specifically economic reasons, it is certainly true that economic exploitation often followed in the wake of military success. In the Greek classical period, for instance, we find Xenophon (d. *c.* 354 BC) writing that 'it is a law established for all time among all men that when a city is taken in war, the persons and the property of the inhabitants belong to the captors' (*Cyropaedia* VII. 5. 73; trans. in Garlan 1975: 69).

It is important, however, to distinguish between economic need and economic greed. There is a world of difference between, say, the assert-ive colonizing activities of the Greeks, particularly in Sicily, Italy, and Turkey from the eighth century BC, and the predatory excursions of the Assyrians which were taking place in the Middle East at roughly the same time. In practice, though, the distinctions were not always that clear. Perhaps nothing is ever done out of a 'pure' motive, and this certainly applies to war. There are many reasons why men resort to violence, and these often become confounded and confused in actual situations. Greed can so easily be rationalized as need when the occasion demands.

The reasons or ostensible motives for militaristic activity in different societies are complicated by the apparent or declared intentions of political rulers and military leaders. Not infrequently, they have used their power – and certainly their success – to enrich themselves and secure favourable positions for their families and friends. Nepotism and even dynastic ambition are common concomitants of rulers with expansionist intentions.

In cases where the military leaders were not themselves political rulers, the military vocation could be a source of mobility for the aspiring careerist. For example, in the Egyptian New Kingdom it was not unknown for a successful general actually to end up as Pharaoh, especially in critical phases of the nation's history, even though, in theory, he was supposed to come from the divinely endowed royal line. Indirectly, military success affected the masses as well. Conquest brought all sorts of beneficial by-products, so the people were usually happy to support a military leader as long as he delivered the goods. Perhaps it was fortunate when such heroes died young, like Alexander the Great; at least people remembered them for their achievements rather than an unproductive old age.

The reasons-for-war issue is further complicated by ideological factors. And here too a necessary distinction must be made. As reasons are different from rationalizations, so reasons are also different from justifications, and justifications are often advanced in ideological terms. It is extremely common, for instance, to find conquest or intended conquest justified in terms of religious conviction or purported revelation. Thus in the Middle Ages, the impassioned preaching of Peter the Hermit helped initiate that series of Christian wars against the Muslims which we still know – rather misleadingly – as the Crusades. They were hardly the heroic endeavours of dedicated knights which some histories have depicted. To what extent their real motives were religious, and to what extent they were political and expansionist, or even acquisitive, perhaps even they were not always sure.

A reactionary variant of the economic expediency argument has been put forward by the sociologist, Stanislav Andreski (1968). He repudiates various kinds of popular explanation as being naïve and simplistic, and is particularly impatient with psychological theories and 'absurd ideas' which argue that all racial animosity is pathological. He has serious reservations on the question of war and cultural relativism, and insists that the basic causes of conflict are reducible to demographic–economic imperatives. He gets right down to what he believes are the fundamentals. It is scarcity that promotes war. Given the overall human situation, struggles for land, wealth, food, women, power, and honours are unavoidable. Struggle is omnipresent because resources are perennially scarce. Therefore, war has a functional importance in ensuring the necessary balance of wealth over population.

A counter-argument, also offered by sociologists (LaPiere 1954), maintains that the land-hunger theory of war is a myth. It is suggested that conceptions of under-population and over-population are mere social evaluations, and are therefore relative to particular situations. Furthermore, it is contended that history is replete with instances of societies that have lived for centuries at near-subsistence levels in areas which, in modern terms, may be regarded as over-populated, without resorting to war on neighbouring peoples who were weaker both in numbers and in technology. With some qualifications, the Egyptian Old Kingdom (c. 2700–c. 2200 BC) would fall into this category, although some of its more ambitious rulers often made predatory raids against the 'non-people' of the Sudan (Nubia) who were hardly in a position to retaliate.

Generally speaking, traditionalist arguments have some cogency, especially when couched in terms of what Andreski calls 'ophelimites', a neologism he employs to denote anything which is desired, and which can presumably be obtained – either directly or indirectly – by aggression. Human conflict is seen as the inevitable concomitant of the struggle for survival, and it will go on as long as men strive for material goods and the intangibles of prestige and social esteem. Indeed, it could be argued that with more and more demands being made upon the world's diminishing natural resources, there will be a reversion to type as men scramble for the limited rewards that remain.

This point calls to mind one further distinction which should be made. We have already seen that we must not confuse the struggle for existence with the struggle for pre-eminence. So if war is primarily concerned with gain in some form or another it is also useful to distinguish between conflicts which arise from 'position scarcity' and those which arise from 'resource scarcity' (Mack and Synder 1970). 'Position scarcity' can be defined as the condition in which an object cannot occupy two places at the same time or fulfil two different functions simultaneously. So, for example, fifth-century Athens, as ostensible leader and benefactor of the Delian League of allied Greek States, could not consistently perform the roles of both protector and oppressor – although she tried to do both. 'Resource scarcity' is much more straightforward. Conflict occurs when contending states cannot both have *all* they want. Mutually exclusive and/or mutually incompatible value-judgements will obviously condition the demand for scarce resources and positions. This is an inevitable consequence of conflict situations (Walzer 1977).

WAR AS A CULTURAL PRODUCT

This view of war and aggression also takes several forms. These tend to stress the nurture rather than the nature side in the perennial debate about primary causal factors, and maintain that aggression and competition are learned rather than inherited. Human biology is de-emphasized, and human culture is seen as an all-important element. The arguments are either psychological in orientation, stressing the formative influences of human growth and development, or sociological with a contemporary emphasis on structural forces.

The *psychological argument* repudiates the idea that aggression is some kind of 'instinct'; indeed, the whole notion of instinctual drives is under something of a cloud in psychology at the present time. Instead, the argument is that aggression is a learned response – like any other learned response – to particular situations. This is said to take place, first, by observation and imitation; so, for instance, cruelty to others is seen and therefore copied – particularly by children. But the evidence here is conflicting. Some research – indeed, everyday experience – confirms this form of the theory, but there is contrary evidence which suggests that some children and adults are *repelled* by the observation of cruelty, and have no compelling wish to imitate such behaviour.

Second, aggression is said to be learned by experience, and again there is evidence which appears to indicate that those who are maltreated as children are also inclined to maltreat others in turn. But this raises the question as to whether this kind of aggression can also be *minimized* by example? Some work done in Tahiti by Robert Levy, an anthropologist from the University of California, suggests that the answer lies with those who act as exemplars. The rising crime rates on the island seem to be related to the fact that children prefer to copy their peers and television stereotypes rather than adhere to the traditional norms observed by their parents.

Not only may aggression be learned by experience, it may also be *induced* by experience. Some research data – especially those of the behaviourists – suggest that it can. The work of Stanley Milgram is commonly cited in this respect. In a now famous series of experiments Milgram has shown that, in certain prescribed circumstances, sets of subjects can be persuaded to carry out acts of ostensible cruelty which are assumed to be contrary to their normal modes of behaviour. These studies in obedience and conformity are somewhat chilling in their implications and suggest that virtually anyone can be induced to act insensitively to other human beings, given an accepted authority, the right conditions, and the appropriate cues (Milgram 1970). Of course, the question which is begged by this is how can aggression be induced if it is not embryonically present in the personality? How can people

11

be induced to be aggressive if the capacity does not already exist?
Potentiality must imply actuality.

There is little doubt that there is a learning element in aggression.
We can see this where aggression is instrumental in the gratification of
need or desire. People tend to repeat those acts which are rewarded;
so if aggression pays – as in certain forms of bullying – then aggression
continues to be employed. Research has repeatedly shown that the
opportunity to aggress, and successfully inflict pain or injury – be it for
material gain or simply for some kind of perverted pleasure – usually
encourages still more aggression. There is certainly very little evidence
to indicate that aggression 'obeys' some form of catharsis principle.
Aggressive acts do not appear to act as safety valves. Unchecked
aggression often stimulates more aggression.

The kindred view that aggression is activated by stressful situations
does not really tell us very much. Aggression may well be elicited by
an appropriate stimulus – say, a frustrating event – but does this mean
that everything that is worrisome or objectionable should always be
removed from our path? Surely learning to cope with problems is part
of the stuff of being human? To argue that aggression simply arises as
the result of temporary frustration in the face of life's obstacles is quite
inadequate. It does not tell us anything about the human *capacity* for
aggression, neither does it tell us what determines either the *degree* or
the *form* of aggression. It may only indicate something of the *focus* of
aggression in particular situations, as, say, with the attitudes of children
to British troops in Northern Ireland. Frustration may be linked with
aggression, but violence is only *one* possible response to a particular set
of circumstances. It does not follow that it should always be 'legitimate'
or even permissible.

Perhaps Leonard Berkowitz has a point when he distinguishes
between defensive and hostile aggression, or Erich Fromm when he
makes a similar distinction between defensive and malignant aggression
(Fromm 1976). In each case, defensive aggression is seen as natural and
creature-like, whereas hostile or malignant aggression is regarded as
something which is particularly characteristic of the human species in
its deliberate and calculated capacity to inflict pain on others. Fromm,
especially, sees malignant aggression as a growing feature of our time
which is occasioned by the increasing alienation of men in an uncaring
and impersonal society.

Such views bring us conveniently to a brief appraisal of the *sociological
argument*. This too takes a number of forms, and has certain affinities
with the economic expediency position which we have already discussed. In general, it too maintains that war is the inevitable outcome
of the interminable struggle for land and resources, but it also links this

with the development of class societies and the emergence of the state as an agent of political control.

The classic Marxist hypothesis is that a highly conjectural primitive communism gave way to the increased complexities of the division of labour and the subsequent development of private property. This, in turn, led to the formation of class divisions with their consequent evils and injustices. War, therefore, is a manifestation of aggression, and aggression is a reflection of the economic inequalities and uncertainties in society. War will presumably cease when these have been remedied and the utopian classless society has been established. Only then will conflict become a thing of the past because aggressive acts will no longer be necessary.

This view envisages war not so much as a product of man's nature as a product of social evolution; the problem is rooted in history rather than the human psyche. Social relations are not a product of human consciousness, but are rather the determinants of that consciousness. Primarily, it is not man that makes society, but society that makes man. The 'answer' to war, therefore, is seen – somewhat simplistically – in terms of social change which would mean the outlawing of classes and the more equal distribution of goods.

Although not without insights, the general Marxist argument has to be suspect. First, the idea that individual consciousness is *merely* a product of social consciousness is without evidential support. It involves a circularity of reasoning which produces an extreme relativism. And second, the utopian vision of the classless society has little to commend it in historical terms. History has plenty of precedents for class conflict but none for Marxist-type classless societies. It has no record of a developed classless society, and anthropology has no knowledge of a society without social differentiation. This has to suggest that the future possibilities for such a social arrangement are, at best, minimal. Certainly, known communistic societies – arguably a legacy of the Marxist idea – show little progress towards such a state.

A related and complementary argument is that the incidence of war is associated with the growth of nationalism, the development of urbanism and the fortress towns, and consequently with the rise of new military elites which were necessary to consolidate and control the new forms of society. Both these views tend to dismiss the idea of war and aggression as something characteristically human, or, as Mosca puts it, 'a constant phenomenon which arises in all human societies from the most civilised down' (Mosca 1939: 29). As yet, there are no signs that social development in either scale or sophistication will necessarily lead to the abolition of war. Indeed, if anything, the evidence points in the opposite direction. As we have seen, in the rare cases where war is not

13

practised the societies in question are invariably primitive and unsophisticated by western standards.

WAR AS A PRODUCT OF MORAL DECLINE

This argument maintains that war derives from the breakdown of the traditional moral order, and the liberating but disorganizing influence of more permissive social norms. It is held that the older identities of estate, class, region, and religion have been eroded by the emergence of the mass society, and that this in turn has precipitated the collapse of a stable moral order. This kind of thesis can be seen in Gibbon's (1979) *Decline and Fall of the Roman Empire*, and has been frequently echoed by historians who have attributed all manner of current evils to moral decline, from the loss of the medieval sense of community to the view that the First World War resulted from the decay of European society after the revolution in France in the late eighteenth century.

The sociologist, Emile Durkheim, contended that any breakdown in the accepted moral order results in both a condition and a sense of 'anomie' or normlessness. People are literally 'without order' (Durkheim 1970). They find themselves in a situation where the old values are disregarded or actually forgotten, and where there are no longer any firm guidelines for personal and social behaviour. This has been a common experience of people since time immemorial. For instance, we find that after the collapse of the Egyptian Old Kingdom, about 2200 BC, one anonymous writer protested that the kingdom had become 'a come-and-get-it for anyone', monarchic authority was ignored, subjects were doing as they pleased, and all restraint had apparently been abandoned. It took some 150 years before normality was restored and control was re-established.

Similar sentiments have been expressed in all sorts of historical circumstances – with more or less justification. Whether they always have substance is still a matter of dispute. What some contemporary observers see as decline, others merely interpret as change – and perhaps much needed change at that. Often, those who make the most vociferous protests are the traditionalists who most regret the challenge to the old order. On the other hand, it may be that their indignation is not without foundation. So another anonymous writer, this time writing with regret about what he regards as the weaknesses and abuses of Athenian democracy, says that

> it is only those departments of government which bring emolument and assist private households that the People care to keep in their own hands. . . . If any mischief should spring out of the deliberations of the assembly [of citizens], the People charge that

a handful of men acting against the interests of the citizens have ruined the state. But if any good result ensue, they, the People, at once take the credit of that to themselves.

(Claster 1967: 45–6)

A further reservation about the moral decline argument concerns the difficulty of establishing any definite connections between any two sets of variables. Some possible correlations have a certain plausibility, but the proposition that there is a connection between moral values – or the lack of them – and the display of social aggression can never be more than persuasive. War can certainly be related to quite contrary types of social value, so it is not possible to say that aggression or non-aggression are *always* and *only* to be found in particular social situations. If, on the other hand, the argument is that war is the result of break-down, no matter what kind of social system is involved, then we are simply dealing with a form of truism. But even here there are problems involved because when a breakdown occurs it is not always possible to establish exactly which is the cause and which is the effect. Does social breakdown *cause* conflict, or is it directly or indirectly the *result* of conflict? Or is it both? The connections between some variables may be arbitrary and fortuitous, and their causal relationship merely plausible rather than conclusive.

WAR AS A RITUAL IMPERATIVE

In this context, ritual may be defined as the expressive aspect of religion, and it is conceivable that war not only has ritual aspects and ritual justifications, but it is sometimes actually waged for ritualistic *reasons* – or what are ostensibly ritualistic reasons. Certainly many pre-industrial societies were apparently impelled to war for what were broadly religious reasons. These do not seem to have belonged to any particular type or area or culture. Ritual war has virtually a universal distribution; it can be found in both simple and complex pre-industrial systems which are often widely separated in both space and time. Head-hunting in New Guinea was a ritual act, though heavily overlaid with status considerations, and the cannibalistic consumption of prisoners among some Amazonian tribes had strong ritual as well as economic conno-tations. Generally speaking, practices of this kind were most developed in more advanced agrarian societies. People who live at or near the subsistence level spend too great a proportion of their time trying to eke out a precarious existence to worry much about ritual warfare. But among settled peoples it is often a different story. They have the time and resources to indulge in ritual strife. Where relative prosperity is confidently attributed to the gods, it is sometimes felt necessary to convince others of one's spiritual good fortune. Therefore, it is not unusual to find historical societies matching god for god on the battlefield. Each deity's claims are aggressively asserted by that deity's followers, and when success is achieved it is not uncommon to find that the spoils of victory include sacrifices to the triumphant deity. So concerning the battles of Rameses III, a pharaoh of the 20th Dynasty (*c.* 1200–*c.* 1090 BC), against the 'Sea Peoples', i.e. tribes of the Western Mediterranean, we read how he crushed their army and scattered their ships with enormous losses, and then how the god Amon, who had granted the victory, received his 'accustomed sacrifice of living victims'. At this all Egypt is said to have rejoiced because of their restored security. Similarly, we find that before the Libyan campaign of Merneptah, the successor of Rameses II (The Great) in the thirteenth century BC, he had a vision of the god Ptah who held a sword before him and commanded him not to be afraid. The result was an inspired and innovatory use of his archers; it is recorded that 'the bowmen of his Majesty spent six hours of destruction among them [the Libyans], then they were delivered to the sword' (Carlton 1977: 188–9).

Conquest for avowedly religious or ideological reasons may take the form of evangelical fervour, as with early – and perhaps not so early – Islam. Or it may take a chillingly 'practical' form as with many Meso-American societies such as the Maya, the Toltecs, and particularly the Aztecs who tried not to kill their enemies in battle, but take them prisoner so that they could be slain on the sacrificial stone as an essential offering to the gods. In the early sixteenth century AD, the Aztecs tried this once too often, this time with the Spanish Conquistadores, and effectively brought about their own destruction. It was the beginning of the end for a distinctive culture which recognized the combination of war and sacrifice as a ritual necessity (Davies 1973).

This overview of war as a cognitive problem has not exhausted the range of explanatory possibilities. So far, we have considered a number of theoretical approaches which have looked at war in terms of key variables such as economic necessity and ritual imperatives. But it may be that we can only explain war in terms of itself. In this sense, it is a little like trying to account for people playing or liking a particular sport. They may offer instrumental reasons which centre on sport as a health-giving, strength-increasing activity. Or they may give social – even moral – reasons which focus on the value of competition or of co-operation and the generation of a team spirit. Yet at the most elementary level they may insist that they take part in sport just because they like it. This has an irrefutable simplicity which is impossible to question. They like it because they like it.

Very similar arguments could apply to war. There is ample evidence that some societies indulge in warfare for 'autotelic' reasons, that is to say they find it – or certain aspects of it – exciting and pleasurable *in itself*. For them, war is a kind of ritualized game, a pastime, an interesting diversion. It is difficult to conceive modern war in these terms, but this has undoubtedly existed in the past. Many early societies spent much of the winter recuperating from war, and planning the next year's expeditions. They welcomed springtime as the beginning of their campaigning season, and looked forward to either the confiscation or the destruction of enemy goods and crops. Societies such as the Dani so regularized and organized their engagements that fatalities were kept to a minimum so that the tribal groups concerned could resume their hostilities on a future occasion.

Other societies have seen war as a kind of proving ground for their young men. Warrior castes have deliberately courted battle in order to test the mettle of the new generation. This mentality is exemplified in such widely different formations as the Zulu impis and the Waffen SS. War is a healthy exercise which tempers the potentialities of both the person and the state. Such accounts are not at all unusual; they can be paralleled from the records of many societies, as we shall see in the ensuing discussion. There is a kaleidoscopic variety to human behaviour, and the reasons, pretences, and justifications for war reflect something of that cultural diversity.

Section II

WAR AND IDEOLOGY

It is a primary contention of this book that war is not just a function of political and economic exigencies, but is also largely determined by ideological imperatives. This means that before we can examine the ways in which war is waged in societies, we must look at the beliefs which are held to justify it. This does not mean that we are going to be able to *explain* war in these terms – explanation, as per the natural sciences, is rarely possible in the social sciences. But it does mean that we can offer more or less plausible theories as to how belief operates in relation to war. After some general statements about belief, the discussion will concentrate on the main theoretical orientations current in the social sciences on the place of religious and secular belief – issues which are assuming growing importance in modern society where so many revolutionary movements are ideologically motivated.

The central concern of this section of the discussion therefore is the relationship between belief and action. The underlying problem is whether belief – intellectualized as ideology – really affects or even determines social behaviour. To what extent are belief-systems dependent or independent variables in the institutional complex of society? That is to say, are beliefs subordinate to the politico-economic realities of the social situation, or do they actually influence action? It is the nature of this relationship that merits study, and which we are going to examine in the context of war and aggression.

What exactly then do we mean by belief, and how is it to be defined? Belief implies the acceptance of propositions or values which by definition are not susceptible of experimental validation. Sets of beliefs which are ideological purport to tell us how things are or were. To this extent, they are modes of self-interpretation, and forms of explanation. As such, they may be both persuasive and prescriptive in that they enjoin certain kinds of behaviour. Religious belief, in particular, can connote more than mere intellectual assent. But it does not necessarily imply the truth or otherwise of the belief-object. The gods may or may not exist. It is the *believing* which is true; the truth-value of the ideology

18

itself may only be significant in so far as it achieves social expression. The belief is innocuous without physical articulation. This text, therefore, takes the view that belief is important because it contributes to the construction and maintenance of our social realities, and it also defines and legitimates our moral and intellectual structures.

Ideology interiorizes institutions and affects everyday practices in subtle ways. But the precise nature of the relationship between ideology and other institutional phenomena still remains an open question. It is impossible finally to demonstrate a direct correlation between a belief-system and any social form or pattern of behaviour. Any argument concerning its 'effects' can never be regarded as conclusive, though its influences may certainly be seen as pervasive. This is particularly evidenced by the determinative perceptions of what is thought of as the 'enemy'.

Here it is very easy to become caught up in the deceptive simplicities and resounding generalities that characterize ideological statements and statements about ideology. In looking at ideology, we are concerned not only with what it 'is', but also with the ways in which it operates. If we consider it, say, in relation to the state, are we to equate it with the ways in which the state thinks about itself? And if so, are we speaking of the way the state actually is (a substantive statement) or the way it would really like to be (a normative statement), or, indeed, how it would like *others* to think of it (a deceptive statement)? In practice, these are often confused both by outsiders and by the members themselves. One only has to think of the varying and contradictory perceptions of Nazi Germany and its policies in the 1930s.

Ideologies are belief-systems which enshrine certain values, and although it can be contended that the need for such systems and the forms they take may be socially derived, the *predisposition* to believe – the 'truth-quest' – may not easily be reducible to simple social explanations. Beliefs attract some and repel others, but this does not necessarily reflect the social position or the emotional disposition of the believer. It is still impossible to know how certain beliefs are derived and how they are appropriated, regardless of whether the beliefs in question are religious, ethical, or merely aesthetic. It is not always possible to say why a view or an idea is elevated to the status of a value which is then expressed as a belief (Parsons 1954). Perhaps some values *are* simple social derivations; courage in battle, for instance, may derive from the need for group survival. But is this also true of *personal* survival? Can group needs entirely explain personal sacrifice? Furthermore, the 'needs'-type argument can involve a logical confusion between function and origination. To say that courage contributes to group survival is quite different from saying that the need for group survival 'causes' courage.

The issues relating to the role of ideology have been overlaid with numerous associations and connotations which have not always contributed to the business of clarification. John Plamenatz speaks of ideology as a 'set of closely related beliefs and ideas, or even attitudes characteristic of a group or community' (Plamenatz 1971: 15). But can we meaningfully speak of ideas which are 'characteristic' of a group? That is to say, can we distinguish ideas which are so peculiar in *essence* (as opposed to the form in which they are expressed) that they can be clearly seen to constitute the differentiae of that group?

Perhaps a more satisfactory definition of ideology is 'a pattern of beliefs and concepts (both factual and normative) which purport to explain complex social phenomena with a view to directing and simplifying [their] socio-political choices' (Gould 1964). Such a general definition does not explicate the many nuances of the term or specify the variety of intellectual systems which have been styled ideologies. Neither does it define the different modes in which they may have been legitimized, nor the internal balance between their factual and ethical components.

Not infrequently, definitions of ideology have pejorative connotations. It has been argued that ideology is to philosophy what superstition is to religion; that, in effect, one man's philosophy is another man's ideology. But it is generally agreed that ideologies are forms of *belief-system* that explain and justify a preferred social order. This social order may already exist or simply be proposed, in which case the ideology may constitute a believed strategy for its attainment. This may generate an emotional appeal which, in turn, may call for some kind of moral commitment. These ethically infused ideals may then help the members of that order to interpret their past, explain their present, and anticipate their future (Christenson 1972: 6). As we shall see, this is particularly evident in military systems which have a strong sense of mission or destiny such as those of the Crusader knights or the Islamic sultanates.

Ideologies, then, are complex belief-systems which involve both empirical and normative elements. For the 'common man', there may be an unreflective confusion between facts and values; but the ideologue, whose approach is far more forensic, will make careful distinctions between diagnosis and prescription. Sometimes, ideologies are systematic and self-sufficient, sometimes they are self-contradictory and internally inconsistent, and their very abstraction detracts from potential mass appeal. In their religious forms, they are frequently exclusive and absolutist. They often consist of beliefs in 'true principles', which are not open to negotiation; in simple dichotomies which distinguish the chosen from the rest – the believer from the unbeliever. They may be reductionist and inflexible, and represent the objectification of

20

personal, group, or even national interests. Their strong inspirational orientations may have little time for logical proofs other than scripturalized validations. Ideologies do undergo development, but they are normally regarded as typically resistant to fundamental change, and both pragmatic and dogmatic when faced with the need to modify doctrine or alter, or adapt – as they inevitably must – to new situations.

On the other hand, ideologies are sometimes regarded as the instruments of change. They can develop as alternative value-systems which emerge in times of stress or emergency, as, for example, the Mau Mau in the Kenya of the 1950s. The fact is that ideologies can operate in either direction. Indeed, this can be true of the *same* ideology; after all, we have only to examine the outcome of so many successful liberation movements to see that the revolutionary ideology of today may be the status quo ideology of tomorrow (Greig 1973).

Values are enshrined in ideologies, and values are really preference statements. This means that their relative merits cannot be scientifically validated. But in institutional terms, they can be 'realized', promoted, and even enforced. It follows, therefore, that although the 'truth' of any particular ideology can never be verified, its potency can be judged in terms of sheer effectiveness. Normal tests of reality may be inappropriate. All that can be examined are its factual assertions; its empirical bases as distinct from its normative prescriptions; the reliability of its promises and predictions; its feasibility and the conditions necessary for its general implementation. At a different level, it is obviously also possible to study its theoretical components; the implicit structure of its ideas, the hidden assumptions, and their compatibilities and incompatibilities (Weiss 1967). But such 'logical' tests can never establish the truth or falsity of these assumptions. It can never be proved that particular ideologies 'cause' particular behaviour, yet the connections have a psychological plausibility. Again, this is particularly characteristic of religious ideologies.

Although interpretations as to the nature and structure of ideologies multiply, the *theories* of how ideology functions are often conveniently reduced to so-called Interest and Strain theories. The Interest (or Realist) view which is most commonly associated with Marxist thought maintains that ideologies are concerned with gain and the preservation of advantage, particularly within political systems. Marx, himself, distinguished between what he termed the material substructure of society and its cultural superstructure, hence his insistence that social consciousness was conditioned by social existence. In effect, he is saying that the way we *think* is conditioned by the way we *live*; it is therefore not belief that affects action, but the need for action that gives rise to belief. In attributing primacy to the material order, it follows that the ideological order is consequently reduced to a dependent variable in

21

the social process (Marx and Engels 1965). Ideology is seen variously as a guise or a weapon in the unending historical struggle for advantage between those who have power and those who seek it (Pareto 1935). The structure of society reflects these interminable conflicts. Ideology, therefore, is an expedient devised by authority systems to secure and justify their aims and policies. It is a contrivance which generates a 'false consciousness' and thus perpetuates a distorted view of the social process. It therefore constitutes a system of related illusions about the state in particular and society in general. This view of ideology necessarily sets it against 'scientific' appreciations of the situation, and, to this extent, it may be seen as a substitute for 'exact' knowledge.

Using the term to denote not the illusion, as such, but the belief or value-system, it is then argued that the ideology of the dominant classes is used to enhance their class interests by justifying the established order to the detriment of the oppressed classes. So, in one sense, ideology is seen as an exploitative value-system which is imposed upon the masses. Yet, in another sense, it is regarded as a contrivance which both mystifies and misleads the masses by encouraging a false awareness of the historical process and of their place in the whole scheme of things. In yet a further sense, it is seen as a pervasive yet vulnerable illusion which is ultimately subject to the practical realities of production relations within society.

The pristine Marxist view has been extensively refined and qualified by subsequent thinkers in the same general tradition. But one thing which divides them is whether ideology should be seen essentially as a form of error or a kind of truth. The idea that ideology is a source of error, and therefore incompatible with science itself, takes a number of forms (Stark 1958: 53). It has been argued that while Marx recognized the situational basis of thought in his political opponents, he failed to recognize that all thought, including that of Marxists themselves, must be subject to the same strictures (Schumpeter 1965). Karl Mannheim has likewise criticized Marx and Marxists for their lack of self-examination and their apparent inability to see that Marxism is also open to ideological distortion. He insists that there are two antithetical urges which lead to distorted thinking; the urge of self-interest which constrains men to maintain the status quo, and the urge which impels men to try to remould society in a new and better image, if necessary by war. The former, he theorized, leads to forms of ideological thinking, whilst the latter – which may be equally mistaken – leads to forms of utopian thinking (Mannheim 1936), and even aggressive expansionist policies. Mannheim insisted that Marx's view that the key to social change was a class rising to power through changes in the character and instruments of production was over-simplified. He felt that any analysis based solely on economic relationships must be inadequate.

Instead, he argued that new and constructive 'syntheses' could be achieved by that relatively classless stratum – the often-underestimated intelligentsia.

What Mannheim does not make clear is how the intelligentsia itself can necessarily remain immune from any form of distorted thinking. A very clear example of how the intelligentsia can itself be susceptible to the prevailing ideology can be seen in the number of German academics such as Otto Ohlendorf and Professor Franz Six who were directly involved in the extermination of European Jewry (Hilberg 1967).

Mannheim is not entirely consistent on these issues. If all values are determined by the situation, how is it possible to remain aloof from such determination? It seems simply to be an assumption that the perceptive being becomes impatient with the strident clamour of conflicting ideologies, and is ultimately disenchanted with them all. Intelligence is thus equated with ideological scepticism. For Mannheim's critics, it is self-evident that these situational arguments are suspect. If circumstances condition thought, why do individuals and groups in similar situations often think so differently? There may be a universality of at least some values, but why is there such diversification in their expression?

Mannheim's 'situational distortion' is but one version of cognitive relativism; other neo-Marxists such as Lukacs opt for a less refined form in terms of class distortion. Lukacs' thinking is rooted in the notion that ideas originate in actual historical circumstances (Lukacs 1971). The problem this raises is to what extent practical considerations can be held to account for the *origins* of these ideas and, presumably, values? A kind of necessity-is-the-mother-of-invention argument. For Lukacs, ideology is a distortion of the truth; a reflection of the economic process which saturates the social consciousness. It is not – as in the more orthodox Marxist tradition – an objective systematized representation of actual social relations embodied in social institutions and practices which facilitate social control.

The view that ideologies are contrived and that ideological pronouncements are, therefore, patently false is open to dispute. There is evidence that underlying the party line of some modern movements is a *believed* ideology (Fest 1972). Ideologies are not necessarily sources of error or distortions of truth which are calculated to deceive the unsuspecting and the politically naïve. Some Marxists have made this very point. Antonio Gramsci, for instance, maintains that the 'truth' of an ideology must be judged pragmatically; has it the power to mobilize political opinion, and achieve historical actualization (Gramsci 1971)? He breaks with the conception of ideology as a simple reflection of economic relations or as a uniform expression of the ruling class. Instead, he sees a differential appropriation of the dominant ideas by both the dominated class and the various groups within the ruling class itself. Ideologies, or forms of ideologies, therefore enjoy different kinds of 'hegemony' in a variety of situations. There is no simple imposition of a uniform set of ideas by one class upon another. Instead, there are various combinations of domination and subordination in given contexts. Action and behaviour are related to everyday ideas – to the social world and its practicalities. Gramsci is impatient with a simple interest view of ideology. Ideologies are not mere 'tricks' to deceive the workers, but have their base in material realities and act as material forces. They can – and do – contain contradictory elements, but, in general, their complex formations are internally coherent. Whatever their 'faults', ideologies – like religions to which they are related – do possess a certain social utility.

Louis Althusser, a modern Marxist thinker, takes up the same ideas. Ideologies reflect the 'ways men live', 'they are rooted in everyday life' (Althusser 1969: 114ff.). 'Human societies secrete ideology as the very element and atmosphere indispensable to their historical respiration and life' (Althusser 1969: 232). He maintains that the various levels of social formations, political, economic, ideological, interact in different ways in their capacity to influence each other, but he recognizes that this interaction can be uncertain and uneven. Here Althusser makes an important distinction between dominant and determinant elements in specific social situations. As a good Marxist, he dutifully ascribes an ultimately determinant role to economic factors, but admits that in actual situations other, possibly ideological, factors may exercise a dominant influence. Thus, say, in ancient societies such as Egypt or Greece, the dominant factors may, in fact, be religious rather than political. War, for instance, may be embarked upon for motives which have little to do with material aggrandizement. No simple primacy can be given to 'pure' economic factors – there is always a complex of motives behind every activity.

Ideology, then, is not false consciousness, it is not – as in traditional Marxism – the basis of a distorted relationship, but of an *imaginary* relationship between individuals and their 'real' (economic) conditions of existence (Althusser 1976). The emphasis is away from a fairly uncomplicated bourgeois conspiracy theory to a view which implies a misapprehension on the part of members of society. Obviously, this misapprehension is encouraged by those who hold power and who wish to manipulate public opinion. But what is not apparent is the extent to which this is, in any sense, a willing misapprehension. The situation, as Althusser represents it, is one in which men connive in their own subjection, co-operate in their own unfreedom. Their unwillingness to live socially authentic lives constitutes a kind of 'bad faith'

24

which reduces them to the situation of mere cyphers in the social process.

Such views are also echoed by other neo-Marxists. Nicos Polantzas, for instance, supports much of Althusser's thinking on ideology. For Polantzas, an ideology is a relatively coherent ensemble of values and beliefs which hide the real contradictions of the socio-economic order from the agents. Its function is to provide cohesion at every level of the social structure, and this it accomplishes by a combination of value-inversion and mystification (Polantzas 1975). One particularly interesting feature of Polantzas is that he recognizes that in any given situation there may coexist a plurality of competing ideologies, one of which may exert a hegemonic influence over the others. Furthermore, he maintains that, in particular systems, the dominated classes may 'live out their revolt' within the framework of the dominant ideology. Thus it follows that in, say, Roman society, the slave-revolts were attempts to secure freedom for particular slaves, not attempts to change radically the social order. In fact, if anything, they were endorsements of that order.

The view that ideologies constitute not so much evil distortions or misrepresentations as forms of – albeit mistaken – explanation, comes close to the type of interpretation which is usually contrasted with Interest theories, namely, Strain theories of ideology. In fact it might be argued that views of theorists such as Louis Althusser really bridge the gulf between traditional Marxists and consensus theorists such as Parsons, and highlight affinities that have already been well-documented (Lipset 1976).

Strain theories see ideologies as a symptom of – or even a remedy for – dislocations in the social structure. In general, they maintain that all societies are riddled with insoluble contradictions which are extremely difficult to resolve. In general, societies are characterized by the desire to maintain stability whilst accepting the need for change; vexed with the problem of how to maintain or increase social efficiency whilst, at the same time, trying to preserve a vestigial humanity. These, in turn, involve yet further problems of precision and flexibility; of how to reconcile the cry for liberty with the stifling necessity of political order.

These issues were not so marked in complex pre-industrial societies where change was slow and hesitant. Questions of humanity and flexibility were usually subordinated to the requirements of stability and social order. Such problems were largely resolved in terms of ideology, and the innumerable frictions arising from them were often contained by ideological imperatives.

In one way or another, all men live 'lives of patterned desperation' (Apter 1964). Thus ideology can be seen as a patterned response to persisting social divisions. On this interpretation the presence of, say, religion in society could be construed as a functional remedy for these problems in that it provides cohesion and consolation, a kind of 'opium of the people'. In this capacity, it may purport to explain these social discrepancies, or it may try to obscure their 'real' nature; or failing this – or even in addition to this – it may endeavour to ameliorate their effects. Thus some societies may well embark upon 'religious wars' in order to distract attention from the inherent weaknesses of the political system. War can have unifying and reinforcing functions which are indispensable in given social circumstances.

Ideology, then, may reflect man's sense of helplessness and inadequacy, and – in its religious forms – may derive as much from his cosmic situation as his social position. And this involves his perceptions of reality; his believed place in the order of things, especially in relation to those with counter aspirations. Thus in pre-industrial systems, particularly, it is not unusual to find war related to perceptions of cosmic competition (Kirk 1973). It is the gods who are really in conflict; men merely act as their agents. Military success or failure, therefore, simply underlines the respective strength of the deities.

It could be argued that most human action is unreflective. Society tends to encourage non-reflection by presenting inadequate sets of choices, and simply indicating approved ways of behaviour. In traditional societies, particularly, there were often no clear empirical references or 'solutions'. So sometimes alternative referents such as religion and myth were found to be effective in given situations. In all societies, the imperfections within the system become too obvious and too great, and eventually various mechanisms are evolved to deal with them. The strains, therefore, are held to call forth different kinds of response, both rational and non-rational. Ideology is regarded as a non-rational response in terms of ideas and symbols. But again, no satisfactory explanation is given as to why people respond to certain symbols rather than others, or why it is that some symbols gain and others lose their force in particular situations.

Ideologies, therefore, usually mirror the conditions in which men live. There is often a suspicious coincidence between the particular ideology which is advanced or adopted and the interests which it reflects. Indeed, it might be argued that ideologies are never adopted, but always *adapted*. That is to say, no system takes over or uses an ideology in its pristine and unadulterated form; it is usually modified – sometimes rather selectively – to suit the needs of the situation or regime. At the very least, the situation will condition its applicatory effectiveness. On the other hand, it is equally – if not more – difficult to sustain the view that all values dissolve into ideology. This strips ideology of any independent meaning and importance. It also shows the weakness of the Marxist position in that economic considerations do not cover all actions. There is no fixed hierarchy of values which insists that men must always prefer, say, economic advantage to social esteem. We will see from the following 'case studies' that ideology does exercise important influences, and does shape the course of human action in discernible ways.

Both Interest and Strain theories of ideology can be criticized on a number of grounds, not least of all for the presupposition that belief-systems are necessarily contrived, false, or – at very best – mistaken. Such explanations – however correct – as to *why* individuals act and think as they do may have nothing to do with the truth or falsity of *what* they say or do. Interest theories, particularly, are open to several objections. In their cruder forms they imply an inadequate psychology; they do not – perhaps cannot – explain *how* or *why* the ideology in question is accepted and believed. They seem unable to span the causal gap between a specific belief and a particular form of social response. In general terms, it is not known why some people sense a natural affinity with certain value-systems and others do not; why some react positively and others negatively to the same ideological stimuli. Interest theories do little to clarify this particular problem. How did it come about, for instance, that in ancient Greece the various warring city-states were prepared temporarily to forgo internecine strife for an armistice celebrated by a festival of Games? The periodic cessation of warfare makes sense in any system, but why in *this* form? And why do we not find this a common practice in other societies? To insist, as Interest theories must, that this was really a device to further the covert interests of a privileged minority is to explain neither the fascination which the Games had for ordinary Hellenes nor the binding solemnity of their ritual performance.

It can hardly be doubted that ideologies *can be* what Interest theorists say they are. They can be contrivances; they often act as exploitative mechanisms – but they are not always or necessarily either of these things. Ideologies can be 'used' to support the hierarchical status quo, to sanction injustices, and neutralize the possibilities for social agitation. But they can also be a source of intellectual enquiry and revolutionary zeal. Even institutionalized religion has been the generative agent of social reform. It can be both cohesive and devisive and to insist that it is any *one* kind of thing is to ignore its ambiguous role in actual historical circumstances. Indeed, there is ample evidence to show that ideologies do condition social relations and that those same ideologies really are believed by exploiters and exploited alike. The argument that 'interest' is a particular form of rational action which derives from a class position does not explain how (1) as a historical phenomenon, an ideology has been formulated, or (2) as a psychological phenomenon, it has been accepted and believed, or (3) as a social phenomenon, it has acquired

27

its power to persuade the credulous and actually influence affairs. In short, Interest theories, even when carefully defined, are inadequate if only because they can be made to cover every contingency, and thereby lose their meanings (Sutton 1956).

In general, ideologies do command attention where other systems of explanation are found to be cognitively inadequate or emotionally unsatisfactory. But the influence of ideologies on the wider social process defies simple calculation. As Jorge Lorrain has argued, ideology 'is one of the most equivocal and elusive concepts . . . in the social sciences' (Lorrain 1979: 13). Ideologies derive from values which, in turn, may be expressed as beliefs. These are not usually susceptible of empirical verification. It is impossible to quantify a value or calculate an influence. It is even difficult to correlate the holding of any belief with a given life-style or a particular pattern of behaviour. But the difficulties involved in trying to isolate the determinative potential of the belief-variable should not detract from its importance. A knowledge of men's fundamental beliefs will not explain everything about their actions in the real world, and it may not always be possible to specify the precise contribution of ideology to the social order, but even though its 'nature' is hard to define, its effects especially in relation to war and conquest are, as we shall see, both subtle and pervasive.

Section III

PERCEPTIONS OF 'THE ENEMY'

INTRODUCTION

In this section of the discussion, we are going to examine the relationship between religious and secular ideas and the conduct of war. In particular we will look at various ideological stances which are taken in relation to 'the enemy'. After this short introduction there is a series of case studies covering twelve substantive areas.

As we shall see, in practice it is not always easy to distinguish between societies characterized by a religious ideology and those motivated by clear secular considerations. And even where mundane concerns seem to be paramount as with, say, Nazism or Maoism, the underlying ideologies may well have quasi-religious overtones. Similarly, it is not always possible to make a simple distinction between predatory and non-predatory peoples. An apparently non-predatory people may, in certain circumstances, become increasingly predatory simply as a survival mechanism. And in particular social circumstances, a relatively non-aggressive people may become expansionistic. This might be said of the Phoenicians of Lebanon who were originally merchant adventurers rather than military adventurers, but who became expansionistic as Carthaginians in a particularly competitive social context. A people with what were initially modest territorial or economic ambitions might well begin to flex its muscles after some signal success against a weaker neighbouring state or – better still – against a rival state which had originally been held in some awe as a stronger foe. An unanticipated conquest can herald unbounded possibilities – as with the Muslim Arabs of the seventh century AD. Similarly, a reputably pacifist people may develop aggressive tendencies given sufficient provocation; this happened with the notably easy-going Pueblos of New

29

Mexico in relation to the Spanish invaders. Successful predatoriness can easily develop into imperialism.

No matter how blurred the line is, therefore, between predatory and expansionistic in some instances, and recognizing that one may shade into the other, there are some societies which have been unambiguously aggressive in both policy and practice, but each had its own individuality, and its own singular motivations for war.

Aggressive activity is generated in a number of ways, and undertaken for a number of reasons. It is, therefore, crude and unsophisticated to insist on seeing aggression as any one kind of a thing. Given that motives are almost invariably mixed, and that the mix differs in different situations, we need to analyse our societies with care. Furthermore, we must not overlook the important distinction – which was first made, as far as we know, by the Greek historian, Thucydides – between the immediate causes of war and the underlying causes of war. Similarly, there is the distinction between aims and policies. The general aims and objectives of a Spartan campaign, for example, may be very similar to those of, say, a Roman campaign, but the underlying policies of the two societies can be seen to be very different indeed.

The societies we are going to discuss display important differences, but all were notoriously aggressive in their own particular ways. The *Egyptians* of the New Kingdom (case study 1) – like, say, the French, English, and especially the Spanish in the New World – were essentially military adventurers, whereas the *Carthaginians* (case study 3) would fall into the category of merchant adventurers who became militaristic almost by default. They developed a taste for empire in special economic circumstances. The *Zulu* (case study 9), who were one of the most aggressive peoples in African tribal society, and who were challenged by the intrusion of the British and the Dutch, may be contrasted with the Americans, who were themselves the intruders in Vietnam. Like the British, French, and other colonizing European powers, the Americans may be regarded as the quintessential military imperialists. Their actions – more recently in Middle America – are strangely reminiscent of those of the early *Athenians* (case study 10) who created an empire ostensibly to impose democratic forms on sometimes unwilling states.

There are certain societies which we must consider that are often thought of as militaristic *par excellence*. But again there are important shades of difference. The *Mongols* (case study 7) were unquestionably one of the most rapacious peoples that the medieval world had the misfortune to meet. They certainly edge out the Assyrians in the ferocity of their campaigns and the merciless treatment of their victims. The *Spartans* (case study 2), on the other hand, were essentially political hegemonists. Above all else, they wanted to be first among ostensible equals. It is said that a Spartan feared nothing except the law. They were a highly disciplined people who have enjoyed a rather bad press; perhaps they are due for popular re-evaluation. They can be usefully compared with the *Romans* (case study 4) who were the great unifiers of the ancient world. Like the Persians before them, they could be amazingly tolerant and flexible on all sorts of issues, but calculatingly and meticulously cruel to those who dared to question their authority. In societies such as these, there was no pretence at furthering ideological conversion, no crusading spirit, but a concentration on hard socio-economic realities – you get what you can take, and take what you can hold.

It is interesting to compare the *Chinese Maoists* (case study 11) and the *Nazis* (case study 12), with their particular predilections for class and race respectively. The Maoists were a revolutionary force, mainly within the confines of their own homeland, who were keen to propagate a civic ideology with ruthless efficiency. There are here affinities with the Khmer Rouge in Cambodia who took political conviction to its 'logical' conclusion by the extermination of their class enemies. It is after this group of studies that it will be instructive to look at the disturbing incidence of massacre and genocide, and the entire phenomenon of 'New Order' politics.

It is here that a consideration of ideology is so important. Religion in particular is often regarded as an exalted abstraction which does not play a direct part in everyday affairs but merely *reacts* to 'real' socio-economic situations. Marx, for example, whilst acknowledging that religion had consolatory functions as the 'opium of the people', also argued that it was just part of the superstructural icing on the substructural cake. Yet, at times, he does not seem to be at all clear about this, and credits religious ideologies with the sinister role of clouding social awareness as well as anaesthetizing people to their social condition. As we have seen, for the contemporary French Marxist, Louis Althusser, religion does sometimes have a dominant role but never a determinant role in society – this is reserved for the supremely important economic factor. On the other hand, for perhaps the greatest of Marx's successors, the German sociologist Max Weber, religion could be influential, and actually determine the course of economic development. He tried to demonstrate this in his monumental but much debated study (*The Protestant Ethic and the Spirit of Capitalism*) which indicated a relationship between the emergence of Protestant Christianity and the rise of capitalism in Europe in the post-medieval era.

Even a cursory survey of the history of war suggests that both these approaches contribute something to our understanding of ideology – and the ways in which it interacts with military practice. As we shall see, this occurs in two main ways: either it acts as the rationale for military attitudes and expansionist policies, even though their effective causes appear to be of a quite different order, or it constitutes the imperative itself. Wars either can be ideological in kind, or are simply explained in ideological terms, or they are most probably a subtle amalgam of both. Here we are going to look at these various forms: each of our studies presents us with shades of difference which actually illuminate the central thesis that ideologies enshrine a complex nexus of values which are expressed as belief, and that belief affects action and is not just the intellectualization of the need for action. Deeds (action) are not always prior to words (ideas). Value-ideas do change things and are not necessarily or always changed by things. This is no more evident than in the practice of war even where it is ostensibly in the pursuit of socio-economic goals. Ideologies can both initiate and validate this activity, and condition indelible attitudes towards the 'enemy'.

It is in case studies 5, 6, and 8 that we are confronted by the phenomenon of religious ideology in its classic forms. In the first of these (case study 5), concerning the early *Israelites*, we will see how the notion of ritual purity provides not only a motive for military action but also a justification for a policy of annihilation. The term 'genocide' would be a misnomer in this context; technically it should only be used to denote a *racial* extermination programme, and this was not the case with the Israelites. They were obviously bent on destroying the 'pagans' of their time, but it is extremely difficult to decide to what extent their motivations were purely ideological and to what extent they were actually territorial – simply clearing the way for an Israelite settlement of the land. This is examined in some detail, and although religious ideology is given a prominent place in the analysis, we will see that mundane considerations cannot be ruled out entirely.

In case study 6, that of the *Crusaders*, we come much closer to what might be construed as 'holy war'. Again, because motives can never be entirely 'pure', we find that material gain is mixed – indeed, perhaps even confused – with religious sentiments. The desire to rid the Holy Land of the infidel was clearly a compelling reason for the Crusades and not simply a justifying principle. But in this case, we find a complicating factor. Here – and this is quite distinct from the Israelite situation – we have the intrusion of knightly codes and martial status which both modified and vitiated the behavioural dimension of the campaigns. The account shows that it is often difficult to square the lofty aspirations of Christian virtue with the actual conduct of the Crusaders; and their treatment of the vanquished was hardly consonant with the noble ideals of Christian chivalry.

Case study 8, relating to the *Aztecs* of Mexico, is quite different. Here we probably come nearest to the idea of pure religious motivation. The Aztecs did not go to war to destroy unbelievers; in fact, most of their enemies had very similar religious practices, though – arguably – they did not pursue them with quite the same rigour and consistency as the Aztecs. Yet the Aztecs did launch military campaigns for religious reasons. These could be construed as wars of extermination, but not in the conventional sense. The primary objective in battle was to secure prisoners to sacrifice to the gods. Again, religion was alloyed with political and economic motives yet, as the discussion shows, these do not really explain the bizarre singularity of Aztec behaviour.

1

THE EGYPTIANS OF THE NEW KINGDOM

The enemy as non-people

Egypt and Mesopotamia are regarded as the world's two great formative civilizations and are consequently designated as 'archaic societies' (Parsons 1966). Both were riverine civilizations, Egypt itself being dominated and sustained by what the Greek historian Herodotus called 'the gift of the Nile'. Indeed, Egyptians spent their time in 'intimate symbiosis with the river'. In a land with negligible rainfall, the annual inundations commencing in July became the focus of practical activity and reverential concern.

Egypt developed in significantly different ways from Mesopotamia. Certain cultural traits suggested that it was not entirely immune to influences from the Tigris–Euphrates area, but the appropriation of these diffused cultural elements in no way seems to have determined the developmental patterns of the Nile civilization. Egyptian society, possibly because of its early relative isolation, evolved its own unique identity and remained culturally homogeneous for the best part of three thousand years.

It is customary – and to some extent useful – to divide the history of ancient Egypt into thirty-three dynasties dating from c. 3100 BC when the kingdoms of Upper (southern) Egypt and Lower (northern) Egypt were united under a common ruler. By Dynasty 3, i.e. c. 2700 BC, with the beginning of what is traditionally termed the Old Kingdom, there was a fully developed and recognizable Egyptian culture, including hieroglyphic writing, monumental architecture, extensive bureaucratic organization under a god-king, all supported by a highly elaborated religious system. The Old Kingdom was the main Pyramid Age. These amazing structures involved a vast labour force which was possibly mobilized on an annual corvée basis. The most impressive of these structures are at Gizeh in northern Egypt and date from the 4th Dynasty. These are the pyramids of Khufu (Cheops), Khafre (whose features may be immortalized in the Sphinx), and Menkaure, and date from c.

2500 BC. The Great Pyramid of Khufu is one of the most incredible structures known to history. It covers about 13 acres and its mass is in the order of 6 million tons. The stone blocks weigh over 2 tons each, and the original limestone facing was so accurately worked that it would have been difficult to get a knife blade between the joins. The pyramid itself, containing the tomb of the king, was the centrepiece of a complex of buildings including two temples and a stone causeway from the Nile some 550 yards long. Herodotus – admittedly writing two thousand years later – says that this alone took ten years to build. The pyramids and their attendant structures are not only a tribute to the considerable – one might almost say, anachronistic – technical skill of the construction engineers, they are also mute testimony to the overarching power and control by the state of all necessary resources.

After Dynasty 6 there was a breakdown in the established social order, possibly due to the rising power of the nomarchs (district governors). There followed a long interval of dislocation, usually designated the First Intermediate period, which lasted for some 150 years. Central authority was restored with Dynasties 11 and 12 (the Middle Kingdom). This revival began in Thebes, and was led not by one of the nobility but by a member of the provincial aristocracy, Mentuhotep, who eventually became king. Little remains of the architectural achievements of this period, especially the famed Labyrinth at Fayum which Herodotus says was the greatest of all the constructional masterpieces, but what there is testifies to the exquisite quality of the workmanship. The Middle Kingdom lasted only about 200 years after which there was another phase of social disruption and widespread unrest when Egypt was invaded by tribes of Semitic nomads collectively known as the Hyksos (Shepherd Kings).

The full flowering of Egyptian culture came with the expulsion of the Hyksos. This heralded the New Kingdom or Empire period (Dynasties 18–20). The economy was buoyant, political organization was stable, and art and literature flourished. Building and architecture generally reached new heights of grandeur, perhaps the most notable achievements being the extensive temple complex of Amun at Karnak which was large enough to contain five European cathedrals. It was the 19th Dynasty that witnessed the building of the gigantic rock temple and figures at Abu Simbel, the inspiration – and presumption? – of Rameses II (the Great). During the New Kingdom the state was at its most powerful – *and* most aggressive. Again the nation's fortunes had been restored by the Theban aristocracy and the capital was actually transferred to Thebes with the founding of the 18th Dynasty. This period, c. 1550–c. 1100 BC, saw the accession of the Ramesside kings and the expansion of the empire into Israel and the Lebanon. Until this time the relatively isolated position of Egypt had presumably made such policies unnecessary. But with the growing need to repel the incursions of would-be invaders and check the depredations of border tribes, it became a short step from defence to offence. The task of reconstruction became one of expansion. Having mobilized the necessary forces to oust the Hyksos and reconquer Nubia and the traditionally held territories, the implementation of an imperialist programme became a natural progression. Tighter control was exerted over the regional governors, and the centrifugal tendencies of earlier periods were minimized by authoritarian government.

By c. 1400 BC, Egypt had extended its empire south into Ethiopia, some thousand miles from the Delta, and had even established indirect trading relationships with central Africa. Its influence was felt as far afield as Cyprus, Canaan, and Syria; we know that it was trading on the Lebanese coast as early as Old Kingdom times, and it may well be that the town of Byblos was an Egyptian colony. Certainly, there were strong commercial ties; with its acute shortage of wood, Egypt needed to import cedar from the Lebanon, particularly, to build ships. There were, however, limits to Egyptian expansion, and it encountered resistance in Anatolia (Turkey) and Babylonia where other powers were periodically exercising their own military muscles.

At the height of its power, ancient Egypt was very much the province of the Pharaoh. In fact, the Egyptians had no word for 'state' and this may have been because all the significant aspects of the state were concentrated in the person of the king. The monarchy was thought to be as old as the world, and although for most of its history Egypt was administered by a vast bureaucracy of officials, it is impossible to divorce the real exercise of power from the position and authority of the Pharaoh. Similarly, there was no equivalent of our term 'law'. Egyptians maintained that 'law proceeds from the mouth of the Pharaoh'. But even the king ruled in accordance with precedent, and his edicts had to conform to the requirements of ma'at (often translated as 'truth' or 'justice'), the principle of eternal balance and harmony which was believed to inform the entire cosmic order. Ultimately, of course, this was very much a matter of interpretation, and the cultural longevity of Egypt testifies to the fact that, by and large, successive monarchs did what had always been done.

There were obvious inconsistencies in all this. The king, as a divine being, though the sole source of law and authority, also relied upon other gods for supernatural help and oracular direction. Furthermore, even god-kings have to delegate responsibilities through a variety of officials. Thus the king worked through the vizier and an army of officials, the requisite members of the military establishment, and representatives of the priesthoods; in all, an extensive and highly centralized organization. But this mediation of divine authority by humanly

36

fallible agents presented a paradoxical situation: its operation detracted from divine absolutism and – depending on the ruler and the circumstances obtaining at any one time – served to neutralize the effectiveness of autocracy. After all, even arbitrary despots can have their edicts 'derailed' by an efficient and determined bureaucracy.

This can be illustrated by one of the most intriguing periods of Egyptian history. In the middle years of the fourteenth century BC, a revolutionary change in religious ideas and practices was elaborated by Amenhophis IV who later came to be known as Akhenaten. Indeed, he and his immediate family introduced a new pharaonic style in art and manners as well as religion. He effectively downgraded the elaborate polytheism of Egypt which included a pantheon of about 2,000 deities, and initiated a form of solar monotheism, the worship of the sun's disc, the Aten. More controversially, he challenged the established priesthood of Amun-Re, the sun-god, who – somewhat strangely – appears to have been regarded as a separate deity. To modern minds this seems rather contrived, but it may be that the difference of emphasis reflected political as well as religious ideas and aspirations. The seat of government was moved from Thebes to a new capital on the Nile roughly equidistant from Thebes, the centre of the Amun-Re cult, and Lower Egypt. This involved the establishment of a new court and possibly a new administration. But archaeological investigation indicates that the new worship probably had little general appeal; the mass of the people still continued with their traditional religious practices.

Akhenaten reigned for about seventeen years, and after his death there was a pronounced reversal in religious thinking. His immediate successor, a young man, Smenkhakare, appears to have died in somewhat suspicious circumstances after a reign of only three years. He was followed as king by his brother, the now familiar figure of Tutankhaten who was only 9 at his accession, and therefore hardly able to exert any real influence on the court or the resurgent priesthood. A counter-revolution was underway, and he changed his name to Tutankhamun – reflecting the movement back to the Amun-Re cult. He too died young, possibly at the age of 19; how – again – we do not know. What we do know is that at this period the memory of Akhenaten was execrated and his religion vilified.

Akhenaten is a difficult person to assess. He may have been little more than a political opportunist who wanted to break the power of the priesthood and restore the practice of absolute monarchy, or he may have been a failed visionary. Whichever he was, his reforms were far from popular, and after his death his city was abandoned, his tombs and temples were destroyed and inscriptions erased. In fact, attempts were made to eradicate all knowledge of Akhenaten and his cult from history, and would have succeeded had it not been for some chance discoveries in recent times.

Records do not tell us as much as we would like about the actual operation of the Egyptian state, or of the many changes that took place over its long history. We do not know that it was hierarchically organized with government control of treasuries, granaries, etc., but with a small measure of autonomy in the 'outer' administrative districts (nomes). Both central and provincial administration were the tasks of the viziers as chief officers of state, one for Upper Egypt, and another for Lower Egypt where there were separate councils of dignitaries. Religious functions, on the other hand, were the special prerogative of the king who was also chief priest, but because he, though divine, was hardly omnipresent, he had to act through his consecrated representatives at the various temple complexes throughout Egypt. Each town of any size had at least one temple, and at the large religious centres there were many temples where the various state deities were worshipped. Each temple was a minor industry. Each had its estates including vineyards, gardens, and servants (serfs?) to tend the land. Some even had their own military and naval personnel in addition to their extensive bureaucracies. The immense wealth of some of these temples, especially those dedicated to Amun, also generated hosts of minor functionaries ranging from cadres of scribes to superintendents of transport, storekeepers, linen-masters, and modest herdsmen and sunshade-bearers.

The king was no mere cypher, and his authority was not simply a fiction. Strange as his divinity may sound to modern ears, there is every reason to suppose that it really was believed to a lesser or greater degree by both officials, whose interests were undoubtedly served by such beliefs, and the laity for whom it was the operative ideology. Yet there must have been some doubts or, at least, rationalizations on the part of *some* members of the community when one realizes that, with one qualified exception, every known royal tomb was violated for its wealth *in ancient times*, despite the awful natural and supernatural sanctions which could be invoked for such crimes. For the unimpressed, religious sanctity clearly took second place to economic ambition.

What could happen as a result of sacrilege can be seen more specifically from a case of believed regicide which took place c. 1164 BC. The Pharaoh in question, Rameses III, may have died as the result of a harem conspiracy in which court officials and members of the royal family were involved. As far as we can ascertain, his death – perhaps by poison – was attributed to 'witchcraft', and the plotters were 'overtaken by their crimes'. The 'lesser' participants had their noses and ears cut off, those more deeply implicated were executed, and those of royal blood were allowed to take their own lives.

Law was not carefully codified, as it was in, say, contemporary Mesopotamia. As we have seen, in principle, the king alone determined the law, but this was operationalized throughout the state by duly convened courts. In theory, the law was constantly 'renewed' by the will of the Pharaoh whilst, in practice, there were accepted regulations which covered specific situations especially in relation to property transactions, inheritance, and so forth. Oppressive treatment by tax collectors and the minor bureaucracy seems not to have been unusual, although they were subject to severe punishments if found guilty of corruption or disloyalty. Little wonder that they were always anxious to declare their probity and conscientiousness. Inscriptional 'evidence' – such as it is – of their blameless service is not an uncommon feature in their tombs, where it functions as a declaration to the gods, and an insurance for the afterlife.

The actual implementation of the law is something we would like to know more about. Judges had a reputation for harsh punishments no matter what class of criminal was involved, although – as we have seen – for highly placed dignitaries some form of 'voluntary' suicide seems to have been imposed for capital offences. Disfigurement was more common for serious crimes, as was also deportation to the mines and quarries where life, as Hobbes reported, could certainly be nasty, short, and brutish. The death penalty appears to have been used sparingly, and was mainly reserved for treasonable offences, particularly rebellion. In general, it appears that the entire politico-economic apparatus was designed to ensure the smooth running and continuation of the current social order. Obviously it was not perfect. This is evidenced at the highest levels by occasional incidents involving assassination and usurpation. In general, though, despite fluctuating fortunes, the traditional system was successfully perpetuated, and during the Empire period this was due in no small measure to the efficiency of the Egyptian military machine.

In such a long-lived society it was inevitable that the military systems of the state could change considerably over time. The military forces of the Old and Middle Kingdoms had a somewhat amateur appearance when compared with those of the expansionist New Kingdom. During the Old Kingdom there was no standing army. The central administration maintained only a relatively small corps of troops to police the capital and to act as a body-guard for the royal family. When large-scale campaigns were planned, the administration had to rely on contingents of militia from the nomes (administrative districts) of the state. Temple police might also be mobilized for military duties, and the whole operation might well be commanded by civic officials with little or no formal military training or expertise. In the Middle Kingdom period, more professionalism was introduced. A small regular army was created, again to be supplemented by local levies which were commanded by high-born officials who owed direct allegiance to the king. Free citizens were enrolled for possible military service in a form of age-set system. Large-scale hostilities were still a thing of the future. War consisted mainly of loosely organized forays into neighbouring territories, sometimes for gain but often to punish raiding tribesmen, especially on the Nubian and Libyan borders.

The Middle Kingdom effectively came to an end, as we have seen, with the invasion of nomadic peoples, possibly from the north-east, collectively known as the Hyksos (perhaps, more correctly, 'rulers of foreign lands'). They dominated most of Egypt from c. 1730 to c. 1570 BC (Dynasties 13–17), and they brought with them certain military innovations, particularly the composite bow and the skilled use of chariots. The eventual overthrow of the Hyksos ushered in a new period of expansionism which led eventually to the creation of the Empire.

During this period both the army and the naval forces were increased. Two large armies were permanently stationed in Upper and Lower Egypt, supplemented by a police force consisting mainly of Nubians. The actual numbers are uncertain, but it is unlikely that the whole army exceeded 30,000 men including contingents from various subject territories such as Libya and Sardinia. The Pharaoh was the supreme commander of the army, but normally authority was delegated to the army council consisting of high-ranking military personnel and officials of state, often including the crown prince. The general staff saw to the day-to-day running of a campaign, but the inspiration for any particular enterprise was duly attributed to the divine power of the king. Even a Pharaoh such as Amenhotep III (d. c. 1360 BC), who had a long and peaceful reign, had – by tradition – to be depicted as a warrior-king. He probably only took to the field once, and this against some wretched Nubian tribesmen who had staged an uprising. But he, or his sycophantic 'biographers', sought to give the impression of a conquering hero without whose example and inspiration the enterprise would almost certainly have faltered. Inscriptions show him riding over prostrate foes in his chariot, and speak of him subjugating foreign lands by the might of 'his valiant sword'. But his aggressive activities did not actually extend much beyond the successful lion-hunt.

Army officers were normally drawn from the upper echelons of educated men who, like the members of the bureaucracy, had been trained for positions of responsibility since childhood. It was possible to be promoted from the ranks; this undoubtedly provided a convenient channel of mobility for able men, especially those from a modest family background. However, it must be pointed out that some evidence indicates that there was some doubt about the desirability of the army as a career. Discipline was strict, life was often harsh and precarious; little wonder that some contemporary texts express reservations about the lot of the soldier. It is perhaps significant that as the Empire developed – and particularly as it declined – there was an increasing tendency to use more and more mercenaries for military duties, an expedient which was later to prove a mixed blessing.

But the military life did have its rewards. Courage and enterprise could be profitable for the successful. Campaigning could often result in the distribution of booty such as women, slaves, and jewellery. Achievement could result in advancement and the allocation of lands, and it is not surprising to learn that in the later Empire certain military leaders actually found their way to the throne itself. This may have been the case with Herihor (d. *c.* 1085 BC) who came from obscure beginnings, rose to become designated 'commander of the Army', and later Vizier of Upper Egypt and High Priest of Amun, and eventually the founder of the 21st Dynasty.

Egyptian soldiers were armed with the usual array of weaponry available in a still predominantly Bronze Age society. The weapons themselves were supplied from state arsenals – a distinctive feature of highly centralized societies – although the actual dress of the troops was mainly determined on a class basis. Protective armour was largely missing from all classes, but officers and high-status personnel were distinguished by emblems of rank. The most important innovation was the introduction of the light war-chariot which was customarily manned by a driver and his armed companion; it was rather a fragile contraption, but quite effective on the flat terrain areas of the Middle East. What seems strange from a modern perspective is that the Egyptians did not have a cavalry, as such, until a much later period. This has been attributed – probably quite wrongly – to the 'fact' that they possibly found the actual riding of horses repulsive.

Campaigning was a somewhat routinized affair in the ancient world. Egyptian military procedures were no exception. Normally it would begin in springtime before the enemy had harvested their crops and when they were therefore at their most vulnerable. The invasion itself would be both a predatory expedition and an impressive display of power which was designed to intimidate other subject peoples. Enemy lands were often plundered and put under tribute, and sometimes they were also put under an obligation to supply scarce goods such as wood and metals on a more or less permanent basis. Sometimes hostages were taken from the nobility of conquered peoples and even egyptianized as insurance against possible further insurrection. Towns were not always razed, nor were their populations always enslaved or massacred, although obviously there were certain infamous cases of indiscriminate slaughter; so much depended on the policy or caprice of the Pharaoh concerned. Amenhotep II (d. *c.* 1406 BC), for example, tells of how he crushed the skulls of his royal opponents and hanged their bodies on a city wall in order to discourage possible rebellion. And how in Syria he single-handedly drove into an enemy stronghold and returned with twenty severed hands hanging from the foreheads of his horses.

The religious implications of Egyptian military activity are all too evident. The mystical cursing of enemies, the triumph songs after victory, all have marked religious overtones. The texts are replete with claims of military prowess, divinely bestowed, especially on the part of warrior-pharaohs such as Rameses the Great:

> At the cry of my despair swiftly the god came to me
> Took my hand and gave me strength
> Till my might was that of a hundred thousand men. . . .
>
> (Murray 1963: 209)

Even allowing for some measure of exaggeration, the conclusion is inescapable that the aid of the gods was sought for all military expeditions, and it was the gods who were to be praised for military success. In practice, this really meant adulation of the divine Pharaoh who was both the 'colleague' and favoured representative of the deities. When hostilities ceased, and peace negotiations began, especially with particularly powerful enemies, it was always done with due religious deference. The gods were dutifully called upon to solemnize the occasion, and appropriate records were kept as witness of their good intentions. So, for example, after the inconclusive battle of Kadesh (c. 1295 BC) against the Hittites, the peace treaty was written on two silver tablets, one of which was taken to Hatti (modern Turkey) and the other to Egypt and laid 'at the feet of Re', the sun deity.

We can see similar sentiments expressed later in relation to the invasions of the 'Sea Peoples' or, as the Egyptian texts call them, 'the northerners in their islands'. These were a loose confederation of tribes who descended not only upon Egypt, but also upon much of the Near East about 1200 BC. They comprised numerous peoples most of whom are not easily identifiable from the texts, but almost certainly included Philistines (Cretans?), Sicilians, Sardinians, and possibly Achaeans (Greeks). It was a time of ominous, restless movements of peoples from the north and west, possibly born of the need for grazing and living space rather than mere plunder. It was also the time of the break-up of Mycenean civilization in Greece, and the period associated in tradition with the siege and destruction of Troy, but we cannot be sure if there was any connection between these events, and, if so, what was their actual significance.

The 'Sea Peoples' overran Cyprus, and parts of Anatolia (Turkey) and Syria. And, no doubt attracted by the rich pickings in Egypt, made at least three attempts to invade by both land and sea between c. 1190 and c. 1185 BC. Indirectly, they also precipitated further hostilities between Egypt and her troublesome neighbours, the Libyans, who the Egyptians called the Meshwesh. These were no ordinary predatory raids; the invaders came with their wagons and families, presumably to stay, and were only defeated with great difficulty by the Egyptians.

The texts are quick to glorify the virtues of the Pharaoh in all this. He is compared with Mont, the warrior-god, as he declares about those who reached the boundary of his territory, 'their seed is not . . . their souls are finished for all eternity. And those who arrived by sea at the river mouths were trapped, pinioned and their corpses butchered. . . .' There is even some evidence that the enemy were sometimes slain as a form of sacrifice, as we hear that god Amun, who granted victory, 'did not fail to receive his accustomed sacrifice of living victims' (Breasted 1906–7: 478).

Military success was one of the primary tasks of the monarch. His achievements were frequently extolled in temple inscriptions, and also represented in artistic form in many victory reliefs. The Pharaoh is not unusually depicted as a giant figure which dwarfs both the enemy and his own troops. The enemy are both symbolically and actually seen as non-people. They are not members of the 'favoured land' but – whether they know it or not – are, nevertheless, subject to the will of the god-king who has ordained their subjugation. The victory is his by virtue of his personal attributes and his divine will.

This, at least, was the theory. The Pharaoh's god-like qualities were calculated to ensure success and make him invincible in military encounters. It goes without saying that this was not always seen to work. Success was not always certain. But even this could be rationalized in ideological terms. Indeed, it could be argued that there was an ambiguous relationship between militarism and religious ideology. On the one hand, military success seems to have been regarded as a proof of divinity, yet there remains a suspicion that this insistent emphasis on the martial prowess and unshakeable resolve of the Pharaoh was a form of compensation for what appears to be some diminution in the acceptance of his divinity, especially in the later days of the Empire.

Regardless of doubts and qualifications, ancient Egypt comes as close as any society ever has to having a system of ultimate explanation. The miscellany of polytheistic religious beliefs were contained and harnessed by the state in the worship of the Pharaoh. Despite the heterogeneity of supernaturalistic ideas, ideological praxis centred on the authority of the king. Policy, particularly military policy, was legitimized and validated in religious terms, and control was actualized through the state in the person of the Pharaoh. It cannot be denied that there *were* conflicts and divisions, sometimes between the priests and the military, sometimes between factions representing different temple hierarchies. But overall, this was a long-lived and stable society.

Egypt's programme of military expansionism was largely conditioned by external circumstances, but the rationale for these actions is inextricably bound up with religious belief. In its early days of relative geographical isolation, it enjoyed a reasonably peaceful existence. Later, partly out of ambition and partly from military necessity, it became increasingly aggressive and imperialistic. Then, having savoured the fruits of power and military success, it pursued determined expansionist policies. This was done quite obviously for the material benefits it brought, but it was also done to preserve the inviolability of its unique and divinely ordained system. How else is one to explain its theological obsessions and the focus of its cultural and artistic achievements? The evidence suggests that the Egyptian system was not primarily cynical and opportunistic, but was informed by the conviction of its own supramundane importance – its mission to maintain the harmony of the cosmic order.

2

THE SPARTANS
The enemy as political obstacles

Sparta, and its unusual social institutions, has exerted a considerable fascination on historians and social theorists alike. Some affinities to the Spartan system can be found in other states which were tribally related such as Dorian Crete, and – strangely enough – in societies widely separated in space time such as the warlike Zulu of the early nineteenth century AD. Yet in its own way Sparta was unique. In many respects, it was deliberately archaic; for instance, it adamantly refused to adopt coinage which it was thought might have a corrupting influence on its people. In a sense, it was a 'closed society', reminiscent in some ways of certain of today's 'restricted' countries. It was apprehensive about innovations that might undermine the fabric of its singular social system. Yet, in other respects, it was regarded as being culturally superior, and was much admired by relatively liberal thinkers in other Greek states. This can be seen especially in the work of the historian Xenophon and the philosopher Plato, who was undoubtedly influenced by its institutions in the writing of his avant-garde treatise, *The Republic*.

The polis, loosely translated as city-state, was the central organizational entity of ancient Greek life. A Greek was known by his polis affiliations; in some states like Athens it was not possible to be a full citizen unless you were born of citizen parents, and impersonation of a citizen by, say, a resident alien was such a serious offence that the culprit could be sold into slavery. Indeed, one of the most powerful sanctions in the social life of a citizen was that of atimia, which could lead to the deprivation of citizenship rights for a designated period. Without the ability to participate in public life, a man was literally without honour in such a status-conscious society. Sparta, however, was not a polis in the conventional sense. Of course, it had political autonomy, but it was unlike many poleis in topographical and architectural terms. It was not the usual walled city with a central acropolis (high town), both of which were customary for defence purposes. Instead, it was a group of villages which formed a kind of large country settlement in the midst of one of the most fertile areas in southern

Greece. It was actually extremely poor in public buildings, and certainly had nothing approaching the impressive temple complex found on the Athenian acropolis. The contemporary observer, Thucydides, wrote, 'If one day all that remained of it were its sanctuaries and the foundations of its public buildings, posterity would find it hard to believe that its power ever matched its reputation' (Thucydides 1972).

Sparta proper was the principal centre of Laconia, and was situated close to the banks of the Eurotas which is one of the few rivers in Greece that does not dry up in summer. It is in a vast valley which is bounded in the west by the Taygetos mountains and in the east by those of the Parnon chain. To the west of the Taygetos, in south-western Greece, lies Messenia, which had been occupied by the Spartans in about 715 BC and which acted as a reserve source of manpower and grain. To the north, Sparta was bounded by the territories of Arcadia and Elis, and to the north-east by the Argolid, the lands controlled by the city of Argos whose citizens were the traditional enemies of Sparta even though they were of the same ethnic extraction.

This entire area, which is cut off from the rest of Greece by the Isthmus of Corinth, is usually termed the Peloponnese. It had been earlier occupied by the Myceneans, the people associated in Homer's *Iliad* with the siege of Troy. But from about 1200 BC, waves of warlike invaders, who came in all probability from the Balkans, brought what is perhaps erroneously known as a 'Dark Age' to Greece. The Spartans were part of this Dorian family of tribes often referred to as Lacadamonians.

In trying to account for the unusual nature of Spartan political and social organization, it is tempting to cite this qualified geographical isolation. But this could be no more than a contributory cause. Other poleis were also relatively isolated, but did not develop in the same way. Also, Sparta did expand into other areas, notably Messenia, Arcadia, and the Argolid, so it was not really that cut off from the rest of Greece. But this expansionism was limited. Unlike some of the large trading poleis such as Corinth and Aegina, Sparta founded few colonies other than Tarentum (Taranto) in Italy and encouraged few settlements other than those on the islands of Melos and Crete. Colonial expansion was extremely common in Greece in the eighth century BC and was usually occasioned by political upheavals, the need for resources and markets, and – not least – internal demographic pressures. But Sparta had no serious population problem because there was no scarcity of suitable land, especially after the annexation of Messenia. Furthermore, its policy of non-colonization meant the retention of the young – who in other states tended to emigrate – and this enabled it to build and maintain a large standing army.

Early Sparta was apparently ruled by a military aristocracy, and seems not to have been very different from many other poleis in its social and political organization. But the records are extremely sparse, and much has to be inferred from later writers. The reforms which changed Sparta into such a singular state are traditionally associated with Lycurgos, who is said to have lived *c.* 650 BC. Lycurgos is a very shadowy figure and his reforms may represent a gradual oligarchic change rather than one man's political ideas. There is always the tendency among some ancient peoples to personify agents of change in order to validate current social practices. These reforms were probably instituted as a reaction to the economic and political prospects that were presented by the conquest of Messenia and the new wealth that the country was beginning to enjoy. Increased prosperity meant pressure from the non-aristocratic elements for a share in the spoils, and this, in turn, threatened a breakdown in the traditional social order with the possible emergence of populists who would champion the people's cause. This was nipped in the bud by the development of a system which was a unique amalgam of oligarchy and selective democracy, and was quite unlike the participative democracy of Athens. The new system effectively reduced the possibilities for disruption, and gave the Spartan state considerable stability. From *c.* 650 BC she established a growing hegemony in Greece, and formed a league of loosely confederated states, with no formal constitution, which was dedicated to the suppression of both tyranny and democracy. Both were distrusted. (Like Socrates, the Spartans regarded one as potentially disruptive as the other.) All this was mainly achieved by alliances rather than military conquest – though possibly with the help of a little intimidation at the margins.

Many of these changes were retrospective in orientation. In effect, Sparta turned her back on the outside world and developed a system which, though not imposed upon her allies, influenced them indirectly in a number of ways. As one writer has put it, Sparta was 'admired but not imitated, an inspiration to political theorists, and a comfort to those who found democracy distasteful' (Andrewes 1976: 66).

The reforms that revolutionized Sparta are reflected in a three-tiered social structure consisting first and foremost of the Spartiates themselves who were known as the 'Equals' (homoioi) but who admitted certain gradations of authority within their ranks. They probably never numbered more than 9,000 yet were the real source of power within the state. In addition there were the perioikoi (literally, the living-around-ones) who were the non-Spartan citizens of largely autonomous communities within the Spartan sphere of influence who were ultimately subject to the dictates of the sovereign state. Perioikoi came in various economic classes and pursued different occupations, but they had to be available for military service should this be required. They also had to confine their interests to the administration of their own local communities as Sparta did not brook interference in its internal concerns. In effect, the perioikoi had to accept any decisions the parent state might make for them, and providing they were politically unambitious they could lead a moderately uneventful existence. But it should also be pointed out that Spartan officials did intervene in the affairs of the perioikoi from time to time, and in extreme circumstances could execute a perioikos without trial. Such was the fate of Spartan satellites.

Finally, there were the helots who were really slaves, though not by purchase or capture, but because they were members of the indigenous race that had inhabited the land when the Spartans arrived. These had been subjugated by the invaders, and henceforth their descendants had been forced to work for the Spartan state. Normally in Greece, slaves were the property of their masters, but helots were merely assigned to masters; they were owned by the state. Also it was not uncommon for slaves in other poleis – especially Athens – to be able to acquire or buy their freedom, but this was virtually impossible for a helot. He paid half his produce to his master, and was subject to considerable abuse and – if some early authorities are to be believed – if he was murdered his death would be considered inconsequential. Their actual living conditions may not have been markedly different from those of poor peasants, but they were always under the vigilant eye of the Spartan secret police, the Krypteia, and it is even rumoured that Spartan youths were occasionally encouraged to kill the odd helot as part of their military training. But helots were also feared. The oligarchy, on their annual resumption of office, formally re-declared war on them as if they were an undefeated enemy. In 464 BC, after a catastrophic earthquake, there was such a serious helot uprising that it took the Spartans, together with a contingent of Athenians, some five years to suppress. On another occasion (425 BC), this time during the Peloponnesian War, the Spartans could not afford a possible stab in the back so they devised a plan by which they effectively eliminated the potential opposition. Helots acted as body-servants to their Spartan overlords in the field, and under certain conditions were actually allowed to participate as troops. Thucydides reports that the Spartans

> offered freedom . . . to those [helots] who claimed to have served them best in war, thinking that those who came forward would be the likeliest to revolt. Some two thousand were selected, [garlanded] and paraded round the temples, as if set free, and then wiped out.
>
> (Thucydides 1972: 313)

Spartan political organization consisted of an unusual four-level hierarchy: a monarchy, an Ephorate, a Gerousia, and an Assembly. Most Greek states had dispensed with kingship ages before, but Sparta retained two hereditary kings who held office simultaneously. They had ritual as well as military duties, and were responsible for much of the administration of Sparta's dependent territories. Then there was the Ephorate which comprised five men, elected by the Spartan Assembly for one-year terms, who supervised the entire working of the state, especially the socialization and training of the young. They were probably the most important executive body in the Spartan system and, although they and the kings swore oaths of mutual co-operation, the relationship between them was sometimes very uneasy. When, for example, the case for war against Athens was debated, the urge for caution by the king was ignored in favour of a counter recommendation by an influential ephor. The king had temporized with his advisers over the decision to go to war; this he tried to avoid, or at least postpone. When the vote went against him, we have the strange situation of Spartan envoys still trying to persuade Athens to yield on certain points – almost as though war had not been declared.

Sharing the administration with the ephors was the Gerousia, the Council of (thirty) Elders of whom the kings were ex officio members. Except for the kings, the members of the Gerousia were all over 60 years of age – a considerable age in traditional societies – and were elected for life by the Assembly which consisted of all full citizens over 30 years of age. At Assembly level, there was something approaching complete equality. The citizens voted on general state issues, yet they were not responsible for legislation; it would appear that they did not actually debate any issues but merely approved recommendations from the higher legislative bodies. This was in complete contrast to the Athenians who debated every issue, and did not really recognize any legislative body higher than its Assembly (ecclesia).

The system thus had a seemingly unbalanced pluralistic quality. It had its monarchy – albeit with reduced functions; a limited democracy in its conception of the Equals – the Spartans themselves; and its oligarchy in the form of the Gerousia and particularly the ephors who were the real power in the land. This strange yet effective combination contributed towards Sparta's famed traditionality and political consistency which continued virtually intact for some five hundred years.

Perhaps the most important underlying value of Spartan society was that of *arete*, a word which is often translated as 'virtue', but is probably more accurately rendered as 'excellence'. *Arete* denoted not so much a general principle as excellence in specific things – in this case, military valour and prowess. It was reflected in popular religion and in traditional myths – especially those related to the culture-hero, Heracles. Quite possibly it had at least some of its roots in the highly competitive inter-poleis situation. State rivalries demanded the possession and display of military qualities and physical courage. For Sparta, *arete* meant being best at the military game.

The selection and training of Spartan youths started from birth. If there was any doubt about a child's suitability, it might be exposed after being presented to its father and a board of Elders. If it survived this test, it was deemed worthy to live. All children spent the first six years with their mothers and at 7 they were segregated, and boys were enrolled in a military company. Here they were in the charge of older boys who, in turn, were supervised by men. They were subjected to very strict regimental discipline which was calculated to harden the body and condition the mind, not least of all to the idea that all others were their military inferiors.

As part of their rigorous training programme, the boys were subject to a number of privations. They slept on rushes and were rarely allowed baths, which were regarded as effeminate; they wore only one garment, and were compelled to go barefoot summer and winter even though many of the mountain passes were often covered in snow during the winter months. They ate very simple food, and were encouraged to steal to supplement their meagre diet, but if they were caught they could be severely whipped. Indeed, part of their training included 'running the gauntlet' of men with whips, and it was not unknown for boys to die from this ordeal. Although virtually illiterate except for some knowledge of music (the flute) and dancing, they were taught to have good manners and always to display the required deferential respect to elders and superiors. In all, everything was done to inculcate what the Spartans saw as manly virtues which included temperance – drunkenness was seriously deplored – fortitude, and, above all, complete obedience.

To modern eyes, the one notable area of inconsistency was that of sexual mores. Sexual inversion between boys seems to have been encouraged or, at least, allowed – although the sources are not entirely clear on this issue. There was undoubtedly a tremendous emphasis on youthful beauty – unsurprising in societies where people age quickly and life expectancy is low, and there were certainly festivals in which boys were the object of attention, and the love of boys was a central preoccupation. But whether actual physical contacts were promoted or whether this homosexuality had a more 'spiritual' quality (as is implied in some of Plato's writings) is difficult to know. Plutarch, a near-contemporary, was also not sure: he suggests that the boys had no *hetero*sexual relations, 'they kept their youthful bloom pure and uncorrupted'. But he does go on to mention mixed wrestling with naked girls, which was perhaps a kind of quasi-heterosexual horseplay. Perhaps versatility was the thing.

Normal sexual relations were certainly expected in adults for at 20 a

Spartan male was compelled to marry. This would seem to put Spartan sexual norms on a par with those of other Greek states where sexual freedom also involved carefully prescribed limits to deviant sexuality. For example, in Athens homosexuality was recognized, but soliciting for boys was a civil offence, and *exclusive* homosexuality was a subject for criticism and ridicule. It was probably most common among military elites, notably in Sparta and Thebes. Youths were said to fight more valiantly in front of their lovers and admirers. In other states, there were no restrictions on sexual relations between legitimate heterosexual partners, but Spartan males lived in barracks and only visited their wives when they could. Apparently this was done surreptitiously with the authorities closing a blind eye to what was going on. The theory was that unlimited coitus was weakening, so if intercourse was only occasional it would produce healthier children. Xenophon even maintains that old men could invite younger men to use their wives to beget children for them; fathers of three sons were exempted from military service, and fathers of four from all 'state burdens'. It was extremely important for a man to beget a son to join the diminishing Spartan elite, and it is reported that Leonidas, who led the heroic but fateful stand of the 300 Spartans at Thermopylae, insisted that he only wanted men for this suicide mission who had at least one son to perpetuate the military traditions.

At 30, a man's training was complete and he was eligible for election to the Equals. If he failed, he was 'blackballed' – literally given a black ball – which marked him out as an inferior who would never be a full citizen. Once admitted to the Equals, he was released from the barracks and given a parcel of land on which he could settle with his family, but he was always on permanent standby for military service.

The position of women in this society was quite anomalous. They appear to have been given more freedom than in many other Greek states. In Athens, ostensibly a more liberal community, Spartan women were a byword for liberty and even laxity, as can be seen from Aristophanes' parody in *Lysistrata* in which the women are seriously advocating the withholding of all sexual favours until their husbands abandoned the war. Yet they are depicted in other source material as completely endorsing the warrior ideal. Their task was to produce healthy sons for the state, and to surrender them as mere children for eventual military service. Men must be taught to fight and die courageously. The greatest shame was to have a son who was a coward and who abandoned his weapons and his comrades; 'Bring back my son *with* his shield – if not bring him back *on* his shield.' The implication being that if he has no shield, don't bring him back at all.

Greek warfare changed relatively little over the centuries. In the early seventh century BC, battles of loose formations occasionally assisted by small cavalry contingents gave way to more tightly ordered phalanxes of heavily armed infantry, or 'hoplites'. There were still lightly armed troops such as slingers and archers who were sometimes imported mercenaries or resident aliens, but the development of the hoplite formations probably represented some democratization of the military compared with earlier times when the cavalry were the elite arm of the forces. As the city-states developed, so did their citizen armies. The ranks of the hoplites consisted mainly of small farmers and shopkeepers, in effect middle-class men who had a heavy stake in the community. Hoplite equipment was expensive and usually consisted of a layered linen corslet, an enveloping brass or bronze crested helmet which protected much of the face and neck, and greaves which were 'sprung' on to the legs. The armament normally included a heavy shield about 3 feet in diameter and perhaps weighing as much as 18 pounds, an 8-foot thrusting spear, and a short sword. The Spartans also wore a red cloak which was said to disguise the appearance of blood and so not demoralize others, but this was normally discarded before battle. They wore their hair long and sometimes – as at Thermopylae – they dressed it nonchalantly within sight of the opposing army before the fighting began, perhaps in an effort to 'psych' the enemy and impress them with Spartan confidence.

Hoplite tactics were really rather crude. Armies advanced in line with phalanxes of eight to ten ranks deep. This could be increased or decreased as the situation decreed. The army might move as a single line or break into columns perhaps sixteen abreast and eight deep. The Spartan's march to battle was often accompanied by flutes, but signals – especially once the mêlée began – were given by trumpet. When the ranks were closed up immediately prior to engagement, each man's shield partly protected that of his neighbour on the left, so there was a tendency for the line to move to the right – a weakness which could often be exploited by flanking movements which rolled up the enemy line. These operations required tenacity and cohesion. Soldiers aimed their long spears at their opponent's chest and throat. When men fell at the front it was imperative that their place was taken quickly so as to maintain the steadiness of the line. A battle was won when through a combination of tactical skill and weight of numbers the enemy line broke and a hurried retreat began.

There was often a frightening disparity between the numbers killed in battle and those butchered in the general rout which followed. When a line gave way, there was a feverish scramble for safety. For instance, just a year after Greece had been saved from a full-scale Persian invasion by the Athenians and their allies at the naval battle of Salamis (480 BC), the Spartans and their allies engaged a Persian army of about 30,000 men at Plataea. After enduring a barrage of enemy arrows while they 'waited for the gods to speak to them', the Spartans launched an attack which eventually annihilated the Persian forces of which probably no more than 3,000 survived the rout. Hoplite warfare did not lend itself to a rapid or easy retreat. Once discipline gave way and weapons were discarded it was every man for himself. There were only the quick and the dead. The cavalry carried out their mopping-up operations with cold efficiency.

Once the Persian threat had subsided, the Greeks once again took to fighting one another, and inexorably the growing rivalry between Athens and Sparta changed to open warfare. The Peloponnesian War which lasted from 431 to 404 BC effectively divided most of the Greek world. Few people wanted to confront the Spartans on land – least of all, the Athenians – so they took refuge behind their city walls while the Spartans took time to ravage the countryside and despoil the crops. On the other hand, the Spartans did not want to encounter the Athenians at sea; with their huge fleet, the Athenians were able to import foodstuffs and make good many of the losses from their fields.

The war dragged on through a succession of uneasy truces, indecisive battles, and indiscriminate massacres on both sides. Eventually, the Spartan forces were victorious and they were able to impose humiliating terms on the Athenians, although nothing like so devastating as some would have liked. Thebes and Corinth wanted Athens destroyed which presumably meant that they wanted to kill all the men and enslave the women and children. This was turned down by Sparta who favoured a more lenient policy. All the more surprising because, shortly before, their leading commander – and subsequent negotiator – Lysander, had ordered the execution of 3,000 Athenian naval personnel after a battle at Aegospotami in northern Greece.

It was a triumph of oligarchy over democracy which was not to outlast the fluctuating alignments of the Hellenic world. Xenophon wrote (*Hellenica*) that the Spartans thought that with the defeat of Athens it was 'the beginning of freedom for Greece' (Xenophon 1949). It was hardly that. They set up a series of military garrisons in what had now become their subject territories. Inevitably this met with considerable resentment and sometimes actual resistance, so increasingly repressive measures had to be employed to maintain order. The unity of Greece and the solution to the Persian problem had to await the arrival of a new conqueror, the precocious and pathological talents of Alexander the Great.

Sparta's empire was short-lived. It was a period of almost perpetual war. It tried to repeat its success against the Persians but with mixed fortunes. The most spectacular enterprise of this period was that of the Ten Thousand (celebrated in Xenophon's *Anabasis*) who tried vainly to secure the Persian throne for the king's brother, Cyrus. A number of those Spartans who survived this epic expedition enlisted with the Spartans in the indecisive Persian campaigns. These military adventures were very exhausting in men and materials, and encouraged sundry coalitions of Greek states to try to neutralize Sparta's military ascendancy – again with varying success. Real humiliation came with the rise of Thebes who introduced new and flexible battle tactics and undermined the traditional authority of the Spartan phalanx. Sparta's dominance had lasted a bare thirty years.

The Spartans – for reasons which are not entirely certain – opted for a militaristic society. Most societies have adopted a 'military way' in so far as they have been prepared to have recourse to military expedients when thought to be necessary. But for Sparta militarism was a way of life. The unique training system which stressed conservatism and unquestioning obedience produced a military elite whose courage has probably never been surpassed, and who dominated Greek land warfare for centuries.

Internecine strife was an ongoing pastime among the Greek states, and certain societies – pre-eminently the Spartans – determined that they were going to be the best at the game. Most of the time they were able to overawe others by their obvious military capabilities. Their very reputation was enough to ensure compliance. It took the exceptional, more powerful states such as Athens or Thebes to stand up to this kind of intimidation, states which – in their own ways – were just as aggressive as Sparta.

The value-priorities of Sparta's military orientations are difficult to assess. Did the valour (*arete*) ideal give rise to the military ethic as a seemingly obvious form of expression? Or, more likely, did the ideal exist to justify a military society? Sparta was not a predatory society in the way that, say, the Mongols or the Assyrians were, nor was it really expansionistic in the customarily understood sense of the term. It did not concern itself primarily with booty or the exacting of tribute, although it *was* hegemonic in that it wished to impose its will on other Greek states and sometimes order their internal affairs. This was particularly so after the Peloponnesian War when Sparta even went as far as setting up military missions in other suspect communities. In a sense this was an attempt to promote a particular political ideology, namely, the abolition of democracy and the substitution of oligarchic forms of government which were deemed to be superior.

Although the Greek world was politically fragmented, it did have a kind of cultural unity in that it used a common language and recognized common cults. So Spartan ascendancy did not mean that there was any marked contempt or disrespect for their enemies among the Greeks. This was reserved for the 'barbarians' (i.e. non-Greek-speaking peoples) outside their borders. But, as is not especially unusual in political affairs,

Sparta could be notoriously inconsistent about its alliances. At one period, the Spartans were the champions of Greece against the invading armies from the east, yet a few years later they connived with the Persians against their fellow Greeks. To be fair, this was not an inconsistency that was peculiar to the Spartans; other Greek states – particularly Thebes – often acted with an eye to the main chance. Neither did it mean that Spartans treated Greeks any better than others. During the Peloponnesian War, they committed some unforgivable atrocities, but again – to keep the record straight – they were often a restraining force on their more vindictive allies, and, on balance, probably came out of it slightly better than the Athenians from whom posterity has mistakenly come to expect more humane behaviour.

In order to pursue their military careers, the Spartans chose to lead the lives of absentee landed gentry. They ensured that their living standards were maintained through the operations of a subjugated serf population, while they concentrated their attentions on the military sphere. Having achieved the status of the finest army in Greece, it had to be perpetuated. Military predominance had to continue. The Athenians had a formidable navy, they also prospered at commerce; the Spartans, on the other hand, excelled by force of arms – this is what they were good at, this is what they did best.

Their whole social and political organization was calculated to perpetuate this tradition. But demographic factors were against them. They simply hadn't enough men. Unlike, say, the Romans, they did not relish the idea of recruiting 'outsiders' into their forces; still less did they like the idea of employing mercenaries – something they could barely afford anyway. Instead they relied on home-grown troops – but this could never make up for their deficiencies. They were a failing minority among a numerous and threatening subject population. On one side they were plagued by the spectre of Messenian political consciousness and their desire for independence. And on the other by the possibility of serf revolts which were said to be the 'nightmare of the hoplite class'. The intransigence of their subject peoples, and the fear of helot uprisings were always a problem to the declining elite. And all this was vitiated by continued anxieties about their precarious relations with other city-states. Their attempt to preserve a rich military caste necessitated in-breeding among fewer and fewer privileged families. In the years immediately preceding their defeat by Thebes at the battle of Leuctra (371 BC), the Spartans were probably still able to field a cavalry of 1,500 and a hoplite force of 30,000 but this possibly included only about 1,000 actual Spartiates. They were a dying breed.

The decline of Sparta is inextricably linked not only with the diminution of its population but also with its persistent archaism. It was defeated by cultural insularity: its unwillingness to change was against the new trends which were taking place in Greece. But perhaps most of all – despite the enviable traits of strength and stability – Sparta's real failure was not to live up to its own imperialistic promise. It posed as a politically superior system and proclaimed freedom from Athenian domination, and then proceeded to oppress those that it had liberated. Greek disenchantment with the realities of Spartan government was enough to dispel something of the ideal of the disciplined and military state.

3

THE CARTHAGINIANS
The enemy as economic rivals

Plutarch, the ancient historian, commented – with undisguised bias – that the Carthaginians were 'a hard and sinister people, cowardly in times of danger, terrible when they are victorious. They hold on grimly to their own opinions, are stern with themselves and have no feeling for the pleasures of life' (trans. Ian Scott-Kilvert, quoted in Harden 1971: 17). This is, of course, something of an overstatement, but then, like virtually all assessments of the Carthaginians, it was the view of an unfriendly observer, in this case a Greek writing long after the great days of Carthaginian power. Similar assessment problems relate to their parent Phoenician civilization. Much of what we know about the Phoenicians comes from hostile Hebrew sources, and almost all we know in documentary terms about Carthage itself comes from her Greek and Roman rivals. But if a society can last for over six hundred years as a viable entity, it must have something to commend it. Admittedly, it is rather a sorry tale. In many ways, the Carthaginians *were* an unsympathetic people, and deserve much of the opprobrium that posterity has seen fit to heap upon them.

Carthage, located not far from modern Tunis, began as a Phoenician colony. The Phoenicians themselves had been a minor maritime power in the Mediterranean since at least the fourteenth century BC. They were related to the Canaanites of the biblical records, and had their chief cities in the Lebanon at Tyre and Sidon. There is some uncertainty about the foundation date of Carthage itself. Archaeology cannot comfortably date the beginnings of the city much earlier than 700 BC, but there is a persistent literary tradition that puts the date in the late ninth century BC, and this earlier date seems to have been generally accepted in antiquity.

The Phoenician penetration of the Western Mediterranean can be largely attributed to the search for relatively scarce metals, especially silver and tin. The small Phoenician colonies that sprang up, particularly on the north African coast, were probably originally safe anchorages *en route* to Spain where these metals were to be found. It is assumed that

Carthage began as a watering-place of this kind, and was later developed because of its strategic position in the 'narrows' of the Mediterranean between the north African coast and Sicily. Later, such settlements became trading centres for Phoenician merchants who – according to the *Odyssey*, at least – had a rather unsavoury reputation for greed and slave-trading. The Phoenicians were intrepid explorers, and during the seventh century BC they founded colonies in Sicily, Spain, and France, and in the sixth century BC the Carthaginians extended their power to Sardinia and Ibiza. The Phoenicians were extremely jealous of their trade-routes, and often took elaborate measures to ensure that they were not discovered. There is an account of how one Carthaginian captain, on finding that he was being followed by a Roman vessel, deliberately grounded his ship and was compensated for his loss – and rewarded for his astuteness – by the Carthaginian authorities (sufets). There were, in fact, already hints of an embryonic anti-Semitism at this time based partly, no doubt, on some accurate information about Phoenician 'closeness' and sharp practices. But hostility probably also arose as a result of Greek resentment that these people were monopolizing potential markets. So the scene was set for an eventual conflict between these two competing maritime societies.

The Spanish silver trade is a case in point. The Greek Phocaeans in the fifty-oared pentaconters were exploring the Balearics, especially Majorca, as early as the mid-seventh century BC, but, as we have seen, it was not long before the smaller island of Ibiza was under Carthaginian control. There is still some debate as to who opened up the metals trade in southern Spain, but the rivalry between Greeks and Carthaginians exerted an increasingly decisive influence on the political and economic history of the 'Western Sea'. By *c*. 520 BC Carthage had virtually put an end to all Greek traffic in these waters by fortifying her settlements at Cadiz and thus blocking access to the Tartessos river and its adjacent mining deposits. Archaeological investigations confirm that after this date Greek finds cease to exist in this area, and it is therefore assumed that the Carthaginians had decided to eliminate all competition and secure the rich silver trade for themselves.

Markets were the life-blood of the Carthaginians, and in *c*. 425 BC we find a huge expedition of – disputably – sixty ships sailing through the Straits of Gibraltar to the West African coast, possibly as far as Sierra Leone. This was probably a colonizing venture, but almost certainly it was also a search for gold, ivory, and slaves.

Phoenician settlements often conformed to a well-established pattern. Colonizers usually favoured offshore islands or small peninsulas which would afford them easy accessibility by sea, and which could be confidently defended from the landward side. Tyre was a typical example, and was virtually impregnable from attack. It is mentioned first in

Egyptian documents dating from the second millennium BC. Originally it was situated on the coast, but was later extended to an island about half a mile offshore. In 585 BC it was subjected to a thirteen-year siege by the Babylonian forces of Nebuchadnezzar after which formal surrender terms were agreed – probably as a face-saving arrangement for the invaders. It finally fell to the Macedonian forces of Alexander the Great who took several months to build a mole out to the island – an incredible constructional feat – and then successfully stormed and sacked the city in 332 BC.

Carthage was built on a promontory surrounded on three sides by the sea. The contours provided a sheltered double-harbour facility which was ideally suited for the anchorage of both merchant ships and warships. The fertile hinterland eventually supported an impressive walled city which was dominated – as in so many ancient settlements – by a fortified hill where archives and treasures were kept, and which also held the impressive temple of Baal-Eshmun which was approached by a flight of sixty steps. Nearby was the senate-house and the adjacent areas were used for residential, commercial, and religious purposes. This was defended by a strong military presence; the barracks are said to have housed some 4,000 cavalry and 20,000 infantry. This entire complex was protected by a series of elaborate fortifications, especially across the narrow neck of the seven and a half mile isthmus which was the most vulnerable point of attack. The advantage was that it was open, flat terrain which made defence reasonably simple. The sheer longevity of the city suggests that the site had been chosen with some care. At the height of her power in the early third century BC, Carthage proper probably boasted a population of some 400,000 including resident aliens and slaves, and compares with Athens at her zenith in the fifth century BC.

In its early days, Carthage was still very much influenced by the mother-city of Tyre, but when Tyre was besieged by the Assyrians in 671 BC, a number of Tyrians fled to Carthage, and it is from this time that the city became markedly independent. By the sixth century BC Carthage was becoming a force in the Mediterranean world, and was entering into treaties with early Rome and the Etruscans, and about 500 BC entertained an embassy from Darius the Great, King of Persia, the 'world power' at this period. From this time onwards, its fortunes were established. It became rich from its extensive trade networks – especially in the Western Mediterranean – until its commercial supremacy was eventually challenged by the Greeks later in the fifth century. It was left to Rome actually to destroy Carthage in 146 BC after a protracted struggle lasting over a hundred years.

Carthage had the unique distinction of being the only non-Greek state to be studied in some detail by Aristotle and his associates in the fourth century BC. And this was simply because it had a constitution – a practice much admired by Greek political writers. Unfortunately, these records are lost, and we now have to infer from later writers exactly what this constitution was and how it worked. As far as we can reconstruct Carthaginian political organization, it consisted of a 'mix' of monarchical, aristocratic, and democratic elements. There is some evidence that it changed during its history, with more power being vested from time to time in the hands of certain influential families. But it was admired, nevertheless, for its balance and stability.

The most powerful figures in the state were the sufets (sometimes translated 'judges') who appear to have acted very much like Roman consuls, whose election also depended on birth and wealth. There seem to have been just two sufets at any one time, and they held office for one year only. Their exact powers are unknown except that they summoned and presided over the senate and the popular assembly, and also seem to have been involved with the administration of justice, although they did not have the authority to declare war or control the treasury. The sufets were aided by a body of officials (including, apparently, a censor of public morals) who carried out the practical day-to-day tasks of state. The senate had several hundred members who were also drawn from the ranks of the aristocracy. They held office for life, and replacements probably took place by simple co-option. As part of the senate there was a permanent committee of senators who were charged with the supervision of everyday affairs.

The citizen assembly itself had limited powers. Issues were often taken to the assembly by the sufets and the senators if they were either problematic or had wide-ranging implications. In general, though, it seems as though the popular assembly was expected to endorse the decisions of the executive. The evidence, such as it is, suggests that ordinary Carthaginians were essentially non-political when compared, say, with the Romans and especially the Greeks. They appear to have been generally submissive to their leaders. Aristotle criticized them for being too preoccupied with trade and the pursuit of wealth, and per-haps, therefore, too concerned to obey the dictates of an oligarchy who represented the financial elite.

In a very real sense, the Carthaginians were a peace-loving people. They were primarily a trading nation. And they were, therefore, keen to protect their merchant interests from upstart intruders, first the Greeks and later the Romans. They were consequently a relatively rich state, but they were also small, too small to counter the interlopers effectively with their own native resources. So their leaders reached the hard-headed conclusion that they could not control a vast trade network *and* embark on military enterprises with only a citizen army. They therefore decided to disband a large part of their own militia, and instead use their considerable wealth to hire a large force of specialist mercenaries from various parts of the Mediterranean world. These included native Berbers and Libyans from the African hinterland, subject Iberians from Carthaginian territories in Spain, all augmented by contingents of mainland and Sicilian Greeks.

At least, this is how it began. But with time it was not just a question of protecting trade-routes and markets, but of defending their sources of raw materials, especially the silver from Spain. The Carthaginians had few natural enemies in Africa; the indigenous tribes were really no match for this prosperous and tightly organized state. The real threats came from overseas, from those who presumed to usurp her trading rights and general political influence in the Western Mediterranean. So the expediency of defence led to the inevitability of offence; it was just a short but perilous step from conservation to conquest.

The Carthaginians seem to have adopted a separation-of-powers approach to military and civil office. We find that although the army was largely officered by Greeks, its generals were normally drawn from distinguished Carthaginian families. But they were not elected to military office as were, say, the magistrates for the year in the Roman republic. And this led to all kinds of anomalies. As high-born citizens, they enjoyed considerable social status, but as generals their political status was, at best, uncertain. The state and its people obviously had ambivalent attitudes towards the military – not an uncommon feature in other societies. They both needed them and distrusted them. The military were the defenders of their interests and the bulwark against their enemies, but they were also a cause for concern, a force that might pose a threat to the established social order. The evidence suggests that in Carthage this very rarely happened; in the field Carthaginian generals were extremely loyal, although it is known that some *former* generals tried to seize office. Successful generals, such as Hannibal (d. *c.* 183 BC) in his earlier days, could be praised by the senate and fêted by the people, and retain their commands for years. But unsuccessful generals could be treated unmercifully, even crucified, for their failure. In 480 BC, coincidental with the battle of Salamis between the Greeks and the Persians, there was a battle at Himera in Sicily in which the Greeks who controlled the eastern area of the island defeated the Carthaginians of the west. Besides considerable losses in men and ships, this humiliation cost Carthage 2,000 talents (about 50 tons of silver) by way of settlement. According to the Greek historian, Herodotus, the Carthaginian general, Hamilcar, who had remained in camp making sacrifices to the gods for victory, threw himself on the pyre and burnt himself to death when he saw his men fleeing from the battlefield. His death – albeit not exactly in battle – almost certainly saved him from a much more shameful execution at home.

Later in this ongoing struggle between the Greeks and the Carthaginians, an earlier Hannibal led an army of Spanish and Libyan mercenaries against the Greek city of Selinus in Sicily and brutally massacred the population, an experience from which the city never really recovered (409 BC). He then initiated a holy war against the Greeks by marching on Himera. The Syracusan Greeks had military commitments elsewhere and were unable to give effective support to their countrymen; a relief force was sent but was only able to evacuate part of the population. Hannibal completely destroyed the city and took 3,000 prisoners who were then tortured and slaughtered in a vast human sacrifice to the 'shades' of Hamilcar. Again, it is noteworthy that when the Carthaginians then went on to besiege the city of Acragas, an epidemic broke out among their troops – of which Hannibal was one of the first victims. The new commander, Hamilco, sacrificed both children and animals in order to pacify the gods who had brought this judgement upon them.

It is difficult to avoid the conclusion that in these instances the Carthaginians had strong ideological motivations. Victims were offered to Baal-Hammon for having granted them victories over the Greeks. The Carthaginian attitude was that when the god favoured their armies he was entitled to his share of the spoils. It was both politically expedient and ideologically acceptable that the defeated enemy should be regarded as subjects for sacrifice. Yet similar practices seem to have been in order for the *reverses*, which were also – presumably – attributable to the negative responses of the god; sacrifices were necessary to appease the god because of the set-backs and epidemics which prevented them from occupying the whole of the island.

The Carthaginian army was organized on much the same lines as those of most other developed societies in the ancient world. The backbone of the infantry was the customary heavily armed foot soldier, very similar to the traditional Greek hoplite. Very important too was their cavalry which was mainly composed of Numidian, and later Spanish and Gallic, horsemen. When Hannibal's army invaded Italy, the cavalry comprised about a quarter of the entire force. The Carthaginians also made extensive use of chariots, possibly with scythed wheels – as was still common in eastern warfare. Diodorus says that as many as 2,000 were deployed in some engagements, but many historians regard this as somewhat exaggerated. Eventually, the use of chariots gave way to some extent to the use of elephants – another eastern innovation, particularly associated with the Indian armies of Porus and Chandragupta in the fourth and third centuries BC. Elephants could be something of a mixed blessing. Perhaps up to a hundred might be used in any one campaign, and they were employed successfully by the Carthaginians in Spain and Sicily. But they were not always reliable. They might easily turn on their masters when frightened, and they were notoriously susceptible to adverse weather conditions; of the thirty that Hannibal took over the Alps in 218 BC, all but one died of the cold.

One particular innovation which revolutionized siege-warfare was the invention of the ballista (catapult) which could hurl stone balls several hundred yards. It is said to have been first developed by or for the Greeks of Syracuse early in the fourth century BC in their wars with the Carthaginians and was certainly used thereafter to great effect by the Romans. Almost certainly it was fear of this weapon that influenced the Carthaginians in their construction of their fortress walls, especially after the town of Motya, in Phoenician western Sicily, had been reduced to something approaching rubble by Dionysus, tyrant of Syracuse, in 398 BC.

Although there is no firm archaeological evidence to support it, ancient testimony has it that the port of Carthage had docking facilities for 220 ships. This reflects not only the mercantile activity of the state but also the size of its war fleets. The people were famed for their navy and for the prowess of their sailors: no doubt a legacy of their Phoenician origins. The rowers appear to have been mainly Carthaginian citizens but there is no evidence – as there is, for example, in classical Athens – that they were members of the lowest social class. Perhaps they took the view that sea-faring was the legitimate duty of a merchant people. It was part of their tradition to serve in the fleet. In battles with the Sicilian Greeks, for example, the tactical superiority of the Carthaginians in their smaller craft was often too much for their opponents, and at Catania, in perhaps the largest sea battle then known, they sank or boarded about a hundred Syracusan vessels and took some 20,000 prisoners.

The Greek-v.-Carthaginian conflicts of the late fifth and early fourth centuries BC afford particularly graphic illustrations of how warfare between developed states was conducted. The Greeks had been in Sicily since *c.* 700 BC when they had gradually subjugated the indigenous tribes, whose origins are largely unknown. The Phoenicians, their closest economic competitors, began their attempts to gain a foothold on the island at about the same time, but Carthage itself does not seem to have made any serious bid for territory until the early sixth century BC. From then onwards there was a continuous struggle for supremacy. There were temporary lulls in hostilities, the Phoenicians/Carthaginians confining themselves mainly to the western side of the island and the Greeks to the eastern parts, but neither side was really content with these divisions.

Syracuse was the most powerful Greek state in Sicily, and its ruler, Dionysus, who had risen from demagogue to dictator, was one of the most colourful and unpredictable characters in classical history. The engagements had a to-and-fro quality of siege and counter-siege with fluctuating fortunes on both sides. Dionysus was able to deploy huge armies by comparative standards, reputedly 80,000 infantry and 3,000 cavalry, with six-storey siege towers for this attack on the island-city of Motya. It is said that when it was taken, the Greeks had little thought of plunder – only revenge for Himera. The carnage was terrible: what prisoners were taken were sold into slavery, except the Greek mercenaries who had fought with the Carthaginians; their treachery could only be expiated by crucifixion – pre-eminently a Carthaginian practice.

At one point, the Carthaginian army appears to have been struck with some kind of plague, perhaps typhus, and this enabled the Greeks to rout the Carthaginians, few of whom survived. The Punic general, Hamilco, who felt himself to have been abandoned by the gods, duly starved himself to death to avoid the ignominy and condemnation that defeat would have entailed. In Sicily, as a whole, the result was stalemate. On balance, the forty odd years of war had really profited no one. It had been extremely costly and cruel with atrocities on both sides. It had certainly brought no benefits to the Carthaginians, who at the end of it all still had no more than their original settlements. Not untypically, they acknowledged the efficacy of the Greek Olympian deities, built a temple to the goddess Demeter, and even hired Greek priests to officiate so that the elaborate rituals would be carried out in the prescribed manner.

This superstitious awe of inexplicable supernatural forces, and the elaborate attempts to placate or condition their seemingly capricious behaviour, is altogether characteristic of the Carthaginians. This is particularly evidenced by their attitudes to ritual sacrifice – especially human sacrifice. The Phoenicians recognized a complex pantheon of divinities, including Asherat, the goddess of fertility, and her consort El, who appear to have been worshipped in Carthage under different titles, Tanit and Baal-Hammon. The Baalim (Lords) were local deities, or perhaps refractions of one main deity which were commonly associated with specified functions. Originally El (Baal) seems to have been a storm-god who controlled the weather and elemental, environmental conditions whose very nature connoted anger and unpredictability. It was primarily to this god that sacrifices were made.

What observers found particularly difficult to understand was that sacrifice took the form of infant 'holocausts' – the burning of children. This was a practice that had virtually died out in Phoenicia but was taken up in Carthage, especially in times of national emergency. Diodorus records how in sheer desperation the Carthaginians sacrificed 500 children of the aristocracy in 310 BC in order to avert military calamity in the perennial wars with Syracuse. Other sources suggest that infant sacrifice was an annual practice, always of male children dedicated by the leading families, which was simply 'accelerated' in times of crisis. Whether there was any legal obligation on the parents to do this, or whether it was a voluntary social act, is still uncertain, but it was a practice that certainly horrified other Mediterranean peoples who were not above a little ritual bloodletting themselves from time to time.

The Carthaginians were quite consistent about the relationship between divine favour and military success; between the endorsement of the gods and national greatness and economic prosperity. It is notable that when they, in turn, suffered these reverses, this did not occasion any questioning of their beliefs, only more sacrifices of children in Carthage to induce their implacable deities to smile on them once again. It was quite in keeping with their ideology that when *they* were defeated they should attribute this to the fact that the gods had deserted them and that the mandate had simply passed to their conquerors.

The critical test for Carthage came when she challenged the rising power of Rome. Already weakened by the interminable on–off hostilities with the Greeks, Carthage now felt herself forced to take on this young and vigorous rival for dominance of the Western Mediterranean. Rome was a potential threat to her monopoly of certain trading concessions, and a danger to her political influence – especially in Spain. At first there were attempts to come to terms; two treaties were signed in the fourth century which were really politico-economic in nature. The second of these specified that 'if the Carthaginians take any city in Latium which is not subject to the Romans, they may keep the property and the captives, but must surrender the city' (Polybius 1981). A third treaty was signed in the third century which was by way of being a convenient military alliance, but this agreement soon lapsed in an atmosphere of mutual suspicion.

The First Punic War (punic, from poeni=Phoenicians, the term used by the Romans for the Carthaginians) broke out when a relatively inconsequential group of Italian mercenaries appealed to both Carthage and Rome for help against the Sicilian Greeks who were trying to wrest back the town of Messana which the mercenaries, the Mamertini, had illegally acquired. The Roman Senate felt no particular obligation to these people but, fearing Carthaginian involvement so near to the Italian mainland, decided to intervene. In this conflict, which effectively began in 264 BC, the Romans were so successful that they decided to break Carthaginian power once and for all both on land and – more formidably – at sea. This entailed the building of a fleet – a new experience for the Romans – and the eventual invasion of the Carthaginian heartland, north Africa itself. Carthage was defeated in 241 BC with a loss of some 500 ships and a reputed 200,000 men. Then Rome twisted the knife: the Carthaginians were also compelled to surrender their Sicilian possessions and pay a huge indemnity to their conquerors.

Carthage then faced a mutiny from its own mercenaries who were demanding payment from a virtually bankrupted government. Rome sympathized with its erstwhile enemies, the Carthaginians, and did a little to help. It was a protracted and bloody business with horrific barbarities on both sides. Roman attitudes then inexplicably changed, perhaps because Rome did not want Carthage to recover *too* quickly. This time the trouble was over Sardinia, and it was no contest. Carthage gave up Sardinia and Corsica, and paid yet another crippling indemnity to Rome.

Carthage gradually recovered and turned its attention to Spain where it began to build a new and profitable empire. Rome, ever willing to listen to appeals for help when it served its interests, became embroiled in a dispute which again brought it into conflict with Carthage. This time the Carthaginians were looking for vengeance and nearly achieved it through the flair and ingenuity of the famous Hannibal, who had the temerity to invade Italy itself (218 BC). One way and another, he lost something like half his army just in crossing the Alps, but was still able to inflict some notable defeats on successive Roman armies.

The Second Punic War was fought in Italy, Spain, Sardinia, and Sicily as well as north Africa. The Romans finally sacked Syracuse – ironically, the old enemy of Carthage – and confiscated the art treasures. At this time they also succeeded in killing one of the great scientific minds of the ancient world, Archimedes, by all accounts when he was still working at his calculations (211 BC). Eventually, they too produced a military commander of genius, P. Cornelius Scipio – later termed Africanus – who wore down what was virtually an unreinforcible Carthaginian army in Italy and completed his conquests with the invasion of Africa and victory at the battle of Zama (202 BC). The ultimate indignity was the infliction of yet another predictable indemnity that was heavier than ever.

Carthage was now forbidden to make war on anyone except with Rome's express permission. This was all very well as long as Rome kept the rules. But when Carthage appealed to Rome for help in a dispute, she idiosyncratically ruled against Carthage, and thus precipitated the final conflict – a very one-sided affair – in which the city of Carthage was laid waste by the unnecessarily vindictive conquerors (146 BC).

4

THE ROMANS
The enemy as uncouth barbarians

Sometimes the Romans are seen as a rather boorish people who were better known for their roads than for their culture. Artistically, they were heavily dependent on the Greeks who preceded them: architecture, building, sculpture, and literature all owed much to their predecessors. Religion, too, rested on a corpus of myth that is largely associated with the Greeks. On the other hand, the Romans made significant contributions of their own, not least of all in the areas of law and administration.

Any consideration of Roman military expansionism must take account of the very long period of time in which the Romans were a dominant power in the Mediterranean area and beyond, which, at a conservative estimate, lasted for about six hundred years. But it is not only the impressive longevity of Roman civilization which matters; the extent of that civilization is also an important factor. By the beginning of the Imperial period, that is, during the principate of Augustus (30 BC to AD 14), Rome had one of the most extensive empires the world had ever seen. At their zenith, the Romans controlled an empire which stretched from western Spain and Portugal to the borders of Iran. By the first century AD, the Roman Empire may have contained about 20 per cent of the world's population, and Rome itself was probably the largest city in the world. It is perhaps worth noting that when so-called enemies of the state were indicted for some offence, they rarely sought exile somewhere else – after all, where could they go? As a punishment, a few might be banished to obscure islands, but it was more usual for those in power to order their deaths, and a number preferred to commit suicide because there seemed to be almost nowhere to which they could flee that was out of the reach of Rome and its client kingdoms.

The traditional date for the founding of Rome is 753 BC. During the early days of Etruscan influence there was a monarchy – the Tarquins – but these kings were ejected c. 510 BC and a republic was established. After the necessary battles for recognition against other Latin tribes, Rome finally came into its own with victories over the Carthaginians in the Punic Wars which commenced in 264 BC. For the next 200 years or so there were further wars of expansion both in the east, mainly against the Greeks, and in the west, particularly in Spain.

As the Roman Republic began to break down in the first century BC with the civil wars, first between the military dictators Marius and Sulla, and then between their like-minded successors Pompeius Magnus (Pompey) and Julius Caesar, the expansionist campaigns continued, especially in northern Europe and – abortively – in the Middle East (Parthia). Eventually, Octavianus (later Augustus) emerged as the obvious leader in Rome, and the Empire or Imperial period began in 30 BC and continued with varying fortunes until the sack of Rome by the barbarians in AD 410. This was not the end, and certainly not for the Roman Empire in the east centred on Byzantium (Istanbul) which survived until AD 1453 when it was taken by the Turks. But by the fifth century AD the really great days were over; in fact, although the 'glory that was Rome' was perhaps at its apogee in the early second century AD during the reigns of Trajan and Hadrian, expansionism had long ceased and a very slow erosion of the borders had set in. The Imperial period was really a time of attempted consolidation of the gains built up during the Republic. As much as anything, it was actually a period of containment of Rome's over-extended territories.

Military organization changed considerably over the centuries, so in the present discussion it is intended to concentrate on that most critical transitional phase in the late Republic when expansionism was at its height. Carthage had been finally destroyed, Greece had been humbled, and Spain had been made increasingly subject to Roman rule. Yet during the first century, Rome became increasingly divided against itself and was not sure of its own directions or certain of its future role in the Mediterranean world.

By this time, too, Roman social organization had undergone a long, and in some ways painful, period of development. The two highest magistrates of the Republic were the two consuls who were elected for one year and given the Imperium, that is, full military and civil power to administer the state. This was done on an equal authority basis, and each had the power to veto the measures of the other, and, of course, those of the lower magistrates. They were men of some political experience, and it was not usual to elect a man to office under the age of 42. Once a consul's term of office was over he was subject to 'examination', in which case he might be impeached for crimes or infractions alleged to have been committed during his administration. Generally speaking the office was monopolized by the nobilitas, the aristocratic patrician families, although in theory the lower classes – the plebeians – had had the right to elect consuls from the fourth century BC. The election was conducted by one of the higher Assemblies of the Roman people (the

Comitia Centuriata), and once appointed it was normal for a consul to spend his year of office in Rome, after which it was not uncommon for him to proceed to the provinces to take up duties as a proconsul. From the third century BC, when Rome often had several armies in the field at the same time, officials might retain their commands for several years. During these campaigns, it was they alone who knew the on-the-spot situation and who were therefore in a position to take executive action. These provisions facilitated the emergence of the militarily brilliant but often quite unscrupulous commanders who characterized the last days of the Republic.

The consulship was the highest prize of Roman political life during the Republic. It was the office to which ambitious men aspired, and it often offered lucrative military opportunities. In the field, the consul had the power of life and death in the army and in the provinces. In cases where cowardice was displayed or suspected in a regiment or detachment it could be punished quite ruthlessly on a corporate basis.

Magistrates might also be elected to the lesser office of praetor. These were not normally under 39 years of age, and were also elected for one year only. During the third century BC, there had only been two praetors, who were mainly charged with judicial duties, but by the end of the Republic (30 BC) this had increased to sixteen. Praetors, too, often had provincial responsibilities, and might continue this work as pro-praetors after their year of office had elapsed. Praetors were assisted by aediles, who were largely responsible for the management of the city itself, and by quaestors whose duties were mainly concerned with financial administration. In addition, there were censors whose civic responsibilities included taxation and property rights, citizenship and, especially, military recruitment.

The supreme council of magistrates was the Senate. Originally, this probably consisted of the leaders of the traditional tribal groups (gentes), but later comprised men from both patrician and plebeian families who had held consular or important administrative offices of some kind. Senatorial rank was thus by selection rather than election. Until the early first century BC, there were some three hundred senators, but this was doubled by the military dictator, Sulla, in 81 BC. The functions of the Senate which were to become seriously curtailed under the emperors were quite extensive during the Republic. It was customary for the Senate to discuss all significant affairs of state before they were brought to the attention of the Assembly. The Senate assigned provinces to consuls and arranged the finances of their administration; it fixed the tribute for dependencies, sent embassies on diplomatic missions, and received embassies from Rome's allies. It also had civic and religious responsibilities; it awarded building contracts, and consulted priests about ritual matters including public festivals. Not least of all, it played a decisive part, once war had been declared, in the direction of military operations and the negotiations for peace. In short, virtually everything the magistrates did was done on the advice or direction of the Senate with the formal ratification of the Assembly.

The Senate was largely the preserve of the Roman aristocracy although in time many provincials were numbered among its members. Large expenses could be incurred in the course of a senatorial career, yet senators were not officially allowed to profit from state contracts or maritime enterprise, although this did occur – sometimes on a vast scale – as with the exploitation in Sicily under the governorship of Verres who was eventually prosecuted by Cicero. There were, in fact, all kinds of opportunities for enrichment, either in the wars – often at the expense of provincials – or through the highly suspect tax-farming system that operated in many subject territories. The tax-farmers, the publicani, were given concessions to raise taxes in the provinces providing they paid the designated amount to the government. It is known that they often over-taxed people in various ways and pocketed the difference; with this extra cash they could then also double as money-lenders. These monies were often levied with great brutality: Caesar (1967) points out how ingenious they were at devising new forms of rapacity including a poll-tax on slaves, equipment taxes, transport taxes, even column and door taxes, 'anything which had a name attached to it provided an adequate excuse for levying money'. Such exactions were particularly difficult for ordinary people to resist because they were done in the name of Roman authority, and were thus a form of legitimized imposition. Unsurprisingly, such a system lent itself to all manner of abuses by unscrupulous Roman officials and their delegates.

The Senate obviously had its weaknesses. But whereas magistrates – including consuls – could only hold office for a year and therefore had a very limited tenure in which to initiate new schemes and carry out new policies, the Senate represented the continuity principle within the system. They alone had the experience and expertise, and the continuation of office which ensured the perpetuation of Roman patrician traditions.

The several Assemblies of the Roman system consisted of either patricians or plebeians or – in some cases – both. The patricians were the elite class and they derived from long-established aristocratic families. In the early days, they claimed the highest offices of state and their superiority was generally accepted and respected. Nevertheless, among the four property classes of Roman society, it was the plebeians who comprised the majority of the citizens, and they had their own special officers, the tribunes, representing their interests in the higher echelons of the state. Tribunes had the power to impose fines on patrician magistrates if it was found that they were acting unjustly. But they could not leave the city during their year of office – perhaps because it was feared that they might act against the interests of the ruling class. Needless to say, the history of these two strata was a long and often bitter one with the plebs gradually winning grudging concessions from a reluctant aristocracy.

The plebeian populations consisted mainly of small farmers who eked out a precarious living on their meagre and often unproductive plots of land. There were artisans engaged in rudimentary industry, but this was essentially an agrarian economy which functioned only fractionally above the subsistence level. As Rome's military conquests increased, there were considerable changes in the economy occasioned by the large influx of foreign slaves. Many of these were employed on vast estates (latifundia) in Italy and Sicily which were able to produce grain at consistently competitive prices. The farmers found themselves undercut by cheap labour, especially from the second century BC onwards when the market became glutted with slaves from the conquered territories. High recruitment for the army also affected the size and efficiency of these small farming units, and owners found it difficult to compete. They often ran into debt, and were sometimes bought out by the large estate owners to increase their already extensive holdings. Eventually many of them joined the swelling ranks of the landless proletariat, and were reduced to casual agricultural labour and the doles of food which derived from the latifundia themselves. It was a spiral of destitution which was ultimately to lead to many of Rome's urban problems.

Rome's expansionist practices do not seem to have derived from any carefully concerted plan or programme. Originally, there was no considered policy of expansion. In the very early days of the Republic, it was simply a matter of survival. Wars were fought against neighbouring Samnites, Sabines, and Etruscans, and also against invading Gauls, just to secure a place in the Latin world. But with success came ambition. In order to extend its territories, Rome inevitably found that it had bigger and better competitors, and this rivalry eventually led to the conflict with Carthage which set it on the path to imperialism.

This discussion is therefore going to concentrate on what was probably the most critical phase of this process when the late Republic was breaking down and there was a very uncertain and violent period of transition. It was a time of opposing warlords and *ad hoc* proscriptions; a time when Rome was busily conquering the world overseas, but was also so ridden with civil strife at home that it took some seventy years of conflict before the problems were resolved. And this only occurred when military dictatorship became respectable and was transmuted into monarchy; when Augustus founded the Empire.

With changes in political structure went changes in military organization. In the early Roman army, recruitment was based upon citizenship. As in so many armies at a comparable stage of development, the aristocracy comprised the cavalry and the remaining property classes were equipped according to the kinds of armour and weapons that they could afford. The very poor acted either as slingers or in a menial 'pioneer corps' capacity. Rome's allies (subjects?) in Italy enjoyed a kind of intermediate citizenship status which put them under an obligation to provide auxiliary contingents, especially of cavalry – in which Rome was rather weak – for Rome's increasingly ambitious military programme.

During the third century BC, after the successful defeat of an invasion by the Gauls, there were modifications in the military set-up. Greek models were adapted; new tactical formations were developed involving the 'coupling' of the units known as centuries, each commanded by a centurion, and these were deployed in more innovative ways. Pay for service was also introduced, and this served to reduce some of the distinctions between the property classes and therefore increase recruitment. Military ranks – especially at the intermediate levels – came to be based more on merit than on wealth or position, although when auxiliaries were raised among the allies, care was taken that they were led by Roman officers. Equipment, too, became increasingly standardized, and the weapons which were to make the Roman army invincible for years to come were adopted for general use: the pilum, a long heavy spear; the gladius, the short cut-and-thrust sword probably of Spanish design; and the large oval shield which was, in fact, changed over time.

The Roman army was nothing if not adaptable, and by the first century BC – in many ways the most interesting and significant century in Rome's long history – further reorganization took place. By this time, Roman arms had crushed both Carthage and Greece, and had been successful in warding off invasions from various hosts of barbarians from the north. Roman military supremacy was now unquestioned, but with increasing power came increasing problems. The legions were being led by aspiring military dictators – ambitious commanders who would brook no rivals. Rome was dominant abroad, but the Republic was beginning to fall apart at home. A struggle had developed in Rome between two political factions, the Optimates (the 'best men') who represented the senatorial aristocracy, and the Populares who represented the equestrian class, the rising rural and urban proletariat and Rome's Italian allies. Eventually there was a social war between Rome and some of her allies which lasted two years, and resulted in a negotiated settlement in Rome's favour, but also gave enfranchisement to the allies. After this, it became a matter of Rome against Rome. It no longer paid to belong to the wrong party or back the wrong military leader. The fratricidal see-sawings of Marius and Sulla are a case in point and were marked by proscriptions and bloodletting on a frightening scale.

Marius, an equestrian by birth and thus a man of the people, was not only a gifted military commander, but something of a populist with particular political ambitions. His reputation was largely built on military success against Numidian (North African) tribesmen in the Jugurthine Wars (111–105 BC) and later against various coalitions of northern barbarians (104–101 BC). He was supported by the patronage of certain influential senators, and – contrary to tradition – was elected consul year after year, but later suffered a temporary eclipse and spent a time in exile in Mauretania. When he eventually returned to power in 87 BC he adopted a much more radical stance, repudiating many who had formally supported him and executing a number of Optimates who were opposed to his political aspirations. He died a year later having just been elected consul for the seventh time. The mantle of military despotism was then taken up by his one-time quaestor, L. Cornelius Sulla, whose politics became increasingly reactionary. He, too, had had notable military success, especially against one of Rome's most notorious enemies, Mithridates of Pontus, a Roman client kingdom in Asia Minor. In 88 BC, in order to extend his own burgeoning empire, Mithridates had ordered the death of all Romans and Italians in Asia, an edict which was taken up with alacrity by his subjects – such was the popularity of Rome – and which resulted in the massacre of some 80,000 people. After crushing this rebellion (85 BC), Sulla punished the people by quartering his army of 40,000 troops on them, and then imposing a virtually unbearable indemnity of 20,000 talents for which – ironically – they had to turn to Roman bankers for loans. When the triumphant Sulla returned to Rome from the east with his legions in 83 BC, he completely disregarded constitutional precedent and had huge numbers of his opponents put to death. These are said to have included some 1,600 equestrians and 70 senators (Keaveney 1982), but this may be a conservative estimate. He confiscated their goods, declared their children and grandchildren ineligible for office, and released their slaves. Such was the penalty in the most powerful state on earth for incautious political preferences.

Sulla, and particularly the less pedestrian Marius, were keen to 'modernize' the army, and this reorganization was both tactical and social. Equipment was modified: the Roman soldier was – in general – more heavily armed and protected, and certainly made more self-reliant in that he had to carry everything necessary for an extended campaign, including cooking utensils and entrenching tools. Furthermore the tactical organization was tightened so that the development of units based upon the century, the cohort (six centuries), and the legion (5,000–6,000 men) could be more flexible at the operational level. The system of banners and standards was also modified. These symbols were central to the whole ethos of military activity; nothing was more ignominious than to desert one's standards, and the threat of losing a standard often galvanized legionaries to greater efforts to achieve a victory.

But just as important was the social reorganization of the forces. As we have seen, the Roman army had originally been a citizen army composed largely of farmers, but as the state grew, wars became more prolonged and more distant, and more recruits were needed. To some extent these had to be drawn from Italian allies who became enfranchised, and from foreign contingents from overseas. Increasingly, the right to serve in the army was extended to the proletariat, and this was formalized by Marius. The days of the citizen militia were over. From this time onward, Rome had what was, in effect, a professional army that was no longer based on obligatory service. Sentimental attachment to the state and its citizens began to decline. The emphasis switched from civic concerns to the profession itself and the profits which might be derived from it. The focus of authority was not the Senate so much as the commander and his personal influence and ambition. The legionary looked to his leader for rewards and for a grant of land – possibly in the provinces – which he might expect when he retired. It was these developments which made possible Sulla's march on Rome, and the subsequent dictatorship of Pompeius and Caesar.

With expansion, it became increasingly difficult to restrict the exercise of power to the traditional consuls and praetors. With the Republic in an almost continuous state of war, it was often through the proconsuls and propraetors who had control in the provinces that continuity of command was ensured. Delegation of authority was also facilitated by the appointment of legati (senior officers), who acted for the consuls in a military capacity. This could be a profitable venture for the ambitious subordinate; Pompeius began a successful military career as a legatus of Sulla who retired to write his memoirs in 79 BC, and died the following year.

Now that Rome was on the military treadmill, conducting both offensive and defensive wars not only in the interests of expansionism but also to contain the conquered at the margins of the 'empire', the scene was set for the power struggles which plagued Rome for a further fifty years. Neither the Senate nor the Assembly any longer had the power to curb the men who had effectively been thrust into authority by the needs of the system. The dangers of civil and foreign wars compelled the Senate to confer military power on men of recognized ability even though they distrusted their ulterior motives. And even this was waived in the case of Julius Caesar, who was something of a maverick politician of no proven ability who was given his first important command simply to get him out of the way for a few years.

It is interesting to trace the careers of some of these men and look at their implications for Roman military ambition. Pompeius first crushed the Populares whom he had once befriended; after accepting their surrender at Mutina, he had many of them executed. The Senate, beginning to sense that they might regret their choice of champion, sent him to Spain where he further distinguished himself against the armies of renegade Populares who had – possibly out of expediency – allied themselves with the cause of Spanish nationalism.

In effect, this was a kind of postscript to the civil war of Marius and Sulla, and gave the continuing pursuit of political ambition the air of legitimacy. This was a time of extraordinary commands, when the Imperium, special authority, was vested in particular individuals who sought military achievement as a foundation for – or a validation of – high political office. There was a reaction to Sulla's measures by those who supported the policies of the Populares, but these met with only limited success. Campaigns were recommenced in Asia after a further insurrection by Mithridates and his followers. But here the Roman commander, Lucullus, although militarily successful, made few friends by his attempts to ease the burden of taxation and debt which had been incurred, as we have seen, because of previous Roman demands for indemnity. Roman financial interests won, and he was deprived of his command in 66 BC. Meanwhile, that much less scrupulous military parvenu was making his way from battlefield to battlefield. Nothing seemed too difficult for Pompeius Magnus.

Perhaps the least laudable episode in the eyes of posterity was that of the campaigns of the slave war, sometimes termed 'the revolt of the gladiators', which lasted from 73 to 71 BC. Slaves had been pouring into Rome in huge numbers. We do not know the exact figures, but we can make reasonable inferences from the few facts that we have. For example, in 177 BC, some 80,000 people were killed or enslaved from Sardinia, and ten years later the Senate ordered the enslavement of the entire population of Epirus (north-west Greece), amounting to about 150,000 people. Public works employed large contingents of slaves, and they were to be found particularly on the latifundia in Italy and Sicily, in the mines in Spain, and in the gladiatorial schools which supplied the circuses. The games might take the form of beast hunts, or the public butchery of criminals or other proscribed recalcitrants (in the later Empire period, these were not uncommonly Jews and Christians), or they might simply be combats between matched pairs of prisoners or between trained gladiators, or between combinations of the two. It was, therefore, not surprising when a group of gladiators led by a Thracian, Spartacus (who may have once been a Roman legionary), broke out of a private training school at Capua and eventually attracted some 90,000 followers to their cause. At first, they had considerable success. In one engagement, two of the legions sent against them were severely defeated, and many of the soldiers fled, leaving their weapons to the enemy. Crassus, a wealthy colleague of Pompeius who had overall responsibility for the campaign, punished the offending units by decimation, a recognized Roman military punishment in which one man in ten, selected by lot, was beaten to death. But the slave army was heterogeneous, ill-disciplined, and not very well armed, and ultimately succumbed to the superior armies of Crassus and Pompeius. After the initial slaughter on the battlefield, the victors lined the road from Capua to Rome with 6,000 crucified survivors, and enjoyed a triumph in the capital – a singular honour afforded only meritorious military leaders.

From this time onwards, Pompeius went from triumph to triumph. He cleared the Aegean and Adriatic seas of pirates, and pursued his conquering destiny through much of the Near and Middle East. He saw himself as another Alexander the Great; no one else had brought so many nations under Roman subjection. When he returned home to yet further celebrations in 61 BC everyone was jubilant. Banners proclaimed 'Pompey the Great has conquered the world', and he led nearly 300 kings and princes in his triumphal processions to prove it.

But it couldn't last. He had celebrated three triumphs; he brought an unprecedented amount of wealth into the Roman coffers, yet within twelve months public adulation began to die away, and he came to be increasingly distrusted by the Senate. They had a number of scores to settle with him, and were less intimidated once he had disbanded some of his units and no longer had an army to support him. Pompeius had effectively become a victim of his own success and his mantle was about to be taken over by a charming but coldly impersonal opportunist 'whose chief claim to fame was his ability to borrow money and to spend enormous sums on public games to increase his own popularity' (Payne 1962). The stage was now set for the advent of Julius Caesar.

Julius Caesar was a very young man – probably only about 18 – during the most turbulent year of the civil wars, but not young enough to prevent his name being added to the proscription lists during Sulla's reign of terror merely because he happened to be married to the daughter of one of the dictator's bitterest enemies. But this was a time when the innocent often suffered along with the guilty – or what despotism deemed to be guilty. Some men divorced their wives in similar circumstances (and some wives betrayed their husbands), but Caesar was not so accommodating and was forced into hiding in order to elude marauding bounty-hunters. Fortunately he was not without influential friends; he eventually received a pardon and soon began to make his way in Roman political life.

The absence of Pompeius, who in the 70s and early 60s BC was away campaigning most of the time, left something of a power vacuum in Rome itself. Crassus who had made a vast fortune, possibly – indirectly – as a result of Sulla's confiscations, aspired to office and military glory, and initially found a willing ally in the ambitious Caesar. Together they tried to counter Pompeius' growing popularity, but when he returned they decided on an uneasy *rapprochement* which – in the short term – served their several yet mutual interests.

This political coalition, or triumvirate, was largely based on 'military force, mob rule and money' (Warry 1980: 160). There was even some strategic intermarriage to cement these arrangements, but despite this politically incestuous manoeuvring, inevitable cleavages began to appear in the alliance. At first, Pompeius was the senior partner, and Caesar had to content himself with a governorship in Spain from which he raised enough money to pay off his most outstanding debts, not least of all those incurred in bribing officials to get him the job in the first place. In 59 BC he became consul, and in the following year he was due for a proconsular appointment, so the Senate tried to fob him off with a harmless province rather than give him the opportunity to win fame and esteem through a military command. At this time, Caesar was relatively untried as an army leader, but he decided to make the conquest of Gaul his own. In middle age, he embarked on a series of campaigns which marked him out as a gifted, strenuous, and ruthless commander.

The Roman invasion of northern Europe was not entirely gratuitous. Italy had long had to face the menace of migratory tribes who threatened her borders, and it could be argued that some offensive operations were necessary in order to check this danger. But it is disputable whether the extent and severity of the campaign can be wholly justified in purely defensive terms. Personal ambition and aggrandizement seem never to have been far from Caesar's mind. Nor indeed was the sheer love of campaigning: the poet Lucan says of Caesar that he was 'furious for war', and one has only to look at the grandiloquent way in which he describes his own success in his *Commentaries* to see that there is much truth in this remark. In clear and dispassionate prose, Caesar graphically recounts how he reduced the Swiss tribes of the Helvetii and the Germanic Suevi, and particularly various combinations of Belgic tribes who stubbornly resisted the Roman incursions, and how he organized punitive expeditions against the Britons who had been lending support to their continental neighbours.

Caesar's *Commentaries*, written some time after the events in question, is the main record we have of these particular campaigns. Because there is no other contemporary material it is difficult to know if his recollections were sometimes at fault, or even whether there are any deliberate distortions. However, what is clear is that there is no real self-criticism – but then this is hardly to be expected in an account which was largely designed to justify his actions to the Roman people. The campaigns were carried out with both skill and pitiless efficiency; particular actions such as those against the Veneti on the Atlantic seaboard and some of the German tribes were tantamount to organized genocide.

Caesar showed great personal courage in these operations, and his enterprising leadership combined with the greater skill and discipline of the often outnumbered Roman soldiers proved too much for the enemy. The Gauls fought with uncoordinated desperation against better weaponry and superior siegecraft tactics with the result that the carnage was often fearful. Caesar tells how on one occasion he let his cavalry loose and killed an estimated 430,000 refugees. Organized massacre of this kind often took place as part of a policy to stem the possibility of further insurrection, though sometimes it was mere retaliation. Caesar reports another instance when 'the name of the Nervii [on the Franco-Belgian frontier] was almost blotted from the face of the earth' (Caesar 1951: 88). Of some 60,000 men capable of bearing arms, only about 500 survived. Failing this, there was always starvation and slavery. When Caesar's legions defeated the Aduatuci, also in Belgium, the 350,000 survivors were all sold into slavery. The gifted head of the Arveni tribe, Vercingetorix, finally led a revolt of the Gauls against the Romans in 52 BC, mainly resorting to guerrilla tactics against Caesar's lines of communication. But after a long siege at one of his fortresses, he was captured, imprisoned for six years, and eventually paraded in Caesar's triumph in Rome with many other notable captives; he was then executed. The Gauls were not exactly noble savages, they could be quite merciless with their own prisoners, but is is disputable whether they merited this kind of treatment.

Many of these figures may well be exaggerations – but that is significant in itself. It can – and has – been argued that Caesar's operations in Gaul were indirectly related to the security of the Roman state. But it can likewise be shown that they were also calculated to increase Caesar's personal wealth and prestige, and give him an established power-base from which to make his future claims to military dictatorship.

By the middle of this fateful century, Caesar's claim to fame equalled that of Pompeius, and this precipitated the inevitable civil war. Crassus, in an attempt to emulate his militarily successful colleagues, had already lost his own life and an army of 30,000 in a calamitous campaign against the Parthians in 53 BC, and it was now time for a trial of strength between his senior partners. Caesar emerged victorious after a protracted struggle with Pompeius which lasted from 49 to 46 BC, and after 'settling affairs' in Egypt, he returned home to Rome where he was assassinated in 44 BC by political opponents, ostensibly because they feared for the future of the Republic.

The social unrest which followed involved the emergence of a second coalition (triumvirate) of political opportunists, and was accompanied by the predictable proscription of political enemies and yet further civil strife. This resulted finally in a showdown at Actium in 31 BC between the main contenders, Antoninus (Mark Antony) – not so fresh from his escapades with Cleopatra – and Octavianus, the young adoptive son of Julius Caesar. Victory went to Octavianus who then assumed the title of Augustus and inaugurated the period we now know as the Empire.

Rome never had such a large army as during the civil wars when there may have been as many as sixty-four legions, and Augustus may still have had fifty legions at his disposal when peace was concluded. Such numbers were no longer really required, and many legions were therefore disbanded. But this could only be done by taking quite radical measures. Money was taken from vanquished opponents, land was confiscated, and military colonies were established in order to settle the veterans. Even the auxilia (auxiliary troops), who were drawn largely from the provinces and who constituted about half the Roman army, were given citizenship on their discharge, and also had to be found somewhere to live. The economy demanded a much reduced military force, but a powerful professional army was still required. There would be many more wars, although, in the main, they were no longer wars of expansion. Those days were over. From this time onwards, most of Rome's energies were to be expended simply on holding the Empire together and retaining what it already had.

In some ways, the Romans are one of the great paradoxes of history. They sought conquest, but also saw themselves as bringers of peace and civilization. They were ready to exploit, but they were also prepared to bestow the benefits of their own culture. Many of their enemies were uncouth barbarians. They did, of course, conquer some cultured peoples such as the Carthaginians and the Greeks, but the majority of their great territorial successes were against the relatively uncivilized peoples on their far frontiers. They vanquished numerically greater armies with their superior skill and equipment, and especially with their military discipline and experience which carried them through some truly daunting campaigns. Barbarians were simply grist for the military mill. But the Romans were also great unifiers, and were prepared to bring others – albeit gradually – into the Roman fold. Provincials and even former enemies could be given a stake in what was arguably the greatest empire the world had ever seen. Yet this had all been accomplished at a terrible cost. Immense sums had been expended and treasures dissipated; whole countries had been laid waste and innumerable people needlessly killed. There was no compelling economic motive, no fight for survival once the very early days of the Republic were past. By and large, the wars had been waged for territory, plunder, and glory, and – not least of all – an intoxication with the exercise of power. As Appian said in his preface to the history of the civil wars, 'I have written this in order that future generations might learn the measureless ambition of men, their dreadful lust for power, their unwearying perseverance, and the countless forms of evil' (Payne 1962: 19).

5

THE EARLY ISRAELITES
The enemy as ritual outlaws

Many societies – particularly historical societies – were informed by a pervasive religious ethic. This often meant that they regarded others as infidels and unbelievers, or – as in the case of Israelite society – as those who were ritually proscribed. Where others did not or could not share their beliefs, they were necessarily excluded from normal, even humane, considerations. The ideological outsider was someone with whom it was not easy to come to terms. Indeed, any understanding might not even be thought desirable except in extreme emergencies or, of course, where the outsiders in question were members of a particularly powerful state. What is especially interesting about the formative phases of Israelite society is whether its considerations were really ideological or simply territorial, and what exactly constituted grounds for a 'holy war'.

In order to appreciate Israelites' attitudes to their enemies it is important to look in broad terms at their social and political organization, and relate these to military systems generally. Only in this way can we see the all-embracing nature of their religious perspectives.

Since early times, Palestine's position in the Eastern Mediterranean had compelled its inhabitants to maintain an efficient war machine in order to maintain independence. This can be seen in the relatively developed armies and fortified cities of the Canaanites and, later, of the Israelites themselves. The very size of the country had always set serious limits on its population, and its natural boundaries made its people exploit its resources to the full. It also encouraged, where possible, the acquisition of further territories, especially to the south and east. This is not to make a case for geographical determinism, but merely to point to the fact that its geographical adjacency meant that Palestine was destined to experience constant pressure from covetous neighbours who – unlike Israel – did not always look beyond immediate economic advantage.

In using the term 'Israelite society', we are thinking of the period covering about 600 years, from the beginning of the tribal settlement in

Canaan in the late thirteenth century BC to the Babylonian conquest in the early sixth century BC. This was a period of varying fortunes for the Hebrews. The Exodus or escape from what was biblically regarded as captivity in Egypt probably took place *c.* 1250 BC during the reign of Pharaoh Rameses II, although this is greatly disputed, some scholars giving a date as early as 1450 BC. The subsequent conquest and settlement of Canaan was followed by the time of the 'Judges' (leaders) which was characterized by both success against the indigenous peoples and disunity among the invading tribes. In certain respects, this was somewhat like the period of heroes (and myths?) found in many other societies – particularly Greek society. It included such worthies as Gideon and Samson – warriors who may well have a real place in history – and their exploits in subduing non-Hebrew tribal groups who were competing for possession of the land.

Gradually, consolidation took place, but not until after there had been a basic change in tribal organization in which heroic leadership reluctantly gave way to monarchy. At first, this was opposed by the priestly caste, but eventually a united kingdom was established under Saul, *c.* 1020 BC. After a rather shaky start, and much scheming and plotting, including a revolt engineered by his son Jonathan and his son-in-law David, he died at the hands of the – by now – traditional enemy, the Philistines. David assumed the throne *c.* 1000 BC and made Jerusalem, which he had wrested from the indigenous Canaanites, his capital. He was followed by his son, Solomon, who expanded Israelite influence even further and brought the nation to the status of a minor Near Eastern power. But this was not destined to last for very long. Wars continued spasmodically against certain resistant peoples, particularly the Philistines in the south who had invaded Canaan about the same time as the Israelites, possibly from Crete, and always threatened the uncertain stability of this tiny state.

This high-water mark of Israelite military and political supremacy was very brief, probably no more than fifty years, during which time the first Temple was built in Jerusalem, and Israel established important political and economic relations with some of her more powerful neighbours such as the Egyptians, the Syrians, and the Phoenicians. When the united monarchy broke down, the kingdom was divided into the ten tribes of Israel in the north and the two tribes of Judah in the south, who, with varying fortunes and intermittent periods of enmity, survived until the re-emergence of Mesopotamian power. The Assyrians destroyed Israel in 721 BC and deported a large percentage of the population, and then the Babylonians – who had defeated a declining Assyria – crushed Judah in 597–583 BC and also deported a number of its people. There was a revival in the fifth century BC with the advent of Persian power when many Jews returned from exile in Babylonia and rebuilt the Temple and the walls in Jerusalem – albeit on a more modest scale.

Canaan–Palestine–Israel, however we wish to refer to it, has always been an area of high economic and strategic importance, principally because it lies on one of the main trade-routes in the Mediterranean and on the main caravan route to Mesopotamia. As such, it has always been vulnerable to attack by more powerful neighbours. So a revival of Jewish nationhood was a precarious affair. After the Persians came the Greeks in the fourth century BC, and after them the Romans who, with growing impatience against the ever-fractious and rebellious Jews, sacked Jerusalem in AD 70, destroying the Temple, and killing perhaps as many as a million of its inhabitants.

Any characterization of the Israelite state must be something of an approximation to the truth. As with so many other systems with a long history, it is only possible to give an incomplete composite picture of its social and political organization.

At the height of its prosperity, Judah–Israel can hardly have had a population of more than a million although some records (e.g. 2 Samuel 24.1–19) suggest that it was much higher than this. While the Hebrews were still a nomadic society, there was simply a division into tribes, including prominent families. But with settlement and urbanization, the structure of the society was transformed. Even so, it is arguable whether there were ever social classes in anything like the modern sense of groups who were consciously concerned to further their own class interests. But there were recognized social divisions. The king's officials constituted a kind of caste which was largely detached from general municipal interests; these appear to have been in the hands of elders in the villages and towns. These elders often held lands from the king and therefore did his bidding, but they also seem to have enjoyed some esteem among the people. In the larger towns where the influence of the councils was particularly strong, we find that the king often found it necessary to negotiate with their most important representatives (Jeremiah 38.24–5). They were men of 'good families', in effect a kind of ruling class of minor – and not so minor – administrators, but they were not a nobility as such, merely the possessors of civic privileges. Closely associated with these were those of military rank, the warriors, who, even if they had little property, owned their own equipment and enjoyed a certain standard of living.

Below these in the social hierarchy were the people themselves. The term 'people of the land' is often used in the Old Testament, and this can mean variously the general body of citizens as distinguished from the priests and nobility, and even resident aliens; much depends on the specific period of Hebrew history in question. A distinction was also made between the rich and the poor; between – broadly speaking –

the independent producers, farmers, stock breeders, etc., and the 'small men', the labourers whose cause was sometimes taken up by the prophets (e.g. Amos 4.1). In order to aid the destitute, the gleanings of the harvest were left, and every sabbatical year the produce was left for their use. However, it would be misleading to equate the poor with a modern proletariat; 'rich' and 'poor' had no overt moral connotations – neither constituted a party or social class in the current sense. Located within this rich–poor continuum were merchants and craftsmen, and outside it – in a special category – the resident aliens, who could hold property but who did not hold full civic rights, and the slaves who were frequently of foreign origin. In the ancient world, slaves were usually either war captives or those who had become slaves through their own or their families' debts. Israel was no exception in this respect, but there is no evidence of any large-scale traffic in slavery among the Hebrews. Indeed, in Hebrew society, slavery seems to have been a relatively humane institution, and the death penalty was prescribed for the crime of abducting an Israelite for the purpose of selling him as a slave. Female slaves came into a special category: they were often domestic servants or concubines, and were not normally released in the seventh (sabbatical) year, as was quite usual with male slaves. Runaway slaves – male or female – were often treated well, in contrast with, say, Mesopotamian society, where they might be either killed or maimed.

The territory that the Israelites conquered consisted of small, sometimes warring, principalities. The Israelites established a very different system based upon twelve traditional tribes which formed a union centred on a number of sanctuaries. When this federation became a national state with the establishment of the monarchy, it inevitably involved the development of new institutions of administration and new systems of allegiances. With the separation of the two kingdoms, Judah opted for divinely sanctioned dynastic succession, but this was slow in coming to Israel where, at first, each succeeding monarch had to be subject to the necessary approval. After the return from Exile, the idea of monarchy was less popular, and power usually lay with the priests under the suzerainty of one or another of the dominant powers. It was really religion which preserved the unity of the nation; the view was that whoever ruled only did so with Yahweh's (God's) authority.

The administration of the state was conducted largely on a tribal basis, with subject territories being laid under tribute, and still sometimes controlled by petty vassals. The main task of local governors, besides maintaining order, was to ensure the collection and dispatch of the necessary revenues for the state coffers. Little is actually known of the fiscal system of Israel or of the resources at the disposal of the state. During the monarchies, there seems to have been no clear distinction between the revenues of the king and those of the kingdom. The king bore all the expenses of maintaining the army, public works, and the like, but he also enjoyed complete control of the monies available. Similarly, there was only a theoretical distinction between the state treasury and the sanctuary treasuries as far as the disposal of revenue was concerned. In times of extreme need, the king would have no compunction in using money from either Temple or palace treasuries. Revenue derived from commercial enterprises, taxes and tithes, tribute money from vassals, besides the produce of the royal estate. Some projects were run on forced labour – a common phenomenon in the ancient world, but it is interesting that the Old Testament makes clear that the small post-Exilic community rebuilt the walls of Jerusalem with *volunteers* and not the forced labour of earlier times (Nehemiah 3.5). In addition, there might be presents from foreign embassies, or special tax revenues which were usually only exacted in an emergency, e.g. to buy off the threats of powerful neighbours such as the Assyrians and Egyptians.

It would be useful, at this stage, to look at the Israelite approach to legal matters. The legislative codes are all to be found in the Pentateuch, the first five books of the Bible; they contain the basic behavioural precepts for religion and morality. There were some variations of time and place, but in general the different versions of the same laws remained the essentials for conduct throughout Israelite history. The Law was the charter of a Covenant with Yahweh and contained all the obligations to be undertaken by the people. It was designed to safeguard the Covenant, and therefore contains many injunctions against idolatry and blasphemy, although its punishments – in the main – are probably more humane than those prescribed by other contemporary systems. There were a number of capital offences, but flogging was limited, and leniencies were shown towards the underprivileged, the poor, the widows, and the orphans. Furthermore, generous exemptions were given from military service. Even the lex talionis, the law of 'an eye for an eye and a tooth for a tooth' – though frightening in its possible applications – only actually demanded proportionate compensation and not the life of the offender.

Jurisdiction might be given by the king, though often through appointed judges, elders, or priests. Justice was usually administered in public, at the gate of the town, or in a holy place or sanctuary. The king gave his judgements in the 'porch of judgement' which was open to all. In a capital case, the prosecution required at least two witnesses, and in the event of the death sentence by stoning, it was these who threw the first stones. If their evidence was proved to be false, they had to suffer the same sentence as would have been given to the accused. According to the historian Josephus, women and slaves were not allowed to give evidence at trials. Even the judge was more an arbitrator than anything else; it was the court that normally made the final decision. Where a decision could not be made for lack of evidence, the accused might be required to take a solemn oath as to their inno-cence (1 Kings 8.31), but there was no casting into the river ordeal as was common in Mesopotamian society. Penalties were often severe: capital offences included sins against Yahweh and against parents, abuses of sexual relations, as well as homicide. Even so, they were probably not as extensive as those found in many neighbouring societ-ies, most notably in cases involving sentences of bodily mutilation. Material restitution or compensation was required in some circum-stances, but there were no prisons as such until after the Exile. Some kind of self-help seems also to have been practised, and was given implicit recognition by law. Asylum was possible for the person who had killed involuntarily, but those who were deemed guilty of premedi-tated murder could be dragged out of a sanctuary and executed, appar-ently without trial (Exodus 21.13–14), or even killed at the altar itself (1 Kings 2.28–31).

The entire land of Israel was technically regarded as being the prop-erty of Yahweh, it was the Holy Land (Psalm 85.2 etc.). A form of feudalism – common in neighbouring states – may have been practised. A fief was possibly given to a local lord or chieftain in return for services which were usually of a military nature. In nomadic times, pasture and watering places were the common property of the tribe, and when the tribes became settled the same system apparently applied to the arable land. The use of the common lands was divided among members of the group who cultivated the land for their own benefit. The annual tithe of the produce that was given to Yahweh and the tithe every third year for the poor attest the ways in which religious laws limited the rights of the human occupants of the land. With the passage of time, however, there was a tendency for the rich to acquire further lands at the expense of others, and the practice of renting of lands began. In this way the rich were emulating the king whose royal estates were managed by stewards and worked by a levy of free men and state slaves.

Ancient Israel has been designated a 'seed-bed' society (Parsons 1966) for the simple reason that, although its influence in its own time was limited, it has had an enormous influence on posterity. This is due pre-eminently, of course, to the contribution its religion has made to west-ern culture and western thought-forms. And it is to religion that we must now turn if we are to have any real understanding of Israelite society.

Ancient Israel was surrounded by nations with polytheistic beliefs, and its strict monotheism was wholly exceptional at the time. Tradition holds that the foundation of Hebrew monotheism dates from the days of the desert wanderings after the Exodus from Egypt. It was then validated by revelations to Moses on Mount Sinai, and subsequently codified as the Law as it is found in the Pentateuch. Various prophetic books and wisdom literature were later added to the historical narratives found in such texts as Kings and Chronicles which together make up the corpus of the thirty-nine books of the Old Testament. This together with the New Testament has become the scriptural basis for religious, moral, and even legal teaching in the entire Judaeo-Christian tradition.

The moral edicts found in the Law have certain features in common with the famous Code of the Amorite Hammurabi (or Hammurapi) in eighteenth-century BC Mesopotamia, but this too may well be based on the even earlier code of the Sumerian Ur-Nammu dating from the third millennium BC. It was not just the specific injunctions of the Law which made it so singular, but the ways in which it was wedded to an unyielding monotheism. There were, of course, periods of spiritual declension when other gods were either worshipped or at least recognized, but by and large the very special nature of the religion was retained. When the priests became too secular in their political roles or became too preoccupied with the need for ritual observances, inspired prophets such as Amos, Hosea, and Isaiah arose to remind the people of their moral and spiritual obligations. Ancient Israel always remained essentially a theocracy.

Perhaps the key to any true appreciation of Israelite religion is to be found in the idea of Election. Indeed, it could be argued that the concept of the Chosen People, that is, the conviction that Israel had been ordained by Yahweh to carry the message of the Law to other peoples, is one of the main clues to any theological understanding of the Old Testament.

Israel owed its sense of national identity to the belief in a special relationship with Yahweh, and it was held that this had been demonstrated in such unique historical events as the Passover and the Exodus. Election and its implications were given formal shape in the Covenant (or agreement) at Sinai where, it is believed, Yahweh revealed his will for the people through the Israelite leader, Moses. This affected every aspect of their social and political life; they saw it as a real event which transformed all of their subsequent history.

The Covenant carried with it both conditions and obligations. The people were to shun idolatry and keep to the social and ritual requirements of the Law. If this was done, Yahweh would vindicate them in the eyes of others – a promise reiterated time and time again by the prophets. Many biblical passages make it clear that Israel's Election was not prompted by her righteousness or merit (Deuteronomy 9.5), but was ordained because of the task which she had to accomplish to be a 'light unto the Gentiles'. This compares unfavourably, as we shall see, with the ways in which some of those Gentiles were actually treated. Israelite religion – not unlike other religions – was subject to interpretation and rationalization, but in its purest prophetic forms it was unique among the contemporary societies of the ancient world.

Our information regarding the military organization of Israel is far from adequate. No single relief or drawing of a military kind has come down to us; perhaps there never were any. This contrasts interestingly with the situation in many contemporaneous societies such as the Egyptian and Assyrian where a great deal has survived. The weapons and remains of fortifications that have been brought to light by archaeology are mainly those of the Canaanites whom the Israelites largely displaced.

It may be that nothing changes in any society quite as rapidly as its military organization because it is affected by so many extraneous factors. Military organization is influenced by changes in governments, and their various policies, by the different kinds of enemy a society is called upon to combat, and, of course, by the relatively slow innovations in armaments and tactics. In the case of Israel there was the other crucially influential factor of religion. Where war is regarded as a sacred undertaking, military enterprise will necessarily take on a particular complexion. This concept may undergo many transformations over time, but it always conditions the nature of war and military preparation.

In their early nomadic phase, the Israelites probably had little real organization. What we know of this, and the subsequent phase of the Judges when the conquest of Canaan was gradually taking place, is preserved in later writings which tended to give the impression of a united force fighting in a common cause. But the source material does vary on this issue. The most complete picture of Israelite military organization can be found in the Old Testament book of Chronicles, and this reflects the state of affairs which we find in the period of the united kingdom and afterwards when the threat from Assyria became an ominous reality.

In the early days the divisions in the army reflected those of the clans. The men were poorly armed and were no match for the Canaanites and other indigenous tribes in a pitched battle, but by stealth and cunning, with small groups of highly trained warriors, they were often able to overcome their opponents. Even in the first years of the monarchy, during the battles against the Philistines, we find that by the stratagems of skilled leaders the Israelites were often triumphant over the superior numbers of their enemies. Sometimes the issue was actually decided between small chosen groups from the opposing sides (e.g. 2 Samuel

2.14ff.) or even between especially selected champions as can be seen in the famous story of David and Goliath (1 Samuel 17).

The first kings of Israel found it necessary to establish a standing army to combat the professional armies of their traditional enemies. The armies were composite units made up of free men, various partisan groups, and even detachments of mercenaries who were not technically free men but who were exempted from certain taxes and forced labour. With increased prosperity, the state was able to develop a chariot force. This was a particular innovation of Solomon, though in this he was emulating the Canaanites and others who had long perfected the use of light two-wheeled vehicles. By 835 BC, in the reign of Ahab, it is reported that the Israelites were able to field as many as 2,000 chariots, although these may have been largely 'bought in' from neighbouring Egypt. These forces were housed in 'chariot towns', and involved considerable supply problems concerning fodder etc.; in fact, excavations at Megiddo have shown that the stables and training areas there probably catered for some 450 horses, many of which may have been imported from Anatolia (Turkey). With the division of the kingdom, these chariot garrisons mainly went to the northern state of Israel, although we find that by the eighth century BC Judah too had built up similar mobile forces (Isaiah 2.7). This was frowned upon by the prophet, Isaiah, who deplored the new dependence on armaments. The chariot force was of no avail in countering Assyrian aggression. In 701 BC, the Assyrian armies under Sennacherib captured every town in Judah except Jerusalem without fighting a single battle in which chariots were engaged (note 2 Chronicles 35.34).

Cavalry was largely an innovation of the semi-nomadic Indo-Aryans who probably emanated from southern Russia. It was never an important feature of the armies of the Near East, particularly Egypt and Israel where horsemen were usually dispatch riders or scouts of some kind. Much later even, in the second century BC, during the Maccabean wars of resistance against the Greek occupying powers, there was no cavalry to speak of to combat the massed forces of enemy cavalry and elephants.

We know relatively little about such things as strategy and tactics. Those recorded for us mainly concern the period of the conquest and the early monarchy when, presumably, the Israelites were dictating the moves. But in the later defensive wars against superior forces, the initiative no longer belonged to the home side. By and large, it was a matter of trying to anticipate the other's moves, and respond in whatever ways seemed possible. We do know that usually the professional or experienced troops fought in the front line, and that the conscripts were held in reserve; when and how chariots were used depended entirely on the situation, and especially on the terrain.

Neither the Bible nor, indeed, archaeology gives us much idea about the weapons used by Israelite soldiers, but it must be assumed that they were much the same as in other Near Eastern armies. Besides various kinds of light defensive armour, there was the sword/dagger, the pike/spear, and, of course, the bow which was introduced rather late in its composite form. This was almost certainly first introduced in Mesopotamia in the third millennium, and probably reached its most refined form among the Scythian tribes of southern Russia in the seventh century BC.

It can be assumed that for the greater part of the history of Israel and Judah, the armies were conscript armies. The men would be recruited by districts which – especially in the early days – would be roughly coterminous with tribal areas. There would be the usual exemptions where men were needed, say, for essential tasks on the land, and there were unusual deferments for newly-weds. In pre-monarchy days, men were expected to bring their own arms, but later on these were supplied from central arsenals. The officers were normally important tribal heads, and the king assumed command of the entire force which was organized in various multiples of ten (i.e. 10, 50, 100, 1,000) – a system which dated back to the period of desert wanderings after the Exodus.

This national army seems only to have been mustered in times of war. Mercenaries may have been retained for more permanent tasks such as bodyguards and guards at frontier posts. Conscription based on a register was, at first, deplored as it was regarded as Yahweh's prerogative to decide who lived and who died. But, as time went on, in the face of more and graver national emergencies, it was increasingly viewed as right and necessary for national salvation.

Towns of any size and importance were normally fortified with walls and ramparts. This was certainly the Canaanite practice, and it was later followed by the Israelites. People were encouraged to retreat to the comparative safety of the towns during times of invasion or attack. These centres were generally impervious to assailants armed only with light weapons, although they might be forced to surrender if their water and food supplies were cut off. Where people could not be starved into submission, the towns could usually only be taken by treachery or by some ruse such as a feigned retreat which tempted the inhabitants to open their gates and give chase to a well-prepared enemy. However, when they were assaulted by really powerful forces, they might fall victim to sophisticated siege engines or other well-tried techniques such as the use of ramps and tunnels. On the other hand, they might be made to surrender through sheer intimidation; this happened when the Syrian forces under Benhadad besieged Ahab's capital at Samaria and forced a capitulation (1 Kings 20).

The Hebrews themselves never used siege engines such as catapults, siege towers, etc., until the Maccabean wars of the second century

BC, and in this they were merely copying their Greek opponents. Nevertheless, the armies of Israel did besiege towns, and here the ethico-religious rules were clearly laid down (Deuteronomy 20.1–20). If the town lay in foreign territory, it had to be offered peace terms, and if the people surrendered, they were still subject to the possibility of forced labour. But if the people refused to open their gates and the town had to be invested when and if it was captured, everything – people and property alike – were regarded as being the spoils of war, and then men might well be put to the sword. Indeed, when the town in question was a Canaanite town inside the frontiers of what was regarded as the Promised Land, all the inhabitants were to be killed without giving them a chance to surrender.

It has been argued that the early wars of Hebrews were really defensive (de Vaux 1973), but this is disputable inasmuch as they were fought to wrest territory from various Canaanite tribes who naturally resented these incursions. Having once taken possession of extensive areas of Canaan, it then became a matter of defending them against both the indigenous peoples and, often, competing forces such as the Philistines. This happened after David's capture of Jerusalem – certainly an offensive action – which was followed by defensive actions against Philistine intervention (2 Samuel 5.17–25). Such actions were a particular feature of the monarchic period of Saul and David, although it should be added that there is no record of any war waged by Solomon. After this, when the kingdom was divided there were wars with hostile neighbours such as the Aramaens of Damascus, especially during the ninth century BC. Both Israel and Judah were also subject to the depredations of more powerful states such as Egypt and Assyria who exacted tribute and taxes as nominal overlords of the land. Subsequently, the two kingdoms had a chequered career under Babylonian, Persian, and Greek domination in which a war of national liberation gave the Jews a breathing space before the occupation and final devastation by the Romans in the first century AD.

Although it was not normally the policy of the Israelite armies to massacre those they had conquered, there were very many exceptions to the rule. Indeed, in general terms, the treatment of the vanquished – by what appears to have been common consent – was pretty awful. At the very least, the fortifications of an enemy town were dismantled. But this was rarely the limit of a victorious army's activities. War had to profit someone, so before a town was burnt it was usually pillaged; property was despoiled, flocks were taken, and even the dead were stripped of their possessions. The possibility for plunder was often the point of the exercise. Men fought for what they could get; they had a right to everything they could lay their hands on (1 Kings 20.39–40) providing – where necessary – the correct royal and ritual donations were made. The king reserved the most precious articles for himself and for the sanctuary.

The Israelites never matched the Assyrians in calculated ferocity, but we find that they were capable of barbarous atrocities, especially when it involved 'holy war'. In the campaigns for the conquest of Canaan attributed to Joshua, the successor of Moses, we find the holy war in its purest form. The warriors had to be ritually cleansed before battle, which included a period of sexual abstinence. After victory, as, for example, at the cities of Ai and Bethel, the final act was the pronunciation of anathema (*herem*) on that which had been taken. All the 'accursed' (literally, separated) living things were put to the sword, almost as a kind of thank-offering for the victory (Joshua 7–9). Similarly, in the subsequent consolidation during the period of the Judges, there were acts of extermination for a mixture of ritual and political purposes. For instance, after Gideon's successful night attack on the rival Midianites, which was much like an elaborate commando raid, we find that there was the mandatory execution of the Midianite chiefs (Judges 7.25) and the incidental – almost casual – trampling to death of 'the men of Succoth' whose only apparent crime was a wish to remain neutral (Judges 8.16).

Once the kingdom had been established, similar policies were adopted. A case in point would be the fate of the Amalekites. Because, ostensibly, they had hindered the passage of the 'children of Israel' to the Promised Land more than two hundred years before, Saul, the Israelite king, was instructed by the priest Samuel in the name of 'the Lord of Hosts . . . [to] defeat Amalek, massacre him and all that belongs to him, do not spare him, slay both men and women, child and infant, ox and sheep, camel and ass' (1 Samuel 15.3 – Moffatt trans.). But apparently, Saul only destroyed what was common and worthless, and kept not only the best livestock for himself but also spared the life of the Amalek king, Agag. This was eventually discovered by Samuel, and such was the ritual authority of the priest, that Saul was reprimanded and told, despite his contrite protestations, that the Eternal had rejected him (1 Samuel 15.26) and that he was no longer to be king of Israel. As a postscript to all this, we are informed that Samuel quickly made up for at least one of Saul's oversights by personally hacking Agag to death 'before the Eternal' at the sanctuary of Gilgal (1 Samuel 15.33).

David, Saul's eventual successor, proved to be more assiduous in dealing with the victims of his raiding parties. And this involved some confusion of loyalties. Whilst operating in the Negev as a kind of freelance guerrilla chief on behalf of the Philistines, the traditional enemies of Israel, he seized the flocks of a particular tribe and 'left neither men nor women alive . . . such was his practice' (1 Samuel

27.9–11). And his son, Solomon, likewise did not always reserve his ire for the recognized enemies of the state; indeed he secured the throne by the common expedient of eliminating rival claimants – particularly his brother Adonijah (1 Kings 2) – and carrying out a few revenge killings, apparently with the benediction of his father. All of which again raises the question of ritual versus political imperatives.

Things did not really improve with the break-up of the kingdom. Various political and religious rivalries resulted in an assortment of bloodletting. This takes us from Zimri, the Israelite king who murdered the entire household of his predecessor (1 Kings 16.11), to the prophet Elijah who ensured the liquidation of 450 prophets of Baal who were functionaries of an imported faith and were, admittedly, doing their best to exterminate the prophets of Yahweh (1 Kings 17–19).

Life was just as precarious for the unwary in the southern kingdom of Judah, where similar internecine struggles for succession also took place. Not untypical is the case of Amaziah who, we are reassured, 'did what was right in the eyes of the Eternal'. After killing the men who had murdered his father, he embarked on a series of campaigns against the Edomites which culminated in the death of ten thousand of the enemy in battle and another ten thousand prisoners who were simply thrown off the cliffs in an act of wanton slaughter. This received no condemnation from the prophets of Yahweh, although Amaziah was severely censured for bringing back Edomite gods which he had adopted, not because they were useless idols but because they had not been efficacious enough to prevent the massacre in the first place (2 Chronicles 25).

And so the sorry catalogue goes on. Even humanitarian acts were as much due to expediency and pragmatism as they were to feelings of mercy. The community stood to gain by keeping prisoners alive: they could be used as slaves or as forced labour. Women particularly could be taken as wives or concubines, and virgins were in particularly high demand as 'rewards' for the fighting men (Judges 5.30). The policy of substituting deportation for slavery, a practice especially associated with the Assyrians and the Babylonians, was never taken up by the Israelites, possibly because their territories were not extensive enough to make it a practicable proposition.

The association between war and religion was particularly common in the ancient world. War was normally accompanied by ritual acts such as libations and sacrifices and a preoccupation with what were considered good and bad omens. It was often believed that war should be waged at the behest of the gods, and certainly that it was carried out with their aid and inspiration. As we have seen, all the institutions of Israel were invested with a sacred character, and nowhere is this better illustrated than in the conduct of war. Not every war was, in the strict sense, a 'holy war' symbolized by the presence of the Ark of the Covenant, although every war had its religious aspects. Certainly, it did not take the form of the Islamic 'jihad' where war is waged in the promotion of a particular ideology. Rather it was the defence of the claims of Israel as a chosen people with a specific mission: as Roland de Vaux (1973: 262) rather protectively puts it, 'it was Yahweh who fought for Israel, not Israel which fought for its God'. In some ways, though, the end result was much the same. Other peoples were oppressed and sometimes exterminated to demonstrate the superiority of a particular people with a particular faith. It was religion – either directly or indirectly – which determined not only how the enemy was perceived, but also the patterns of conquest and the mode of occupation of his territory. One's enemies were the enemies of the faith, and this was evidenced by the ways in which others treated the people of that faith. To those who competed for a place in the Promised Land there was, at first, only one response – war. Later, for good or ill, the tribal groups reached an uneasy accommodation with their neighbours, a policy dictated by both tolerance and expediency.

When the situation changed in the subsequent divided monarchy period, the opportunities for aggression were neutralized by the powerful forces ranged on the borders. The view that 'Yahweh your God . . . marches in front of you [and] will fight for you just as you have seen him do in Egypt' (Deuteronomy 1.30; Revised Standard Version) had to be modified in the light of political exigencies. The armies of Israel and Judah, even in coalition from time to time with other states, were not enough to ward off the incursions of the highly predatory Assyrians and Babylonians who, to use the imagery of the prophets, descended like locusts and devoured the land. The Israelites had originally taken the land by force at the behest, so they declared, of their god. Eventually, after an uneasy occupation of some twelve hundred years, they were removed by the superior forces of those who did not come to settle but to plunder and despoil, or – like the Romans – to administer the territory as just another intransigent province.

There is some evidence – both biblical and extra-biblical – to support the contention that at least some tribal groups of Hebrews (Habiru?) occupied Palestine in pre-conquest days. But it was the conquest itself which established them in strength in this much coveted country. The question of their 'right' to the territory will go on being debated. What we can say is that, despite the means employed, it is probable that only a people imbued with such religious zeal and a steadfast belief in a divine decree could have developed the necessary endurance not only to cherish and sustain such an ideal, but also to keep that hope alive over the tragic centuries.

6

THE CRUSADER KNIGHTS
The enemy as unbelievers

As we have already seen, religious ideology is an extremely potent force in human affairs. What people believe affects what they do. To see the enemy as unbelievers may be an irrational basis for hostility and even cruelty, but it has frequently seemed to justify this kind of treatment. Ideology has a cohesive quality; it unites people in a common belief – no matter how 'false' that belief may be – and this may well metamorphose as a common cause or crystallize around a common goal. This is a process which can be seen very clearly from a study of the Crusaders in the Middle Ages.

Long before the Norman Conquest, the disruptions brought about by the barbarian invasions, especially from Scandinavia, had given rise to a new class of knights. These were, in effect, professional fighting men who possessed their own horses and accoutrements of war. The need for defence was acute and pressing, and consequently by legal grant from either kings or nobles – or sometimes by informal usurpation – more and more land was given over to support these 'new men' who might be mobilized at the local or national level. So by the Conquest, Europe could boast a comparatively numerous knightly class who acted as protectors of society as a whole. This all had to be paid for, but it was not all done at the peasants' expense. There was growing economic development and quite rapid urban expansion; new industries and agricultural improvements resulted in the emergence of rudimentary capitalism, and with it some degree of political consolidation.

The Middle Ages are commonly associated with feudalism which, in turn, tends to be seen in terms of the manorial system where an estate was cultivated by peasants for a local lord in exchange for small strips of land for their own use. It is also linked with what is technically termed a seigneurial system where full administrative and judicial authority is localized under *one* person who also controls all economic rights in the area. But neither of these is peculiar to feudalism only as can be seen, for example, in Spanish America. Strictly speaking the term 'feudalism' connotes far more than this. European feudalism was a

95

system of feuds or fiefs, given as compensation – in a contractual arrangement – for military services rendered by chiefs or lords and sub-let by allotments to their subordinates or vassals. It is thought to have originated after the wars in the eighth century AD between the Franks and the Saracens. The victor, Charles Martel, decided to copy the Mus-lims and increase the numbers of his cavalry. This necessitated the confiscation of many church lands in order to provide forage for the horses. And these lands were given as endowments (estates) to nobles and knights in exchange for a pledge of military duties. Failure to comply automatically meant the forfeiture of the lands. In what was then only a rudimentary money economy, gifts of land constituted a kind of payment for services rendered.

At the first level, the contract was between the monarch and the nobility whereby they agreed to supply soldiers – particularly mounted knights – when required on condition of a generous benefice or fief. A benefice involved income, whilst the holding of a fief was very much bound up with status and honour. Furthermore, a benefice need not be hereditary, and might not involve political powers at all, and was more usually associated with the clergy rather than secular vassals. A lord could revoke a benefice or promote a benefice-holder; this was not the case with a fief which always involved land held by the vassal for the lord. Each swore obligations to the other; it was hereditary on both sides, and the 'contract' was renewed when an heir took over, and new oaths of fealty were sworn. Although, for instance, in France the lord had the authority to freeze the rights of a vassal, he could not prevent him from passing on the fief to his heir – but the vassal certainly could not pass it to anyone else. There were mutual bonds of rights and duties that were recognized by both sides.

European feudalism also involved an estate system of stratification, the term 'estate' being a legal category – in practice, somewhere between a class and a caste – which allowed for minimal social mobility. There were exceptions to this as is evidenced by the considerable mobility in the lower orders of knights in English feudal society. There was no high degree of rational economic organization; entrepreneurs were discouraged where there was arbitrary rule and interminable power-struggles. Merchants and traders tended to constitute a rising class within this hierarchy, and there was an appreciable degree of decentralization of judicial and administrative authority. This was vested instead in an autonomous nobility; consequently we find that in European feudalism there were no highly organized bureaucracies. A complex administrative machine was largely unnecessary, and probably could not have been sustained anyway. So in the absence of strong central government, every man who had anything worth having had to worry about whether he had enough strength to keep it. In these circumstances, the powerless submitted to the powerful for protection, and this meant to their local lord.

A key stratum in an estate or feudal system is the priesthood, and this presents us with certain anomalies in relation to medieval society. There must surely be some doubt as to whether the founder of Christianity would have recognized very much of his teachings in the policies and practices of the medieval Church which, in many ways, was enveloped in the political anarchy that affected society generally. Some of the abbeys and bishoprics were in a sorry state: the higher clergy often acted as feudal lords, and many of the lower clergy were ignorant and illiterate, giving rise to the suspicion that they were little more than dealers in spells and incantations. Yet despite all this it remained a centralized organization which kept alive the essential ingredients of the Christian tradition. Although riddled with benefice practices and nepotism, it was still the great rationalized mechanism of administration in medieval society, and eventually it was to become a salutary counterweight to the increasingly monolithic power of the state.

The Church was also a welcome channel of social mobility. People of intellectual capacity found a niche in its structures and advancement through its activities. Indeed, the Church was the only repository of learning of any kind in medieval society. There was no education outside the Church; salvation – both intellectual and spiritual – was only to be found within the Church. Consequently, men of ability such as Peter Abelard, who was both promoted and persecuted by the Church, could find within it their ambition and their vocation.

What must never be underestimated is the power of the medieval Church. Its wealth alone was colossal – although the idea that it owned about a third of European lands is almost certainly an exaggeration. During the eleventh century, an energetic programme of reforms was initiated which aimed at establishing its true independence from any form of secular rule. The papacy, under Popes Leo IX and Gregory VII, began the conflict which was to influence European history, in one way or another, for several hundred years; the struggle to create a papal sovereignty to which all Christendom was subordinate. But in trying to extricate itself from the domination of secular rulers, the papacy had to take upon itself the mantle of secular power. In its efforts to supplant secular authority with spiritual authority, it merely succeeded in instituting a morally questionable ecclesiastical authority. Inspiration had inevitably succumbed to institutionalization.

Despite the inconsistencies and ambiguities of organized religion, the life of the spirit was still important to many ordinary men and women. It may have been mingled with superstition and an undue reverence for ritual and relics but it evidenced the moral concerns which were very much alive in the community. In general terms, medieval man had little time for original ideas or speculative thought. The Church had always taught him the essentially evil character of the material creation. His body was just a temporary habitat for the soul, so it had to be kept in permanent subjection lest it became contaminated by fleshly lust or worldly ambition.

This all made for a static society in which change and innovation were regarded with apprehension and even suspicion. Yet within this apparently unyielding structure which derived its authority from the unquestioned verities of Scripture, there was a moral and intellectual concern – a spirit of enquiry which sought coherence in a reasoned faith. It may, therefore, be no coincidence that it was just at this time that the politically astute Pope Urban II called for a Holy Crusade. This enterprise was to be led by the nobility and the knights, and it is to them and their ethos of chivalry that we must now turn if we are to appreciate what has been cynically described as 'that total apparatus of elegant futility'.

The idea of knighthood as the bulwark against social disorder is a central theme of medieval literature. This justified the knight's right to lead, and sanctified the use of arms; although the right to bear arms was not enough – they had to be used correctly in what was regarded as a worthy cause. Knighthood, as such, was originally bound up with personal status rather than economic (i.e. landholding) status; but with the passage of time, the warrior caste increasingly reflected the demands of the feudal order. Indeed a warrior in his capacity as a vassal might hold fiefs from several lords but swear special allegiance to only one to whom he would give homage in precedence to all others. This naturally affected the ways in which he could be mobilized, especially for such ventures as Crusades.

There were also the special demands of medieval warfare. Weaponry and horses were expensive, and only the prosperous were able to equip themselves in this way. So a new 'class' was created; a kind of military bourgeoisie. But knighthood was not necessarily confined to the nobility, though men of low birth were rarely knighted. Knights tended to come from well-established families with recognized feudal responsibilities, and by the end of the twelfth century, knighthood and nobility had virtually become synonymous terms. Gradually knighthood became a hereditary right. Knights were not only warriors, but often also landowners and administrators as well, and their legal status as 'knights of the shire' made them key figures in local and central government. In fact, in France the 'king's service' was one of the bases of bureaucracy, and knighthood became the key to a political rather than a military career. It was developments such as these that seriously undermined the strictly feudal basis of knighthood by the early fourteenth century.

In their heyday, however, the knights' primary functions can be seen in essentially military terms. Their predominance was virtually complete in the eleventh and twelfth centuries when the economic monopoly of agriculture had not yet been challenged by the growth of the towns and the development of industry. Political power was almost entirely based on force of arms, and knightly influence increased with the waning authority of central government. Monarchs were not infrequently at loggerheads with their nobles, and it was perhaps to counterbalance the unflagging aspirations of successive secular rulers that knightly institutions appear to have enjoyed the unqualified blessing of the Church.

In effect, it was the Church that 'made' the knight. As part of the consecration ceremony, the knight's sword was laid on the altar as a symbol of dedication; it was then sanctified by prayers which called upon God to ensure that its bearer would use it successfully against 'the scourge of the pagans . . . and other evil-doers'. By the twelfth century, this simple service of dedication had become an elaborate ritual that involved the blessing of each piece of armour, and the ceremonial brandishing of a sword with the invocation that it should never be used in an unworthy cause. The candidate was given a light token blow with the hand or sword – a mysterious but essential part of the service – and presented with his spurs and, where appropriate, a banner, and then duly declared a knight. There was a return to simplicity when knighting took place in the field immediately before battle. This was not unusual for poor squires who could earn more as knights, and it would possibly ensure that they were handsomely ransomed in case of defeat. More commonly, however, knighting in the field took place *after* battle as a reward for valour; even the Black Prince 'won his spurs' this way.

Whatever form this solemn act took, in submitting to it the knight had effectively become a member of a quasi-religious order which acted as the secular arm of the Church, ostensibly to protect it and to defend the weak. It was carefully controlled so as to exclude undesirables from the knightly ranks. A peasant could hardly aspire to knighthood, but it was not unattainable for a man from the lower gentry. On the other hand, it was not easy for, say, a merchant; making money by trade had always been a suspect occupation.

What probably distinguished the knightly ethos more than anything else was the notion of honour. In theory, a knight's word once given could never be retracted, although a vow could be annulled by ducal or royal command. Exceptionally, this only occurred where someone had made a rash or trivial promise as happened with the Duke of Burgundy who overrode a vow made by one of his knights that he would not turn his horse's head back until he had killed an infidel. For knights generally an oath was sacrosanct. The very concept of honour had a mystique and a solemnity which could be neither defined nor denied. Honour was the key to the chivalric code, yet its applications were shrouded in ambiguities. Perhaps its 'essence' can best be discerned in particular circumstances or settings, as in the Arthurian romances or the *chansons* of the medieval troubadours; it can also be seen in the tournament ethic and the knightly attitudes to women. But, complementarily, its inconsistencies were all too evident as well, particularly in the organized barbarism of medieval warfare, not least in the Crusades.

The techniques of warfare had shown some advances from the crudities of the Dark Ages. These were especially notable in the use of cavalry. Horses were now shod – a great improvement on rough terrain. And the development of the stirrup – an innovation of nomadic Asian tribesmen – made it possible to use a heavy lance by reducing the probability that the rider would be unhorsed in the charge. There was also the development of the long-bow and the cross-bow which greatly increased the distance at which the initial engagement could be fought. These had a devastating impact on warfare, and they were condemned by Pope Innocent II in AD 1139 as a 'deadly art, hated of God . . . which should not be used against Christians and Catholics'. At this high-water mark of crusading zeal, it is worth noting that non-Christians (infidels) are conveniently excluded. Not least of all were the changes in protective armour which became more all-enveloping yet allowed the warrior to fight either mounted or dismounted. Ultimately, it became so heavy that a *reductio ad absurdum* situation was reached in the fifteenth century when knights had literally to be winched on to their steeds, and once unhorsed were at the mercy of lightly armed troops.

In the Crusades themselves it is interesting to compare the tactics employed by the Franks and the Turks. The Franks relied on their heavily armed knights to force a breach in the enemy line. Timing was crucial. If the attack was mistimed, the elusive Turkish cavalry would scatter and then counter-attack the now vulnerable Franks who had lost their tight formation. The Turkish cavalry were essentially mounted archers who had great speed and agility. They were no match for the Crusaders in hand-to-hand combat, but usually they could maintain their distance and often wreak havoc on the ponderous and more easily exhausted knights.

When wars were not available, there was always surrogate military activity. Medieval tournaments were like mimic wars, but it would be misleading to suppose – as some chroniclers have suggested – that medieval wars were little more than mimic tournaments. Admittedly, the scale of warfare was comparatively small by both earlier (e.g. classical) and later standards; most medieval armies rarely numbered more than 10,000 men, of whom less than a fifth would be knights. Pitched battles between evenly matched armies were relatively rare; Henry II, for instance, never fought a battle in the whole of his life. Battles were risky affairs, and were not normally undertaken without very careful deliberation. It has been argued (Barber 1974) that although war was a kind of unreal game for the professional warrior, it was also much rougher and bloodier than is often believed. Strategies were limited, and tactical innovations were few, so the general approach to battle followed a fairly predictable course. But it was not all cut and rush by a mêlée of colourfully accoutred knights. Considerable skill was displayed in the choice of terrain and the disposition of the forces, as well as in the use of the weaponry itself.

The general strategy in much medieval warfare was concerned with the control of the countryside. The common directive was, 'First destroy the land.' In practice, this meant manoeuvres designed to deprive the enemy of their fortresses. Thus a great deal of time and effort was expended in siegecraft, and a typical knight might well spend more of his active life in sieges – either as an attacker or a defender – than in actual battles. Even so, it was rather unusual for a well-fortified town to be taken by direct assault; intrigue and betrayal were not uncommon solvents of resistance. Knights, by both temperament and training, were rarely inclined to a defensive role, and it was their relative lack of discipline which often had disastrous consequences, especially in the Crusades. Their encounters with the infidel, whom they were often disposed to treat as their military inferiors, sometimes led to rash and reckless attacks which resulted in unacceptable losses. A typical example was the Templar Gerard of Ridfort who impulsively decided to engage a large Muslim force at Cresson in AD 1187 and ended up as only one of three survivors. Tactical prudence and a greater willingness to listen to sage advice might have prevented a number of catastrophes of this kind. Yet not even defeat was always enough to curb the impetuosity of those who felt themselves to be fundamentally superior to their enemies. *They* had the stomach for it, they had the knightly *esprit*, and they alone had right on their side – ultimately, they believed they *had* to win.

The conduct of war was conditioned by its context, and the exercise of chivalry was graded in accordance with the social position of the participants. The ground-rules were normally established at the outset of any engagement, although circumstances might decree that these were subsequently ignored. For example, pillaging and burning were technically forbidden between Christian states, but in certain conditions this might be waived, as can be seen where commanders were either unwilling or unable to restrain their troops in the final stages of a battle.

Amidst all the anger and confusion, soldiers might be let loose – say at the culmination of a siege – to ravage the town and take revenge upon the enemy. Normally sieges were governed by quasi-legal provisions. If a siege had been formally declared the besieged were in a position to make terms at any point prior to the storming of the town. If they refused and were defeated, their goods and possibly even their lives were forfeit. It was entirely up to the discretion and disposition of the conqueror whether this power would be exercised compassionately. Technically, churches and clergy were immune, but even this discriminatory concession might well be ignored in practice. This can be seen in the invasion of Cyprus by the Crusader Reynold of Chatillon who became Prince of Antioch. Regardless of the fact that the citizens were Christians who had helped the men of the First Crusade, he decided to sack the island even though it was really part of the Byzantine Empire. For three weeks his troops carried out a campaign of pillage and murder; shops were looted, animals stolen, and property burned. Women were raped and the old and the very young had their throats cut. Nothing was sacrosanct, not even the churches. Chivalry took second place to sheer lust and brutality.

Alternatively, devastation might occur where there was an unintended escalation of hostilities. This happened on one occasion in the interminable battles between the French and the English, where what began as an expedition to intimidate the local population, ended as the battle of Poitiers. Usually, the conditions of a medieval battle were understood from the beginning. At the battle of Crécy, for instance, before the fighting began the French signalled that no quarter was going to be given, and all prisoners would be killed. In other engagements, where it was understood that quarter and ransoms would be allowed, the combatants often fared reasonably well; it was the non-combatants who suffered from the rapacity and devastation of the contending armies. A contemporary account records:

> The march begins. In front are the scouts and incendiaries . . .
> after them the foragers to collect the spoils. Soon all is tumult.
> The peasants hurry back from the fields with loud cries . . .
> shepherds drive their flocks into the woods to save them. The
> incendiaries set the villages on fire, and the foragers sack them.
> The terrified inhabitants are either burned or led away . . . for
> ransom. Fear sweeps the countryside. Wherever you look you can
> see helmets glinting in the sun, pennons waving in the breeze . . .
> horsemen are everywhere.
> (From the 'Chanson des Lorrains', quoted in Gillingham 1978: 118)

It was comparatively rare for a captive with some social standing to be slain where lucrative deals for their return could be arranged. But the fate of the common people was altogether a different matter, and massacres could occur as the result of uncontrolled aggression or simply as the outcome of a calculating and cynical expediency. Things changed somewhat in the later Middle Ages, notably during the Wars of the Roses, when it was the nobility who had the most to fear, especially from their fellow nobles.

War to the death was usually reserved for the infidel. Christians, despite the conviction that theirs was the true faith, were often very apprehensive about Islam. At the Council of Clermont in 1095, Urban II spoke of 'our tiny portion of the world . . . pressed by warlike Turks and Saracens [who] . . . hope to devour the rest'. This directly derived from the prevailing attitudes to Islam and all that it represented. Yet, interestingly, this varied considerably at different levels of society. In the literary and scientific communities, there had been profitable contacts with Islam since the eleventh century, and these became quite developed in the next two hundred years. So we find that during the period of the Crusades when Muslims and Christians were enthusiastically slaughtering one another for ideological reasons, some members of their respective intelligentsia were sharing ideas on all manner of erudite matters ranging from medicine to astronomy. Similar contradictory attitudes can also be seen in the same period in the relations between Christians and Jews: at one level there was co-operation – especially in works of translation – but at another there were hysterical outbursts of violence towards the Jewish communities in several European cities.

There was undoubtedly an economic dimension to the Crusades. The Asia of Islam was seen as a place of incalculable wealth and exotic delights – besides being a haven of the unconverted. Lesser knights and impecunious adventurers alike found the prospect of overseas riches both alluring and exciting – even if it was all something of a gamble. Greed was tempered by uncertainty. Later, after there had been some limited successes, more campaigns became necessary to try to retain that which had already been possessed.

It was, however, the religious factor that was probably most important. Avarice was accompanied by a righteous indignation at the Muslim desecration of the 'Holy Places'. Christians wanted to curb what they saw as Muslim abominations in Palestine, and liberate their shrines which they felt had unique Christian significance. In the furtherance of this cause, they were promised absolution and remission from sins. At the inauguration of the First Crusade in AD 1095, Pope Urban enjoined the Christian states to cease squabbling among themselves for temporary territorial advantages, and to concentrate on seeking eternal glory in an expedition against the infidel. So the rewards that were offered to those who took the cross were considerable. On a profit and loss basis, they could hardly lose. At the most mundane level, while they were on crusade, their property was taken under the protection of the Church, and the repayment of any debts they owed was postponed until their return. As a bonus, there might be rich pickings from plunder and 'appropriation' in the Holy Land. For some – perhaps for many – what was more critical was that they were granted a plenary indulgence which freed them from the terrors of purgatory and hell, and held out the promise of eternal life in heaven. According to Bernard of Clairvaux, a great contemporary divine, they were being offered 'an amazing bargain that [they] could not afford to miss'.

The development of such ideas is interesting to trace. The traditions of the primitive Christian Church appear to have been opposed to war of any kind, but things changed after the adoption of Christianity as the state religion by the Roman Emperor Constantine in the fourth century AD. By the fifth century, perhaps under the pressure resulting from the barbarian invasions, the notion of the 'just war' had evolved. Within another hundred years, the idea that it might be legitimate to wage war for the forcible conversion of the unbelievers was being discussed, and by the eighth century this had become politically feasible. So by the time of the first Islamic invasion of southern Europe, mass was being said before battle and saints' relics were being carried as a mark of piety and as a form of spiritual insurance. The era of the soldier-saint had arrived.

The faith and the growing wealth of the Church had to be protected, so there was an increasing involvement of the Church in secular affairs. State interests became ecclesiastical interests, and some popes actually marched to battle alongside the troops. The defence and promotion of the Christian ideal became a sacred duty, and the warrior who espoused the cause received the endorsement of the Church. This does not mean that the clergy encouraged unqualified expansionism or normally resorted to warfare to advance their interests, but it does mean that in numerous situations, most notably those concerning infidels – Muslims and possibly Jews – necessary violence might be sanctioned.

Given that the necessary rationale had been evolved, it is instructive to look at the ways in which it influenced the origination and progress of the Crusades themselves. The Muslims had held Jerusalem since AD 638, but it was not until the Church of the Holy Sepulchre was destroyed by a particularly fanatical caliph in AD 1009 that Christians became really alarmed. A new climate of opinion developed; uncertainty bred suspicion, and this eventually generated even more hostile attitudes among Christians. The papacy had already sponsored expeditions against the Muslims in Spain some thirty years before the First Crusade began, and had encouraged other quasi-religious causes such as that of the Normans *vis-à-vis* the English in AD 1066. It was therefore quite in keeping with ecclesiastical policy to initiate and support a campaign against the Muslims of Outremer (a term literally meaning Overseas which was popularly applied to Palestine). The response was overwhelming, yet the expedition itself was marked by unexpected disappointments and disasters, and one suspects that it might have been abandoned long before it was had it not been for a virtually unshakeable conviction that it was divinely inspired. But it was also marked by a mindless cruelty which cannot easily be squared with the much vaunted code of chivalry. For example, in one of the earlier sieges at Antioch, the Crusaders were welcomed by the Greek and Armenian citizens who hated their Muslim overlords, and who were only too willing to join in the massacre which followed the fall of the city. It was a barbarous affair in which no one was spared, and Turkish women and children were butchered along with their men. By midday not a Turk was left alive, and the streets reeked with the smell of rotting flesh. Another infidel stronghold had been won for Christ.

If anything, the subsequent carnage at Jerusalem in AD 1099 was even worse. The Crusaders had been camped in the desert for a month and for some time had been suffering from hunger, thirst, and disease. Frustration, anger, and questionable convictions combined to bring about yet more wanton slaughter. Nothing was regarded as being too bad for 'the pagan cattle', the 'unbelieving black-faced brood'. They were seen as hated of God, profaners of Holy Places, and incorrigibly degenerate. The Crusaders killed every man, woman, and child whom they could find in the city. The massacre went on unremittingly throughout the day and night and even included some Jews who were herded into a synagogue and then burned alive. It is testified that when the Crusader chaplain, Raymond de Aguilers, visited the Temple next morning he was hardly able to move for the corpses 'which reached up to his knees'. In fact, the only people who were known to have escaped were the governor and his bodyguard who had paid the chaplain a huge bribe and surrendered a considerable treasure. When it was all over the triumphant Crusaders went to the Church of the Holy Sepulchre to give thanks for their great victory over the 'servants of anti-Christ'.

The First Crusade can hardly have been considered a success, and eventually a Second Crusade became necessary. Thanks largely to a fervent sense of mission generated by the eloquence of Bernard of Clairvaux, various armies set off for the Holy Land from AD 1146 onwards. As usual there were fratricidal tensions among the Crusaders themselves, particularly between different national groups. In making their way to Palestine, they were plagued by logistical problems and difficulties over supplies. They had either to buy what they needed or to rely on the generosity of those through whose territory they had to pass. But not infrequently they just decided to live off the land, and this simply meant taking what they wanted when they wanted it. Consequently there was the kind of pillaging and atrocities among the indigenous peoples – who were often Christians – that was normally reserved for the infidel. This happened, for instance, when the Germans got out of hand in Byzantine territory; their killing and looting even included the burning of a monastery and the murder of all the monks. Further anomalies can be seen in the treatment of one class by another. After defeat by the Turks in AD 1148, there were not enough ships to evacuate the whole army, so the French embarked the king and his retainers and the best part of the cavalry (knights) whilst the infantry had to make their own way as best they could. Deserted by their leaders, many died from disease, and many more were picked off by marauding Turks. A final campaign to take Damascus ended in failure, and the Second Crusade petered out amidst bitter rows and recriminations.

The Third – and perhaps best known – of the Crusades was probably also the best organized and best led of all the ventures to the Holy Land. Although its nominal leader, Frederick Barbarossa, died accidentally *en route*, it was ably but divisively generalled by Philip Augustus of France and Richard I (Coeur de Lion) of England. Their opponent was the fabled Saracen leader, Saladin, who had recently annihilated a Christian army at Hattin. Other Crusader-controlled cities had soon surrendered including Jerusalem in AD 1187. Both fortunately and unfortunately for the Europeans, Saladin had a reputation for never breaking his word to either friend or foe, which was unusual even by Muslim standards, and earned him enormous respect, especially among his enemies. When he made promises, they were kept, so when he promised the lives of those captured after his siege of Jerusalem, it was honoured by his troops. But, by the same token, he had all the Hospitallers and Templars who were captured at Hattin killed without giving them a chance to be ransomed, and it is said that he watched the slaughter with a joyful face because it was an act of purification.

Keeping one's word has its problems, at least it did for Coeur de Lion. As the epithet suggests, Richard was a man of considerable prowess and personal charisma; unlike Saladin, he was physically impressive – the personification of the warrior-knight. Nor were his virtues all of the machismo variety; his chroniclers speak of his great sensitivity to the arts, especially music and poetry. But he also had his dark side. Even before the Crusade, he had shown how his enemies in France ought to be treated: blinding and drowning were quite fit punishments for rebels. And this was only an indication of what was to come. After the siege of Acre, Richard vowed that he would kill all the prisoners if they were not ransomed in the prescribed time. When Saladin was apparently unable to raise sufficient money on time, Richard had 3,000 captives led out and massacred, and only spared their commanders – possibly for ulterior reasons. One eyewitness says that the soldiers delighted in the butchery as revenge for their comrades who had died in the siege, and perhaps also for those who had been coldly exterminated by the Muslims at Hattin.

So after all the reciprocal slaughter, nothing was really achieved. The failure of the Third Crusade was particularly significant because even though the great national leaders of Christendom had made common cause and had commanded a greater army than ever before, they were still no nearer success. The Fourth Crusade which followed was even more of a disaster because the overall objective became lost among the welter of subsidiary aims. There was an inevitable clash between the various interested parties which involved the commercial gain of the Venetians and Italians, the imperial ambitions of the Franks, and the hopes for ecclesiastical reunification between east and west which were vainly entertained by the Vatican. Ultimately nothing was gained except the papal excommunication of the entire Crusade.

Despite the almost predictable failure of further Crusades, the ideal was still retained. It could be argued that they were really only a manifestation of papal ambition in the Near East and an attempt to extend ecclesiastical power in another secular domain. Yet this tends to overlook the response of knightly chivalry and the resonance which these ventures had among the common people. Eventually there were murmurings about their purposefulness, but the prospect of the liberation of the Holy Land and its sacred places retained a considerable popular appeal. They also had the diversionary function of forcing men's minds away from their parochial squabbles by giving them a greater cause and a nobler objective. But their main problem was the disparity between principle and execution. The ideal of the Crusades was reasonably unambiguous, but its actual implementation was riddled with anomalies.

This discussion has tended to stress the shortcomings of the Crusaders, their national differences, their mixed motives, and, above all, their brutality. But very similar accusations could be made against the Muslims; in the calculated cruelty stakes there would be very little to choose between them. Furthermore, we can see the internal dissension which vitiated their whole approach to war. This was particularly marked among the Europeans, and we are often treated to the spectacle of Christian slaughtering Christian ostensibly in the pursuit of a common religious goal. Finally, in the thirteenth century, we have the irony of finding Muslim Saracens ousted by Muslim Turks, who, as Mamelukes, had taken control of Egypt, and Christians in league with Mongols in an effort to neutralize Muslim power. These wars culminated in the destruction of the Abbasid Caliphate in Baghdad with the general massacre of its inhabitants, and the invasion of Syria which became a vassal state of the Mongol empire.

So the outcome of the Crusades was a far cry from the glorious ideals which had originally inspired them. Similarly with the noble institution of knightly chivalry. It became increasingly elaborated and was ritualistically organized with codified – even mystical – rules and regulations. Gradually it degenerated into little more than a social code – a means of distinguishing the fighting aristocracy from their peasant inferiors. At first, this code mitigated some of the extremes of feudal society, but eventually the knightly class became a victim of its own ideology.

Knighthood was a relatively closed system with limited fraternal possibilities for those outside its orders. It thrived within its exclusive *métier*. In its own way it reflected the dichotomous attitudes of medieval society with its simplistic division between believers and unbelievers which culminated in the theory and practice of the holy war which might be justly waged against the infidel. In the eyes of the Church, the lives of unbelievers were of little account. They were doomed to hell anyway, and there might even be some virtue in accelerating the process. 'The Christian glories in the death of a pagan', said Bernard of Clairvaux, 'because thereby Christ himself is glorified' (quoted in Gillingham 1978: 183).

For some knights religion obviously acted as a convenient ideology to justify their material ambitions. Others were suffused with a genuine religious zeal. Yet the literature makes clear that it would be a mistake to settle for such a simple distinction. Men can rarely be categorized in this way – and this is certainly true of the knights. The majority were clearly rapacious *and* religious, superstitious and commonsensical. They *were* avaricious, they *did* want to line their own pockets, and seek out lands and titles for themselves. On the other hand, they could still be exultant when they believed that they had discovered the lance that had pierced Christ's side, and still clasp bloodstained hands in prayer in the Church of the Holy Sepulchre after the butchery of Muslim prisoners.

The Crusades were not really undertaken because of either resource or position scarcity. Nor were they directly waged in the promotion of an ideology, or in the attempted destruction of a rival ideology. No efforts were made to convert the Muslim; it was not a question of the Islamic 'submit or die'. The Crusades and the Crusader ideal were directed towards the elimination of strategically placed adherents of a faith that threatened to engulf the known world and whose territorial acquisitions happened to include the most sacred shrines in Christendom. In the furtherance of these aims there was a happy coincidence of motives. Greed and glory make a potent combination – and there was always eternal bliss as an added incentive. There is nothing better than serving God and Mammon at the same time.

7

THE MONGOLS
The enemy as effete degenerates

With the possible exception of the heavily armoured mounted knights, the feudal armies of medieval Europe were no real improvement on the armies of classical times, whereas all kinds of revolutionary innovations were being developed in certain contemporary Far Eastern societies. In China, for example, forms of gunpowder were being made as early as the ninth century AD by rather esoteric Taoist alchemists, and within a hundred years primitive flame-throwers were being used. By about AD 1000, simple bombs and grenades had been developed, and so had incendiary arrows which were launched from wheelbarrows. In effect they were a rudimentary form of mobile rocket from which the proto-type of the barrelled gun evolved in the twelfth century. There was no heavily armoured cavalry in China, the strength was in the infantry, and these weapons merely supplemented the conventional arsenals, and their proving grounds were the interminable wars against the Mongols.

By the thirteenth century, the Mongols may have had the best army in the world; its organization and training, its tactical principles and structure of command were quite different from those of their opponents. Indeed, they probably had more in common with the bar-barian hordes that had ravaged Europe in the fourth and fifth centuries than with the effete civilizations which they regarded as ripe for conqu-est. In fact, there is a sense in which it is possible to view history, down to the fifteenth century, as a long-drawn-out struggle between nomads and city-dwellers; between the hardy tribesmen and the cultured but indulgent urbanites.

The societies of wandering herdsmen do not normally produce writ-ten histories; only a few folk-memories remain, embedded in the tra-ditions of their victims – the developed peoples that they have conqu-ered. Even from these it is hard to assess the amount of human suffering caused by the great waves of barbarian invasions, although it has since become fashionable in some quarters to entertain a more generous appreciation of these peoples, looking upon them as vigorous invaders almost deservedly taking over the remains of a decaying civilization. This kind of reassessment may apply to the early Aryans and the later Arabs, and even the Teutonic invaders of the declining Roman Empire, but it is hardly true of the Mongolian tribes who poured out of the wastes of central Asia to devastate the continent and beyond.

The original home of the Mongols was in the region of Lake Baikal, and in their early days there was little to mark them out from other Asiatic nomads of the eastern steppes. They formed an essentially feudal society; each tribe was led by a khan with a group of lesser 'nobility' who, in effect, constituted a kind of ruling aristocracy. The tribes were divided into clans, each of which established its own independent ordu (English=horde) or camp in which each family occupied its own yurt (tent). Even for the better placed families, life was hard – especially in winter – when the most important consideration was their survival, and this meant the preservation of the herds. It was nothing for tribesmen to spend several days, sometimes without food, searching for pasture and game, and men developed hunting skills in this constant competition for existence. Prior to the emergence of the Mongols as a united force, the commonest way to increase the size of herds was to steal animals from others, so the hunters also developed their warrior potential in frequent inter-clan raids. And these were not confined to the acquisition of cattle and horses, but extended to the capture of able-bodied men as slaves and presentable women as wives, as the rules of this polygamous tribal society forbade endogamy, that is, marriage between clan members. Loyalty and endurance were encouraged, and any show of weakness was not tolerated among clan members, and certainly not in their enemies to whom the Mongols could be ruthless in the extreme.

These loose and fluctuating alliances among the tribes changed with the advent of Chingis (Genghis), a clan leader, who united the tribes in AD 1203 and assumed the title of Khan three years later. By an impressive combination of force and persuasion, he brought about a high degree of co-operation between the tribes. Loyalties were widened by interspersing clan members among different units of the army, and other previously alien tribes were incorporated into the structures of this new military society. In this way, bonds were strengthened, and fidelity to the central authority was reinforced. Chingis enforced a code whereby it became illegal to hold other Mongols as slaves, and theft and kidnapping both became punishable by death, as were also spying, bearing false witness, black magic, adultery, and sodomy. Tribal cohesion was a necessary part of the military ethic. As he put it, 'The greatest joy a man can have is victory . . . to conquer one's enemies . . . to reduce their families to tears . . . and make love to their wives and daughters' (quoted in Fryer 1975: 130).

111

All men over the age of 20 except physicians, priests, and those who cared for the bodies of the dead, were liable to call-up for military service. When messengers brought the orders to mobilize, trained men would collect their weapons from the armoury of their ordu, select their horses, and set out to join their units. The army was divided into multiples of ten: no one of these might leave the others, and no one was allowed to abandon a disabled comrade. Above these there were squadrons of a hundred, regiments of a thousand, and divisions of ten thousand which had leaders appointed by the Khan himself. These, and the senior army commanders, the 'eleven orloks', carried authorized insignia of office which were instantly recognizable by the largely illiterate troops. There were well-organized groups of support personnel such as Chinese and Persian physicians, supply and communications sections, besides the auxiliary units of engineers and artillery. But the main arm was the cavalry which may have numbered – at its height – a quarter of a million men. Mobility, not gunpowder, was the secret of Mongol success; they relied on the extraordinary speed and paralysing savagery of their horsemen to achieve the victories which instilled such terror among the neighbouring peoples.

The cavalry was divided into heavily armed and lightly armed units. All were well equipped with fur-lined clothes and boots against the winter, with differences in trim and decoration according to rank. A heavily armed trooper wore a helmet and coat of mail with a cuirass made of ox-hide and iron scales, whereas a lightly armed trooper might only be protected by lacquered leather strips or just a quilted coat. All wore loose undershirts of raw silk which, in conditions of limited hygiene (bathing was forbidden by Mongol rules), virtually rotted on their backs. But the shirt was very important as it was often capable of 'trapping' a penetrating arrow in such a way that it could be effectively removed without making the wound much larger. Each man carried a leather covered wicker shield and a lasso, and a dagger was strapped to his forearm. The lightly armed troops also carried a small sword, and the heavily armed troops a scimitar, axe, or mace together with a 12-foot lance. All men carried two bows which were unquestionably their most important weapons. One was for short range, and the other – a composite bow with a pull of some 120 pounds – was a formidable weapon by any standards. It was made of horn and wood, and had a more impressive performance than the famed English longbow, having a range of about 350 yards. In addition, each horseman carried quivers containing sixty arrows of various kinds: armour-piercing arrows, incendiary arrows, and even whistling arrows for communication purposes. Needless to say, training with such equipment began at an early age, and mature warriors were able to use these weapons with terrifying skill.

In effect, every man was an independent ordnance unit, carrying everything he needed for both welfare and warfare from his cooking-pot to an inflatable waterproof saddle-bag which could double as a crude life-jacket when crossing rivers. Even his indispensable horse was thickset and strong, and was purposely bred for its courage and stamina. Herd instincts were deliberately fostered by training so that both mares and stallions would follow each other to battle. Different army units liked to have distinctive colour combinations in their horses, but white was reserved for the nobility. Each man probably had at least three horses, and although these appear to have been relatively well treated, it could be argued that the warriors literally lived off their mounts. The mares – which were prized for their versatility – supplied milk, and both mares and stallions were bled for sustenance, and eaten when necessary. Horses, therefore, provided everything that a warrior needed to survive, but a horse that was ridden in battle was not normally used for food, and when a warrior was slain his favourite horse was usually killed too so that their spirits would 'ride together'.

By law, a man was trained from boyhood to become a warrior. He was instructed in archery and horsemanship, and took part in the 'great hunt' which in practice involved the whole army and took several weeks to complete. In both training and warfare competitiveness among the warriors was encouraged. No man was regarded as fit to command unless he had first served in the ranks, and appointments and promotions were made strictly on the basis of merit.

One of the most outstanding features of the Mongol army was its unity of command. Enemies wondered at the almost inexplicable co-ordination which was achieved over wide expanses of terrain. It was actually accomplished by a complex signalling system using coloured pennants during the day and burning torches at night. This was combined with an extensive courier service with regular, well-maintained staging posts. Couriers had their bodies bandaged for support against the rigours of the ride. They might cover as much as 120 miles in a day over rough terrain, sometimes actually sleeping in the saddle. On occasions they were prepared literally to ride their horses to death to ensure that vital messages were delivered.

When it took to the field, the most common tactic of the Mongol army was to engage the enemy with its lightly armoured troops before bringing up the heavy cavalry. This might be done in one of two main ways, either by engaging the flanks at a distance with flights of arrows, or by trying to break the enemy's main line by 'suicide' tactics of frontal assault and retreat. This left the enemy in some disarray and therefore open to an attack from the heavily armed cavalry which more often than not proved decisive.

Expansionism means that armies have to master siege operations, and the Mongols became increasingly sophisticated in the use of artillery. They employed various forms of catapult and ballistae to hurl rocks and incendiary bombs. There is no evidence that they actually used cannon, but towards the end of the thirteenth century they were using gunpowder balls and primitive bamboo rockets which though apparently inaccurate and unreliable were quite frightening and sometimes actually destructive.

Chingis Khan first launched his army against the Chinese saying, 'Let's kill all the men who are taller than the axles of our wagons.' The Chinese relied principally on their foot soldiers and on their excellent fortifications. Many of the cities were walled against attack (later – towards the end of the fourteenth century – these were monumental and dwarfed their European counterparts with walls as much as 70 feet high and 50 feet thick at Nanking and Sian), but even these and the Great Wall itself did not deter the invaders. For a time, the Mongols had a working agreement with the southern Chinese, but still took some eight years to defeat the Kin dynasty in the north after seasonal depredations of the countryside. A vast tribute was paid and, as part of the humiliation terms of capitulation, Chingis had demanded 500 boy slaves and 500 girl slaves in addition to a herd of horses and large quantities of silk and gold. The emperor hoped to buy off the Mongols but simply succeeded in fomenting a rebellion among his own supporters, whereupon he had to flee to the south. The success of the Mongols was complete, and in 1216 Chingis married into the royal family.

The southern Chinese took much longer to subdue. The reasons are largely geographical: the Mongols were used to operating in the steppes, in northern fastnesses, not in rice fields for which their horses were not really suited. Also the population density was far higher, and the people fought with considerable courage – some cities withstanding sieges for several years. But in the end they too succumbed to Mongol tenacity.

Their army operated like a modern panzer force. They appear to have moved twice as fast as their enemies, and were often victorious when the odds were at least two to one against success. The Mongols sometimes spread rumours among their enemies that their numbers were far greater then they really were. This often gave them a real advantage. Yet in most of their campaigns they were actually outnumbered by their opponents. In their initial onslaught on the Chinese they had an army little more than 100,000 strong, about a quarter that of their enemies. Even at the height of his power, Chingis probably deployed a force not much larger than this. The core of the army was the Imperial Guard of 10,000 men which was formed after a sifting of the entire Mongol horde. To be a mere private in this elite unit was the equivalent of being a commander in any other Mongol regiment. They expected no mercy from their enemies, and they certainly showed none to their enemies. The inhabitants of some Chinese cities, for example, were massacred to the last infant. All captives west of the Great Wall, except artisans and scholars, were put to the sword. Sometimes even the cattle and other animals were slain in a seemingly purposeless orgy of killing. The army probably won less by fighting than from the horror it inspired in its enemies.

Their success was undoubtedly based on superior skill and tightness of organization. But it also had a strong psychological dimension. The Mongols aroused abject fear in most of their enemies – and not without reason.

The Mongols knew little of culture or the arts. Arguably they would have been content to see much of China as grazing ground for their herds, but they were astute enough to realize that the efficient organization of the ancient kingdom meant a continuation of the tribute which they demanded. They therefore encouraged a modified administration and allowed life to go on much the same as before providing there was no hint of rebellion. Although they had turned many a city into a wilderness, they somewhat incongruously fostered religious toleration – perhaps because it was regarded as 'harmless'. Indeed there was a real measure of freedom so long as subjects obeyed the laws of their masters, but a complex and demanding system of exacting taxes increased their sense of subjugation. The Mongol generals had advocated exterminating most of the northern Chinese, and turning their lands over to grazing, and it was with some difficulty that their chief minister persuaded them that it would be more profitable to impose taxes than to slaughter the inhabitants (Dawson 1972).

Chingis had a restless conquering spirit. He reputedly claimed to have a divine mission to subdue all peoples. So he turned west, to the rich pickings to be had in the developed Islamic empire of Khwarizmian which stretched from the Persian Gulf to the Himalayas. The Mongols were not deterred by the army of nearly half a million men supported by cohorts of trained elephants. They were more concerned about another empire with full treasuries that was ready for devastation. The fabled magnificence of the shah and his court was a byword in the east, and the supposed impregnability of his domains bred an overconfidence that was to prove disastrous. As usual, the Mongol intelligence was excellent, and an expedition was mounted using widely separated columns whose marches eclipsed those of Hannibal and Alexander the Great. By a cunning series of diversionary moves, Chingis disguised his true intentions, and when the main thrusts came from three different directions, the shah's territory was severed, and he was forced to flee to his western territories still pursued by the Mongol army, and ultimately died of exhaustion. Eventually countless cities were captured and mercilessly looted including Bokhara, Tashkent, and Samarkand. In the mosques, Chingis had himself proclaimed the Scourge of God. Everyone had good reason to fear him: only technical experts who could be of use to the Mongols were spared; the remainder of the population was slaughtered. It is said that at Herat there were over a million corpses; huge pyramids of skulls were left to warn any surviving enemies that resistance was useless.

Chingis Khan must go down as one of the great warriors of history. His territories were so great in breadth that – as he put it – it took a year to reach their centre from either end. With the help of competent officials he administered his vast but unwieldy empire with considerable skill. Trade continued, the arts and medicine were still encouraged, and the Yassa, the Mongol code, protected certain freedoms – particularly freedom from religious bigotry. But there was a price – an awful price – to pay for Mongol domination, and to achieve it perhaps as many as 18 millions were massacred in China alone.

Though occupation policies differed with places and people, they accentuated cultural differences in China by introducing a form of caste system. Mongols naturally comprised the highest caste, other non-Chinese (Persians, Turks, etc.) the second caste, and the Chinese the third and fourth castes who were subject to curfew and generally had an inferior legal status. They could not bear arms and merited little compensation in the case of murder. According to Marco Polo, the whole population of Chinkiang was massacred in reprisal for the Chinese killing of just one small group of drunken Mongol soldiers.

There was no real pause after Chingis's death in 1227. The Mongol hordes rolled on. He left three 'recognized' sons, the second of which, Ogdai, succeeded his father and was accepted by the Mongol tribes. The policy of expansion continued, and everywhere it was the same story. There were campaigns against the not entirely suppressed Chinese. Revolts were put down in Georgia and Armenia, and Mesopotamia was so ravaged that it was little more than a desert for six centuries. The Mongols now held vast territories in the east: Korea, Burma, and parts of Iran and Afghanistan. In the west, Ogdai and his nephew and future king-maker, Batu, ravaged Russia from Moscow to Kiev, perpetrating the most fearful atrocities everywhere. From Russia in 1241 they turned to Hungary and Silesia with similar results, and it seemed as though nothing could prevent Europe from being overrun. But at this point there was a reprieve. Europe was spared a predictable fate because Ogdai drank himself to death. This precipitated a crisis in the succession which postponed the intended invasion indefinitely.

Europe seemed largely deaf to the appeals of those who were immediately threatened, and indifferent to the pleadings of its more far-sighted nobility who sensed the true extent of the danger. The pope might have been capable of mobilizing a crusade had it not been for other political preoccupations. He piously pinned his hopes on the possible conversion of the Mongols and sent friars to the Great Khan, Batu, in 1245. Needless to say, this mission failed, although it did provide the west with more information about Mongol culture and possible Mongol intentions.

After a period of consolidation under more of Chingis's successors, expansionist activities were recommenced, and in 1258 the city of Baghdad fell; here the ferocity of the Mongols was such that not only was the last of the Abbasid caliphs tortured to death, but perhaps as many as three quarters of a million of his subjects suffered as well. Muslim power now seemed to be irretrievably ruined. Yet within a few years the Mongols had their first serious reverse. The army that was sent against Egypt in 1260 was defeated by the Mamalukes, and this led to a resuscitation of Islam and to the liberation of Syria soon afterwards.

With the advent of Khublai Khan, a grandson of Chingis, a more constructive period of Mongol rule began. Khublai himself became a Buddhist, and education and the arts were encouraged. A much admired system of courier communications was established, roads and canals were built and restored including the Grand Canal which stretched for a thousand miles, and a new capital was built at Peking. But the taxes were still demanding and the labour levies were increasingly resented. There were numerous uprisings, and within fifty years of Khublai's death the empire had begun to break up. The successful overthrow of the conquerors in China and the establishment of the Ming dynasty heralded the end of this phase of Mongol power.

In their time, the Mongol's success had been phenomenal. They had carved out one of the greatest empires known to history. Generally speaking, they preferred the riches of Persia, India, and China to the comparative poverty of the west in the thirteenth and fourteenth centuries. Consequently, neither Chingis nor his successors – including the later Tartars under Timur – made any permanent impression on the west. But by giving a semblance of unity to Asia, they did facilitate a degree of contact between the east and the west. Asia had been less politically fragmented than the west, and this meant that the invaders had only to strike a critical blow at its huge settled empires to reveal their military impotence. With the initial shock of invasion they were paralysed and really had no answer to the terrifying efficiency of the Mongol armies. Chingis had once said that 'to crush your enemies and see them fall at your feet, that is best', except that in this case the 'enemy' was rarely a threat to anything but Mongol expansion and greed.

But the Mongol empire could only be ephemeral. There was no

unifying ideology to bind its disparate elements. True, it had its code, but this had nothing like the force or universal acceptability of, say, Islam. It was an empire that was hastily won – carved out by the sword among weak peoples of a superior cultural level. It was ultimately based upon naked force and had no real foundation except fear. Mongol rapacity took, but put little in its place. Unlike the rulers of other great empires, the Mongols contributed little to the civilizations they conquered. For a time they were adequately administered, but the devastation was such that real recovery was slow and painful. Wherever the Mongols rode they left ruined economies and political wastelands. Although they once dominated from the Danube to the China Sea, they left no permanent legacy. When their power waned they eventually returned to the obscurity of the steppes, and there is now only the remote memory of a very efficient killing machine which once cast its lethal shadow across half the known world.

8

THE AZTECS
The enemy as ritual fodder

There has never been a system of institutionalized human sacrifice which compares with that of pre-conquest Meso-America. It is not known just how it arose or by whom it was first introduced or established. It was certainly known by the Maya in southern Mexico, Honduras, and Guatemala, probably before their classic period from about AD 300 to about 900. But among the Maya, it seems to have been used sparingly, mainly in times of great emergency or national disaster. Human sacrifice may well have been characteristic of the early Olmec civilization which flourished in the area of Veracruz in the first century BC, but it did not become really extensive until much later, around AD 1000, with the emergence in northern Mexico of the Toltecs and their successors, the Aztecs.

The Spanish – admittedly a biased source – estimated that the Aztecs sacrificed about 20,000 people a year. But it was not just the scale on which it was practised that was so horrendous, it was also the mode of sacrifice and the ostensible reasons given for it which both horrified and intrigued the Conquistadores. The complex rituals, which were well documented by Catholic priests soon after the conquest, showed that sacrifice took a number of forms, including strangling, decapitation, and execution with arrows. But it was the strange yet widely used practice of extracting the heart of a living victim and offering it to the gods which was such an unusual feature of Meso-American society.

The rationale for human sacrifice was linked with Aztec history and cosmology. Their traditions indicate that, after a long series of tribal wanderings which were punctuated by uneasy alliances and sporadic warfare (somewhat reminiscent of the early Israelites), they finally settled in the valley of Mexico under the guidance of their tribal god, Huitzilopochtli. Their capital of Tenochtitlan (Mexico City) was established c. AD 1325 amidst swamps and shallow lakes which were partly drained and 'sculpted' with considerable ingenuity. This inhospitable territory was skilfully farmed and eventually supported about 40 per cent of an estimated valley population of a million people. Efficient provisioning was possible by the reclamation of the swamps, by terraced irrigation, and by the ingenious creation of artificial island-like gardens (chinampas) in which were grown the staple crops of maize and vegetables. Every acre had to count. It was only through a system of intensive cultivation that labour could be released for specialist – often cultural – occupations, or diverted to public works such as roads, and temples with their paved, open plazas.

The modern Mexico City has been largely built over the old city of Tenochtitlan which covered about 5 to 6 square miles. Excavation is therefore difficult, and has to be carried out when and where circumstances allow. However, what can be ascertained is that the Aztec capital was divided into four quarters which intersected at a great walled plaza, about 500 yards square, which was dominated by the stepped pyramid temple some 150 feet high. This was surmounted by blood-caked shrines dedicated to Huitzilopochtli and the rain-god, Tlaloc. The plaza, which included other temples and administrative buildings – perhaps some eighty in all – was the centre of the main religious rituals and festivals. Outside this enclosure were the markets and the common dwelling areas. According to eyewitnesses, the entire central layout gave the impression of light, colour, and space, a tribute to rational planning. It evidenced an immense architectural effort all expressing religious themes. The Conquistadores found the total effect overwhelming: 'we saw pyramids . . . that looked like gleaming white towers . . . a marvellous sight'. But on further investigation, they were repelled by the shrines. When they examined the figure of Huitzilopochtli at the summit of the pyramid Templo Mayor, they found a grotesque idol decorated with gold, precious stones, and seed pearls, but even the pervasive aroma of copal incense could not disguise the overpowering stench of the dried blood which had been splashed all over the walls.

The precinct also housed the ball court, the military arsenals, musicians' schools, and guest accommodation, but did not contain the ruler's palace and administrative offices; these occupied some 6 acres that had been carefully differentiated from the ritual area. In effect, Tenochtitlan presented a Venice-like appearance. There were at least six main canals through the city besides a maze of major and minor waterways. An impressive system of dykes and causeways connected the city with the shores of the lake beyond which there was a rural area dotted with farming communities. Considerable activity and a seemingly limitless supply of unskilled labour had combined to construct a capital that was known throughout pre-conquest Meso-America.

The government of the Aztec state was hierarchically organized. Control lay with the ruler who was selected from a leading family by a highly placed elite of nobles and priests. In practice, there were strong dynastic elements in all this: a successor was usually related to a deceased ruler – perhaps a son or brother – but he had to be vetted and approved for his personal and political qualities. His coronation was a momentous and solemn affair, involving ritual bloodletting, fasting, and prayer over a period of four days. As supreme ruler he controlled a number of separate – sometimes semi-independent – rulers (tlatoani) in a confederation of allied and vassal states that really constituted an Aztec empire. He had the power to appropriate labour, land, and resources, and allocate them at will. He was the ultimate arbiter in matters of law as all appeals went to him for final judgement. Preeminently, he was responsible for defence and the waging of war to subdue enemies and to take prisoners for sacrifice.

The ruler governed with the aid of four advisers who were all members of his own family. These operated through a council of 12–20 further nobles and a military committee. Except for his immediate entourage, the ruler lived in something like splendid isolation, in a palace set among gardens and aviaries, taking his sumptuous meals virtually alone, attended by members of his harem and entertained by jesters, hunchbacks, and singers. He alone was permitted to wear cotton in the palace; others might attempt to but only on pain of death. Even nobles were not allowed to look him in the face; they had to approach him barefoot with abject obeisance, attired only in common dress, of wool or maguey fibres. Indeed, it was they who carried Montezuma in his litter to his first meeting with the Spaniards, and who threw their cloaks in front of him lest his feet touched the ground.

In practice, the government consisted of two interlocking bureaucracies: the secular bureaucracy of officials, judges, and tax-collectors which comprised the general administrative machinery, and the religious bureaucracy of priests and their assistants who exercised extraordinary influence within the system. The power of the government was both pervasive and decisive. Punishments for crimes and even what we might regard as moral infringements were swift and severe. Not only was homicide punishable by death – usually either by hanging or stoning – but so were theft, military disobedience, and adultery. In their policies towards vassal states, the Aztecs operated a repressive system designed to ensure an ongoing flow of tribute into the state coffers. These contributions of quilted garments, cloaks, feathers (much used in all forms of decoration), gold, and cacao (cocoa), were a continual burden to these subject states. Perhaps most resented was the tribute of workers for state projects, and particularly slaves to satisfy what has been described as 'the insatiable maw of the gods' (Fagan 1984).

Besides tribute, the Aztec economy was sustained by a highly organized network of commerce, both within the empire, and outside with the neighbouring states with which the Aztecs often had rather strained relations. The currency of trade was normally pieces of copper and cacao beans; bronze and iron were unknown, and gold and silver were only used for decorative objects. Craftsmen who worked with precious metals and stones – and particularly with feathers – were highly esteemed, and there were guilds to perpetuate and guard this kind of expertise. Merchants, too, were an important 'class' within Aztec society; they were even allowed to hold their own ceremonial feasts and sacrifices. Their entrepreneurial role left them free to conduct elaborate trading arrangements, and they sometimes acted as diplomatic and even espionage agents on behalf of the state. In reporting back what they had witnessed abroad they became an invaluable source of information for the military strategists. They were often the best people to discern the rumblings of revolution in the Aztec dependencies, or to bring back intelligence which indicated that yet another foreign state was ripe for invasion.

The social structure of Aztec society followed a fairly conventional pattern. Stratification was based on birth and occupation, and, although there was some mobility through personal achievement, the astrological birth omens of any particular individual were held to determine his future life chances. The main distinction – as in most traditional societies – was between nobles and commoners. It has been argued that one of the main weaknesses of Aztec society was that it was top-heavy with priests and nobility who were creaming off the best of the available resources. This may well be the case, and it probably generated resentment among the poorer classes who had little chance of redress for any actual or supposed injustices. On the other hand, the nobility were subject to special applications of the law. The ruler could make his own disciplinary arrangements just for them, and there were even occasions when he had members of his own family executed for quite minor infringements. It is probably always true that those who have most to fear from arbitrary despotism are those who are closest to despotic power.

At the other end of the social scale were the commoners and the slaves. The commoners consisted of free peasants who were very poor, and who sometimes paid tax/tribute in goods, but more usually in the form of manual labour or military service. There were also landless serfs who were – for various reasons – deprived of descent group (calpulli) membership, and worked on estates for local lords. They were also liable for military duties, but were exempted from paying tribute. At the bottom of the social ladder were those who had become slaves, possibly through debt or the inability to pay tribute, or perhaps because their parents had sold them into slavery. They were allowed to own land and to marry, in which case their children would be born free. They might even earn manumission, but one suspects that their chances were rather slim as they were normally engaged in extremely menial work, sometimes actually doubling as pack animals. There were lucrative slave markets in Mexico which were always prepared to negotiate terms with the estate managers and, of course, with those who felt that they had no alternative but to sell either themselves or their families into slavery. A very special type of slave was the war captive who was often destined for sacrifice because his life was already forfeit to the gods.

The literature on Aztec society gives the impression of a hard-working people characterized by conformity and moderation. This was enhanced by their structural arrangements in which kinship was a critical factor. Most people belonged to a descent group which might number several hundred members, and which would generally have its own temples and their attendant schools. This was the basis of territorial organization and of military recruitment, and had its own elected headman who reported regularly to the tribute officers for orders about labour and services to the state. Kinship recognized primary patrilineal obligations, although due emphasis was given to matrilineal concerns. But there were ambiguities. Polygyny was practised, but normally only among the nobility; perhaps the distinction served to reinforce a sense of social distance between the respective social orders. There were moral strictures against prostitution, and a strong emphasis on female virginity and the sanctity of marriage. Women could own property and enter business contracts, but their main task was seen as the care of the home. Generally speaking, they commanded considerable respect in Aztec society and those who died in childbirth were accorded a reverence second only to that given to warriors slain in battle. Yet among the nobility they might be expected to follow their deceased husband as a voluntary act of renunciation.

Socialization processes were carefully ordered and monitored among the Aztecs. Children were reared into what was regarded as a strange and uncertain world; life was hard and discipline was unremitting. There was considerable regard for age and seniority. Children were taught to respect and obey their parents and elders. By extension, this meant the authorities and the gods as well; all was calculated to produce and maintain a conforming and co-operative society.

Boys customarily worked from the age of 5 in the fields and on public works, but also had an elementary schooling. Girls, on the other hand, received little formal education outside the home, so in domestic terms they were ready for marriage in their early teens. Both boys and girls between the ages of 12 and 15 attended the 'house of song' which was attached to the local temple. Here the curriculum consisted largely of music, singing, and dancing, as preparation for their part in the religious festivals. Much was done by rote learning. Except for a kind of pictographic script which was interpreted rather than actually read off the codices, the Aztecs were not literate in the commonly accepted sense of the term, and this meant that children were required to memorize and recite the 'essence' of the texts. Boys of the nobility received a higher training, especially in military matters, and were sometimes encouraged to accompany warriors on their expeditions. This was complemented by manual labour in the fields and on public works, and rounded off with the necessary religious instruction. Again, discipline was harsh; minor offences were severely punished, and serious offences might even merit a death sentence. Compulsive gambling – which was apparently a common vice – might well lead to slavery as the result of debt.

Probably the feature of Aztec society which most fascinated and repelled the early Spanish explorers was their religion. What the Conquistadores could never resolve was the apparent contradiction between the cultural sophistication and architectural grandeur on the one hand, and the frightening nature of many of the religious rituals on the other, particularly the practice of human sacrifice. Furthermore, there seemed to be a serious moral inconsistency between Aztec industriousness and sobriety and the unfeeling way in which they treated others. These issues require some investigation as they are inextricably bound up with the nature and purpose of war.

The Aztecs inherited a number of religious ideas which were common to various parts of Meso-America. There were traditions associated with the northern and very ancient city of Teotihuacan, the 'place of the gods', which was founded about a thousand years before the Aztecs appeared on the historical scene. Teotihuacan, which set the pattern for Tenochtitlan both in layout and in temple construction, included the incredible Pyramid of the Sun which was over 200 feet high and almost 700 feet at the base. Its society displayed ritual features which provided a legacy for the Aztecs, especially the worship of the rain-god Tlaloc and the culture-deity Quetzalcoatl, the feathered serpent who appears to have been revered as a Lord of Creation, in one guise or another, throughout Meso-America.

To these and the extensive pantheon of deities, the Aztecs added Huitzilopochtli, the god of war, possibly via their immediate predecessors, the Toltecs; this god became their supreme tutelary deity. Huitzilopochtli (literally, 'the hummingbird wizard') became increasingly identified with the sun, with military ambition and expansionism, and the souls (hummingbirds) of those who died in battle. Since the bad harvests of 1455, human offerings had multiplied considerably in order to ensure the fertility of the land. This necessitated almost continuous warfare to guarantee an adequate supply of victims. And when the Temple of Huitzilopochtli was dedicated in 1487, the ruler, Ahuitzotl, gathered hundreds of prisoners-of-war for sacrifice. To these were added hosts of slaves ordered from visiting chiefs. The festivities and the bloodshed went on for five days in which it is recorded that several thousands died in honour of the god and for the glory of the Mexica.

The Aztecs developed highly elaborate forms of religious symbolism. Life was seen as a dream; the real world lay beyond. Men simply existed to serve the gods, and their destiny was largely determined by their mode of death. Their cosmology was therefore concerned with those natural forces which were believed to be beneficial to mankind. Complementarily, it tried to allay or repel the forces that were feared. It had no marked redemptive or ethical elements which are characteristic of 'high' religions. Instead, it concentrated on devising complex and symbolic rituals which would ensure that the divine powers would work for the public good. This, in turn, was associated with a cyclical view of history. As part of their corpus of mythology there was a story, preserved on the great, 24-ton sacrificial Stone of the Sun in the temple of the war god, which depicts the cosmos locked in a never-ending struggle between the forces of good and evil. This conflict had already destroyed four suns, and the present, or fifth, sun merely represented a temporary world order which had to be sustained by human sacrifice. This same idea was also reflected in the companion myth which told of the sun being devoured by a monster of the deep who then disgorged it, a not uncommon theme in ancient mythologies. The Egyptians had an account of how the sun-god, Ra, traversed the heavens in his ship-of-millions-of-years, and did battle every night with Apophis who lived under the earth, but rose triumphant at every dawn. The marked distinction between the Egyptians and the Aztecs, which some bizarre theories suggest are connected, was in the ritual forms which were held to ensure celestial stability.

Cosmologies are rarely coherent affairs. People seldom work out the exact relationships of one myth to another, or one myth-character to another – as, say, in the Greek myths. This was no less true of the Aztecs, although some attempts were made to rationalize the sequences of the many religious festivals. The calendar year of 365 days was distinguished from the sacred year of only 260 days; each week had its own specific deities, and there were some gods that were particularly associated with the day whilst others were associated with the night. The great Aztec ceremonies were based on the calendar or solar year which was composed of 18 months of 20 days plus a 5-day 'unlucky' period when there was fasting and lamentation; people destroyed their furniture, pregnant women were shut up lest they changed into animals, and children were kept awake in case sleep would cause them to turn into rats. Most of the ceremonies involved sacrifice of some kind. For example, during the 8-day feast to celebrate 'the adoration of the ripening corn', women were required to wear their hair loose, presumably as a form of sympathetic magic to symbolize the healthy plant, and a slave girl – impersonating a goddess – was slain. Only after this were the people allowed to eat the new corn. The calendars coincided in 52-year cycles, at which points time was seen as having 'ended'. This was regarded as potentially cataclysmic. The whole created order was in jeopardy. People were filled with apprehension, demons might be let loose which would destroy the world, and so the appropriate steps had to be taken to avert the impending catastrophe. Needless to say, these steps involved self-immolation, personal penance and mutilation with knives and sharp spines, and yet more human sacrifice.

The understandable fear that the Aztecs had of natural and supernatural forces – 'of the gods who laugh at us' – involved them in the most complex rituals. These were organized and carried out by a hierarchy of several hundred priests who appear to have been both respected and feared by the bulk of the population. Children – including some girls – could be dedicated to the priesthood from infancy, and trained for their vocation at the temple schools. Adult priests continued to live within the temple precincts, although some did not make lifelong vows but served for a limited period only. They dyed their bodies black, did not cut their hair, and practised sexual abstinence. In addition to making the customary prayers and offerings they were particularly punctilious about penance and the accompanying self-mutilation. The records suggest that they were given to supererogatory bloodletting, thrusting spines through their ears, lips, and tongue to attest their devoutness.

In effect, the priests constituted the state literati; they were the teachers of the sacred law and traditional lore, and the interpreters of signs. They combined the functions of diviners, magicians, and sorcerers. They had to be meticulous in adherence to the rules of good behaviour which were strictly enforced on pain of hanging. Quite apart from the main ceremonial occasions, they were required to offer incense four times a day and five times a night, besides making quail sacrifices every morning. They often had a military role, and were allowed to take prisoners of their own for sacrifice, although normally it was only the high priests – chosen by the ruler or his advisers – who actually wielded the sacrificial knife.

Almost all the principal Aztec festivals included human sacrifice. It was regarded as having been ordained by the gods. Usually the victims were either slaves or warriors taken in battle; the blood of warriors was predictably thought to be more efficacious than that of slaves. Sometimes, at specific ceremonies, women and children were also sacrificed. Whoever the victims were, they usually had very little choice in the matter, although on occasions there were sacrifices of a voluntary nature. In general, the mode of sacrifice required that the victim was led to the summit of the temple pyramid where he was pinioned by four priests whilst a high priest ripped open the chest with an obsidian knife, tore out the still pulsating heart, and offered it symbolically to the god. The body was usually then thrown ignominiously down the temple steps where it was often dismembered, the skull sometimes joining others on the temple rack.

All manner of ritual refinements were involved as a whole array of gods had to be honoured and placated at the appropriate times. Furthermore, the 'instrumentality' of sacrifice was only thought to be effective if the correct symbolism was employed. So, for example, in the ceremonies in honour of the fire-god, prisoners of war and their captors took part in a rather macabre dance after which the prisoners were bound and cast into a specially kindled fire. Before death, they were wrenched out with large hooks and, as a last ritual requirement, and as a kind of merciful *coup de grâce*, the hearts were torn from their blistered bodies. In a rite in honour of the sun-god, a captured warrior might be tethered to a circular stone, armed with dummy weapons, and required to fight a mock duel with selected eagle and tiger 'knights' – elite Aztec troops – in which he was inevitably killed. This was held to symbolize the triumph of the sun over those malevolent forces which threatened to overwhelm it. In yet a further ritual, this time in honour of the Tezcatlipoca (Smoking Mirror), the chief god of the pantheon, a particularly brave and handsome captive was selected as a surrogate deity a year in advance. During this period, he was fêted by the people and treated like a ruler before being sacrificed with great jubilation and feasting. In deference to his ascribed status, his body was not cast down the steps, but his head still joined the other skulls spitted on the rack beside the temple. Yet more attenuated forms of symbolism character- ized the bizarre rites associated with Xipe, the god of seedtime and planting. After sacrifice, the victim was flayed and his skin was worn by the priests for twenty days. In this there seems to have been some symbolic representation of new growth; the god of spring was honoured and 'stimulated' by the flayed skin which became the covering of new vegetation.

The fertility theme in Aztec religion was much more poignantly expressed in the rites relating to one of the principal deities, Tlaloc, god of rain. In this case the victims were children who were painted black, adorned with simple ornaments, and either drowned or decapi- tated. Young children were preferred as their crying on the way to sacrifice was regarded as particularly propitious; there was held to be a magical correspondence between the expected rainfall and the amount of tears shed.

Where dismemberment of the victims took place, there appears also to have been some ritual consumption of the flesh, presumably in the belief that to partake of the victim is to partake of his nature and attributes. So if he happened to be an esteemed warrior or a surrogate deity, his flesh was particularly beneficial. There is a theory that war was really conducted by the Aztecs for this specific purpose (see Harris 1978). The view holds that the common people were short of meat-protein, and that the flesh of sacrificial victims helped to make up for this grave deficiency. This has been largely refuted by many modern authorities as being quite unnecessary as dogs and turkeys were a regular part of the Indian diet. Anyhow, the evidence suggests that it was not the common people who shared in these delicacies but the captors who saw them as part of their prize.

As we have already noted, human sacrifice was not peculiar to the Aztecs, but can be found in many antecedent societies, but it was refined and institutionalized by the Aztecs as part of their state policy. All the evidence shows that it flourished with the expansion of the empire. Indeed, the pursuit of aggressive policies became an increasing obsession as attempts were made to obtain yet more victims to please the gods and make the Aztecs a greater power. Warfare was the most effective way of securing a tribute of slaves and prisoners for sacrifice, so the Aztecs became locked into a syndrome of conquest, sacrifice, and more conquest in order to fulfil their destiny.

Immediately prior to the Spanish conquest, war had become the prime *raison d'être* of the state. Boys were socialized for war from birth, and mothers who died in childbirth were themselves regarded as warriors by the state because they had been trying to produce warriors for the state. The greatest exploit was to capture at least one enemy in battle; until this time youths could only wear a fibre cape, and might even be subject to a certain amount of derision. These 'virgin' soldiers wore a lock of hair at the nape of the neck which was not cut until they had taken their first captive; after this they were allowed to grow their hair long over the right ear as a form of display. Seasoned warriors were entitled to wear special regalia and to share in the booty of a victory which, in effect, often meant sharing the body of an enemy. Military prowess was an avenue of social mobility, and successful warriors might rise in the hierarchy and join the elite societies of, say, eagle or jaguar 'knights', and attend military councils. In the higher echelons, there seems to have been no clear distinction between civic and military offices. War chiefs and their subordinates appear to have been civic dignitaries.

Military service was compulsory for free men. There were officials who were responsible for recruitment and training, and usually the regular Aztec forces were supplemented by drafts from vassal states. This was necessary in order to make up the appalling losses which came from almost continuous warfare. In one battle alone, it is recorded – perhaps with some exaggeration – that 20,000 were killed, including 80 per cent of the elite troops.

The army was organized in bands of 20, 200, and 400, though smaller detachments were commonly used for scouting and reconnaissance. The larger divisions were commanded by clan and tribal chiefs. Troops were equipped with very rudimentary weapons such as swords, clubs with obsidian blades, feather-decorated wicker shields, and helmets with plumes. Their armour was in much the same category: quilted cotton soaked in brine to give it some small degree of resilience, though, interestingly, the Spanish were quite impressed with how light and effective this form of body protection could be. These armaments were supplied from central arsenals which were maintained in many of the larger towns.

Military expeditions usually took place after the harvests, and were relatively short affairs for simple logistical reasons. Transport was the problem. There were no beasts to drag or carry the food and equipment so everything had to be borne by the troops themselves. Furthermore, it was not considered prudent to live off the lands of the vassal states *en route* for fear of inciting revolt, so the actual campaigns usually only lasted a few days. This all made siege operations virtually impossible; but then few towns were actually fortified, being mainly dependent upon their strategic positions for safety. Defensive strongpoints such as temples were very difficult to take, and once some prisoners were captured the attack would often cease and the army would retire. Sometimes temples were destroyed, but usually sacking and looting were discouraged. It was enough to win the battle, to take some captives for sacrifice – the more high-ranking, the better – and to reduce the enemy to tribute. This was the object of the exercise. On occasions, policy demands would go further and the worship of Huitzilopochtli might be instituted, but normally the conquered state was allowed to retain its own government and its own customs providing it paid its dues every eighty days. Refusal or rebellion meant swift and frightening reprisals.

When the Aztecs had to face the Spanish Conquistadores they were overwhelmed by an entirely different battle strategy. Although the Spaniards themselves only numbered about 600 men, they were able to deploy horses and cannon, which were altogether unnerving to the Aztecs. In addition, they had the aid of Indian allies who hated their Aztec overlords more than they distrusted the Europeans who had made a very shrewd assessment of the Mexican situation. The evidence suggests that the Aztec empire was beginning to creak immediately prior to the conquest; the tribute-oriented nature of Aztec imperialism had made them a lot of bad friends and discontented neighbours.

Very strangely, too, the arrival of the Conquistadores coincided with predictions concerning the return of the culture-god, Quetzalcoatl, and this initial identification of the Spanish with the gods temporarily neutralized Aztec hostility. When the rapacity of these only-too-human invaders became evident, the war began in earnest. But obsidian-bladed clubs and wicker shields were of little use against Spanish steel, and the cut-and-rush tactics of the Aztecs in trying to take prisoners were no match for the disciplined expertise of their enemies who fought ferociously to avoid the certain fate of Aztec captives. In the end, probably no more than 60,000 of the 300,000 defenders of Tenochtitlan survived.

The Aztec ideology of war and death is, in some ways, reminiscent of that of traditional Japan. War was not only a duty, it was a privilege. Successful warriors were fêted and praised, but the valiant death was the ultimate act. Young men were enjoined to 'die like blossoms'. An Aztec poem applauds the ritual: 'there is nothing like death in war . . . so precious to the Giver of Life. . . . My heart yearns for it.' Warriors were primed for death from the sacrificial knife. When captured they were well received and well treated, virtually as guests, in preparation for their great day. To attempt an escape – normally the duty of a good soldier – was considered an act of cowardice. When killed, it was held that their spirits journeyed to the sun and then returned to earth as hummingbirds. Civilians, who did not have such a heroic end, were not so honoured; they had to travel through the nine layers of the underworld to the void of the ancestors, and even this was regarded as hazardous for those who had not led lives of requisite piety.

As the gods grew more ravenous, so more campaigns had to be mounted. When there were insufficient victims from legitimate warfare, the Aztecs contrived tournaments to ensure that supplies were maintained. The 'Wars of Flowers' were festivals of fighting held in honour of the Aztec deities, and could be either intra-state or inter-state affairs which involved the best fighting men available. These ceremonial combats sometimes escalated into genuine hostilities if there was an underlying political rivalry, but their main purpose was not to maintain a precarious balance between contending states or even to display the prowess of their warriors; it was rather to provide yet more sacrificial fodder for the gods.

The Aztecs were a militaristic society, they coveted lands and goods, and saw military activity as the best – or easiest – way of achieving these things. Furthermore, they were a highly status-conscious people. They had come from nothing, and they were out to show the neighbouring tribes that they were a power to be reckoned with. Theirs was not so much a question of resource scarcity as position scarcity. They wanted a place in the Meso-American sun. But none of this completely explains their history and their culture, and particularly the bizarre beliefs and practices associated with them. These they shared – to a greater or lesser degree – with many of the neighbouring peoples, but in their case it was much more highly developed. For them, war and sacrifice were something of an art form. One was not possible without the other. War affected all their other institutions; indeed, all other institutions were subordinated to the need for war. They believed that it was a passion awakened by the sun to ensure its own continuance. The sun could not survive without its diet of human hearts, so the capture and sacrifice of prisoners became a ritual act.

In trying to make sense of all this, it would be a mistake to think that religion here provides a form of *post facto* explanation. Religion was not a dependent, but an independent variable – it really determined actual courses of events. Similarly, it would be misleading to think of religion as a means of self-justification; for the Aztecs, the requirements of the gods were clear and self-evident.

To interpret these practices in purely economic – possibly Marxist – terms would be a mistake. The economic argument does not explain why war took the form it did, nor why human sacrifice should be so institutionalized when the enslaved and the prisoners might have constituted an invaluable labour force, as they did in so many other pre-industrial societies. For the Aztecs, war was an ideological imperative. Indeed, in one sense it was virtually war without aggression. It was a dispassionate, sometimes artificially contrived undertaking, as in the Wars of the Flowers, which had admitted political benefits but was not waged simply for political reasons. It was a cosmic as much as a commercial enterprise. It had supramundane as well as mundane implications. The rationale was not just that the Aztec nation must survive and flourish, but that the future of the whole world was somehow dependent on this particular sacrificial activity. The sun must be replenished with blood, or *all* would die. Thus the enemy was not regarded as an infidel or an inferior who had to be exterminated at all costs, but a valiant opponent who, when captured, was greeted rapturously by the people who would benefit by his death. A sacrificed enemy might ensure that the cosmos would endure for just a little longer.

9

THE ZULU
The enemy as colonial intruders

The question as to whether specific social practices are generated by particular environmental conditions or identifiable politico-economic exigencies is of special interest to students of warfare and aggression. There is also the question as to whether specific social practices are related to cultural diffusion or independent development. These are intriguing problems which admit of no clear or generally acceptable answers, and both are particularly relevant to the Zulu situation. Here we have what was originally a relatively insignificant clan which consciously developed an unusual form of social organization early in the nineteenth century with the deliberate intention of subduing their immediate neighbours and carving out a minor empire for themselves in south-eastern Africa: a policy which eventually brought them into confrontation with the Dutch and British intruders who presumed to contest their supremacy.

Anthropological and historical evidence – such as it is – points to the fact that the indigenous inhabitants of southern Africa, the primitive Bushmen (San) and the Hottentots (more correctly, the Khoikhoi), were gradually ousted by invading bands of Bantu from central and East Africa from about the time of our Middle Ages. From what we can gather, the Bantu had no more respect for these nomadic peoples than the Boers and the British had after them, despising their uncertain, 'stone age' existence. Some were made serfs and others migrated westwards to the desert of the Kalahari and beyond to eke out their precarious living from grubs, rodents, and occasional game.

Folk-myths and travellers' tales give us some idea of the settlement patterns of the Bantu. They were divided into a number of not always harmonious tribal elements, and it was from a minor clan of the extensive Nguni people that the Zulu derived as a distinct social grouping. The Nguni, a generic term which included the Xhosa, the Swazi, and the Ndebele (more popularly known as the Matabele) as well as the Zulu, were mainly pastoralists who also did some tilling, hunting, and trapping. They spoke a variety of dialects and their clans were largely

autonomous political units of disparate sizes; some contained only two
or three hundred people, whilst a few clans had several thousand. They
lived in circular kraals, loosely fenced enclosures, which comprised
cattle pens and dark, cockroach-ridden bee-hive huts that housed patri-
lineally organized extended families. These kraals varied considerably
in size, and could range from modest settlements housing, say, a patri-
arch with two or three wives, together with his unmarried children and
his married sons and their families, to a huge enclosure, perhaps a mile
in diameter, for a king or paramount chief. These vast kraals would
include accommodation for an extensive entourage including a harem,
indunas (senior officers) and servants, and a personal bodyguard who
– particularly in the case of the more despotic kings such as Shaka –
might also double as a corps of executioners. At the height of Zulu
supremacy, there were a number of specifically designated military
kraals which housed various combinations of Zulu regiments, and were
sometimes dignified with colourful names such as the Place of Endless
Worry, or – more ominously – the Place of Killing (Bulawayo), which
was Shaka's headquarters kraal.

The division of labour in Zulu life was characteristic of most pastoral
societies. Women were occupied with agricultural and domestic chores,
and men were concerned with herding and hunting, and, of course,
developing and displaying their prowess as warriors. The training of
the young highlights the clear differentiation between the sexes. Girls
assisted their mothers; boys, on the other hand, were subjected to the
most rigorous training and initiation within their age-set system in order
to prepare them for their place in this warrior society. Girls were also
organized in age-regiments, and were technically regarded as wards of
the king. When male regiments were disbanded after completion of
the period of service, their corresponding female regiments were also
dissolved and their members given as wives to the retiring warriors.
Those on active duty were forbidden to enter into permanent sexual
relationships under pain of death. It is little wonder that the Zulu are
sometimes referred to as 'black Spartans'.

Military valour was a prime determinant of prestige and was reflected
in the regalia that a warrior was allowed to wear. But wealth was also
important. In what was, in effect, a propertyless society, a man's wealth
was largely assessed in terms of the size of herds. Cattle was the
nearest thing to currency in Zulu society, and payment in cattle was the
recognized form of bride-wealth (lobola), the 'gift' that was made in
exchange for a wife. Cattle were prized for their milk and their hides
rather than their meat, although it was customary to kill them for ritual
sacrifice. They were not normally bred for their quality but it did become
a practice – one might almost say an artifice – to breed them for their
colour. It is said that cattle-keepers could distinguish every one of their

beasts, and some kings liked nothing better than having their herds paraded before them. An early visitor to Shaka's kraal, Henry Francis Fynn, counted one herd of precisely 5,654 cattle, but no one believed him because he hadn't used his fingers in making the calculation. Cattle was the main form of booty from inter-tribal warfare, and it is estimated that some hundreds of thousands were taken in this way. At the intra-tribal level also, when, say, someone was executed for some real or imagined offence, it was the confiscation of their cattle that was the real prize. It is worth asking how many of the accusations of witchcraft at the highest levels, for which the punishment was automatically death, were actually made with a view to increasing the size of the king's herds.

In the pre-Shaka era, the military system of the Zulu was relatively simple. There was almost continuous warfare but – from what can be discerned – it was conducted in a somewhat casual way. Objectives were usually immediate and therefore limited. Disputes were frequently over cattle or grazing rights, and forces – such as they were – fought as unrehearsed groups in the interests of their tribe or clan. The contest itself made few concessions to strategy or tactics, but was usually decided on the basis of numbers. Bows and arrows were rarely used; the main weapons were throwing-spears which could be hurled with accuracy for some 60 or 70 yards, a knobkerrie which was a kind of club, and a large ox-hide shield. The conflicts themselves were often prearranged, and warriors were frequently accompanied by their families whose supplementary duty was to yell support from the sidelines. The battle usually began with an exchange of taunts and insults followed by threatening movements of the 'line', all calculated, of course, to intimidate the opponents. The outcome was often decided by a successful charge; afterwards some kind of settlement was made in terms of cattle and land, and sometimes captives were duly ransomed. In these pre-expansionist days, it is said that crippling damage was rare and extermination unknown. Kraals themselves were not defensible; it was quite a simple task to erect a new enclosure elsewhere. The worst that could happen was that a clan might be forced off its land and compelled to find living space elsewhere – an omen of things to come.

This all changed with the development of Zulu power. The amaZulu, 'the people of the Heavens', began as a small clan, and by the time their neighbouring clans to the south were first encountering the Boers, they may have numbered only about 1,500 people occupying a territory of about a hundred square miles. At this time, they were known to be a contentious people, but there was no hint – as yet – of a will to rule; they were still very much overshadowed by other, more powerful tribes.

There had been several generations of minor Zulu chiefs before the

advent of Shaka, the main architect of Zulu power. He was the illegitimate son of one such chief and a girl from an adjacent clan. In Zulu
society, certain forms of sexual indulgence were permitted outside marriage, but they were not supposed to result in illegitimate births. This
particular liaison was eventually regularized (iShaka was the name of
the supposed intestinal beetle which was conveniently held to account
for menstrual irregularities), but Shaka's mother was never really
accepted by either clan – a matter which Shaka himself never forgot.

Shaka was born in about 1787 and because of his domestic circumstances had something of a chequered childhood. He apparently
developed a powerful physique which he was later to display when
opportunities arose, but there is a certain amount of indirect evidence
to suggest that he may have been a latent sexual deviant. Despite his
huge seraglio he was most probably impotent, as there was not one
recorded heir among all of his 1,200 women. Whether, or to what
extent, this can be held to account for his cruelty and capriciousness,
is still a matter of debate. The story is told of how, on one occasion,
Shaka decided to test the 'piety' of one of his regiments who had been
away campaigning, and had therefore been deprived of sexual relations
for some time. The warriors were lined up naked while hundreds of
scantily dressed girls danced provocatively in front of them. Shaka
warned the men that those who had erections would be executed.
Many of them – physiologically at the mercy of their autonomic nervous
system – began to erect despite their fears and were urged by the girls
to hit their own penises in order to detumesce rapidly, but, apparently,
without much success. Consequently, some were executed (Ritter 1967).

Shaka served his apprenticeship in the age-set system, and eventually
in one of the regiments (impis) of the dominant Mtetwa clan. It was
here that he came to prominence, and here that he honed and refined
his military philosophy which was to shape Zulu thinking for the next
seventy years. Basically, he disparaged the idea that a battle was simply
a show of force for some kind of tenuous or temporary gain. Warfare
was really about terror and annihilation, a killing game for permanent
stakes and lasting supremacy.

Shaka began with probably no more than 300 warriors, and turned
them into a superb but completely ruthless fighting machine. As other
tribes were conquered their young men were pressed into service or
executed if they refused. By the end of his reign in 1828, he was capable
of calling on some 40,000 warriors for increasingly arduous expeditions.
His overall strategy was the subjugation of the surrounding tribes, and
this required a whole new outlook on warfare which had to be inculcated in the young from their earliest years. Boys were recruited from
the age-set system into regiments from the age of 14 and socialized as
warriors. They might be transferred or regrouped, but one way or

another, they would stay with a regiment until they died in battle or were disbanded in old age. They lived and fought as cohesive units, and could not even marry until they had been 'blooded' in battle, and only then with the king's permission. As a kind of interim coital substitute, forms of external 'intercourse' were sometimes allowed with particular girls, and might even be mandatory after battle – possibly as a form of compensatory ritual act.

Training was hard and basic. Sandals were discarded; Shaka tested his troops on thorn-strewn ground, and executed all those who did not stand up to the test. The impis learned to move at the trot, and a trained regiment could travel fifty miles a day and then fight a battle at the end of it. (Later, their British counterparts thought they were doing well if they could do twenty miles in the same time – admittedly with more equipment.) The throwing-spear was largely replaced by a shortened, broad-blade assegai (iklwa) which could be used over-arm for stabbing, but was more commonly used under-arm much like a sword. Even the shield was used as an offensive weapon. The Zulu practised hooking over their opponents' shields in order to immobilize them preparatory to the deadly thrust of the assegai under the left armpit. Any Zulu who were wounded and unable to walk were liable to be dispatched by their comrades where they lay. Warfare was dispassionate and functional.

The general attack formation of the Zulus became known as the 'buffalo head'; the most experienced regiments (the head) mounted a frontal attack whilst the younger regiments (the horns) attempted an encircling movement. The reserves (the loins) were ordered to turn their backs on the battle until required, otherwise it was feared that they would be overcome with excitement and join in anyway. These tactics – rudimentary as they seem – were carried out with great skill and tenacity, and were a considerable improvement on anything that had gone before. Certainly they were extremely effective against other African tribes, and initially against both the Boers and the British.

As Zulu power was increasing, there was a developing population problem in south-eastern Africa deriving from the unfavourable ratio of people to land. Suitable grazing ground sets limits to a pastoral economy. Added to this was the fact that white intruders were now encroaching on the lands to the south, establishing 'movable borders' with the indigenes to the north. This already difficult situation was then greatly exacerbated by Zulu expansionism. This had a knock-on effect throughout the entire area. The effects of Zulu depredations were catastrophic. Tribal war was waged on a scale never before experienced, and its unprecedented ferocity left countless dead and homeless. When the Zulu targeted a particular group, the result was usually a massacre, and this caused neighbouring peoples to flee their lands in terror. Huge numbers of refugees were on the move; the breakdown in traditional clan structures was such that over vast areas – extending to several thousand square miles – not a single permanent kraal existed. Foraging and plunder were common, and many people were reduced to cannibalism. In one particularly well-known case, a woman clan leader led her people, numbering some 50,000, and their herds to the south, and hundreds died daily in their desperate search for better living conditions.

This period of South African history became known as the Mfecane (or Difaquane), 'the crushing' of those peoples who did not – or would not – become incorporated in the Zulu kingdom or who were indirectly affected by Zulu policies through the aggression of others. It lasted for some ten years, and virtually depopulated what later became known as the Orange Free State. It is generally estimated to have involved the death of up to two million people by slaughter and starvation. Later, when the Boers moved northwards, it is said that they found fertile lands 'peopled by more skeletons than living natives' (Roberts 1977).

Eventually both the Boers and the British were also affected. The human debris of this chaos inevitably spilled over the traditional boundaries, and the colonialists at last became aware that they had a formidable potential enemy in the interior.

Parts of southern Africa had been explored by the Portuguese before the Dutch set up shop with a small trading station in 1652. By the following century the Boers (literally 'farmers') held extensive territories with farms commonly covering 5,000 to 7,000 acres. The primitive Bushmen were particularly vulnerable. Having suffered the incursions of the Bantu, they were further decimated by disease and the depredations of both the Boers and the Hottentots. Expansion was not legally curbed until 1780, and with certain – albeit temporary – restrictions on immigration there was an increasing tendency to turn to black labour. Much of the basic manual work, therefore, became the task of the natives who were looked down on not so much because of their colour but because of their culture. Their pagan ideas were particularly despised, especially their extravagant and – so it was felt – unfounded obsession with witchcraft. White repugnance was genuine enough, but it is now difficult to know to what extent this acted as a *post facto* rationalization for the near slavery to which many of them were eventually reduced.

The British began to settle in strength at the beginning of the nineteenth century. They still had no very clear idea of what was going on in the interior, although the reverberations of tribal conflict were becoming all too obvious. The Zulu impis were now virtually unstoppable. By 1820, they were waging war simply for the sake of it. Conquered warriors were often invited to swell the ranks of the Zulu regiments whilst frequently women and children were slaughtered. They had now recruited so many warriors that they were often engaged in more than one campaign at a time, and some of these further and further from the tribal heartlands.

Shaka's policies inevitably led to schism within the Zulu nation itself. His one-time favourite and protégé, Mzilikazi, broke with him and fled north with a band of warriors and – unforgivably – some of Shaka's herds. Hurriedly and aggressively he forged the great Matabele nation. He had learned his trade well, and became as feared as Shaka in the lands he dominated. The Matabele approach to war and conquest was typically Zulu in thought and execution. Indeed, there is a sense in which they became more Zulu than the Zulu, an elite among the indigenous Shona peoples, a state within a state – effectively a state which existed solely for war. They 'ate up' the tribes that stood in their way; killing the old and useless, and absorbing the young into their impis. In this way they expanded: looting cattle and women, and extending their power throughout the territory we now know as Zimbabwe.

Zulu conquests had fearful repercussions throughout the Transvaal and beyond. The Swazi, who had preceded the Zulu as a native power, adopted some of the military innovations of the fully developed Zulu system. Even the remnants of those who had been conquered by the Zulu were impressed by the success of Zulu tactics and used them in carving out new areas of influence for themselves elsewhere. So, for example, the defeated Ndwandwe peoples took these ideas and practices as far afield as Mozambique and central Africa. Indeed, a whole series of states came into being with recognizably common features, all – in one way or another – following the Zulu model. It was not that they all were keen on expansionism *per se*, but they were political pragmatists – this seemed the only way to survive.

Shaka himself was becoming less subject to any kind of restraint, and took on more and more the persona of the arbitrary despot. Executions were a daily occurrence and might be carried out for no better reason than that a courtier had sneezed in the king's presence or had made him laugh at the wrong moment. He appeared to become increasingly indifferent to the amount of pain he caused, and frequently had groups of his own warriors executed for what he regarded as either military or 'personal' failure. On one occasion, for example, he was so convinced of adultery among his own isiGodlo girls, that he had 170 warriors and girls put to death, and killed some of their suspect progeny personally. During a witch-hunt, he 'tested' women by asking which ones owned cats; 300 gave the wrong answer and were duly killed. When white visitors remonstrated against the bludgeonings and impalements, Shaka was both puzzled and unmoved. Instead, he expressed his horror of imprisonment which he had learned was an integral part of the British penal system.

A not entirely untypical example of Shaka's bizarre behaviour was witnessed by Henry Francis Fynn who was being entertained at the kraal when the king's mother, Nandi (the 'Great Female Elephant'), died. Shaka ordered everyone to cry, and anyone who was found not to be lamenting with the appropriate enthusiasm was referred to the executioners. The whole affair became so out of hand that the mourners turned on one another, and a general massacre ensued in which Fynn estimates that some 7,000 people died. Eventually the funeral went ahead, and Nandi was given ten maidens who were buried alive to keep her company, and a regiment of 12,000 warriors was set to guard her grave for a year and given 15,000 head of cattle to keep them supplied. Shaka ordered that no crops were to be planted for a year, and all milk was to be poured away. All women found pregnant were to be executed together with their husbands, and all who had shown a dereliction of their duty in not attending the king during his grief were likewise turned over to the executioners. It was a full three months before these arbitrary killings and meaningless 'rituals' were finally called to a halt.

When the inevitable encounters did take place between the colonialists and the natives, they were characterized by caution and uncertainty. At first, hostility was muted. The Zulu were naturally apprehensive, but also curious. They had only the haziest ideas about European civilization; indeed, there was a half-held belief that the whites came from the bottom of the sea where they collected beads, and occasionally rode to the surface on great animals with white wings (ships?) which fed on ivory. Shaka initially welcomed whites to his court; he wanted to know more about King George and his empire, and he was predictably interested in demonstrations of European technology, especially guns which proved so effective against elephants that he invited his visitors to join him in his campaigns.

For their part, the British were impressed by Zulu power and the extent of their domains. Early visitors to the king's kraal were obviously surprised by its 1,500 huts and its huge standing army. They had certainly seen nothing like this before. There was some minor trading, but when it came to specific negotiations for land there was a great deal of misunderstanding on both sides as to what was actually taking place. The confusion really lay in the difference between rights to *use* and rights to *own* the areas in question. And once occupation had actually taken place, notably at Port Natal, there was a greater influx of white settlers and further encroachments began. The clash between the cultures became inevitable.

Shaka had already voiced his suspicions that King George might attack him, and an argument about this had led to the peremptory execution of eight of his indunas. The problem became even more difficult for him when he planned expeditions that would take him further south where white settlements were well established. He knew that this would bring him into direct conflict with King George's subjects, and he actually contemplated a mission to the king. Whilst this was failing to materialize, the British and Boer forces had had their first serious clash, not with the Zulu directly, but with some of those tribes displaced by Zulu aggression. The contestants were drawing closer together, and when Shaka was eventually assassinated by his own brothers in 1828, the scene was set for a decisive encounter with the colonialists.

Shaka's successors were really not much better than he had been in the treatment of either their own people or those of other tribes. They were not so determined as empire-builders; they had no need to be. The Zulu nation was their inheritance. But in the niceties of control and the exercise of government, there was not much difference either in attitude or in technique. Shaka's immediate successor, Dingane, was as cruel as he was incompetent. He effectively signed away the future of the Zulu nation when, after informally ceding certain key areas of Natal to the ever intrusive Boers, he invited them to a farewell feast and amidst the celebrations ordered his stamping warriors to 'kill the wizards'. Not one Boer survived, and this was followed by a general massacre of Boer families which was attended by horrific atrocities to women and children. But it sounded the death knell for the Zulu. The Boers brought in reinforcements and broke the power of the Zulu at the battle of Ncome, afterwards known as Blood River, in which some 3,000 Zulus died for the loss of only 4 wounded Boers.

Dingane was unsurprisingly assassinated and was followed by another brother, Mpande, who was 'more self-indulgent than zealous' (Roberts 1977) – a king whose ruthlessness was tempered by a love of the good life. He consolidated his own position by murdering other possible claimants to the throne, together with their families. He dexterously side-stepped any unnecessary conflicts with the Europeans, but in order to keep his impis gainfully employed and also maintain the impression of himself as the warrior-chief he ordered attacks upon more vulnerable native peoples such as the Swazi.

By this time the Zulu kingdom had become somewhat circumscribed. In the earlier days, Shaka could almost certainly have crushed the white settlements, but for various reasons was reluctant to do so. Dingane came into conflict with the colonialists, but by now they had become more securely entrenched. Mpande avoided any direct confrontation with them despite the fact that their incursions had progressively reduced the size of the traditional Zulu territories. Mpande lived to uncharacteristic old-age, having survived by a policy of guile and pass-ivity. He had even encouraged rivalry between his sons, an expedient which led to one of the worst massacres in Zulu history when Cetsh-wayo, already an accomplished warrior, defeated and butchered his opponents including 6 of his brothers and some 23,000 of their followers and their families at what came to be known as Mathambo – the Place of Bones.

In so many colonizing situations there comes a point at which the indigenous population feels that it has taken as much as it can. Someone has got to take a stand – even if it is something of a fruitless gesture. In the case of the Zulu, it looked as though they did have a remote chance of success, and the triumphant Cetshwayo lost no time in pre-paring his regiments. He could now deploy an army of 50,000 men, even more than Shaka, and there is little doubt that he wanted to emulate his uncle, but history was against him – he was just too late. It was now 1872; more and more British settlers were coming into Natal, and there were also the Boers to the south. All were apprehensive about the huge Zulu force on their borders. The British wanted to come to an understanding with the Boers and establish some form of federal government in South Africa, but they knew this would only be possible once they had dealt with the Zulu. The political juggling was taking place in an atmosphere of increasing tension and mutual suspicion.

Hostilities were eventually precipitated – as so often – by a trifling border incident which technically violated the treaty which Cetshwayo had made with the colony at Natal in 1878. This supplied the British Governor of the Cape, Sir Bartle Frere, with a convenient *causus belli*. Cetshwayo's excesses were the ostensible reason for this invasion of Zululand, but even at the time it was pretty well recognized that this was part of an encroachment policy of divide and rule which the British found surprisingly difficult to implement.

The Zulu were given an ultimatum which left them a mere thirty days to disband their army and effectively capitulate to British demands. It was an impossible situation, and war was formally declared by the British in January 1879. Their confidence in an early success was shat-tered at Isandhlwana when Lord Chelmsford's force was overwhelmed and massacred by a surprise Zulu attack. Chelmsford, the British com-mander-in-chief, was away at the time on a reconnaissance expedition and returned to find the camp virtually obliterated. At much the same time a desperate action was being fought at Rorke's Drift where a handful of men were holding off a huge Zulu impi. Despite a shortage of supplies and the meagre protection of improvised barricades they survived against all expectation. They lost 15 men for the loss of about 350 warriors, a disproportionate expense which the Zulu commander felt unable to sustain. The victory of this small garrison led to the award of eleven Victoria Crosses, more than for any other single action in the British Army. The British took their revenge in March when they defeated a large Zulu force at Kambula. Although this battle involved the death of some 2,000 Zulus, it was indecisive as far as British objectives were concerned. There was still considerable dissatisfaction at Chelmsford's handling of the situation, and it was in July, at the point where his recall was imminent, that he achieved a spectacular success over the Zulu forces at Ulundi, the site of the royal kraal, where their impis were finally defeated.

This was really the end of Zulu power. There were some desultory – almost poignant – incidents after this when Cetshwayo's son, Dinu-Zulu, tried to assume the mantle of kingship and revitalize Zulu power. He sought the alliance of the Boers who effectively cheated the Zulu of their territory as a condition of their help against some neighbouring tribes. The Boers then poured into the territory and dispossessed native farmers of their lands and livelihood. The Zulu then appealed to the British who, in turn, negotiated with the Boers to limit their boundaries, and the rest of the country became a British protectorate in 1887.

The struggle was now over. To some extent, the Zulu were the victims of their own aggressive and expansionist practices. The chaotic situation which they helped to create in south-eastern Africa encouraged a winner-take-all ethos in which they were eventually the losers. When confronted by superior powers, in weaponry, technology, and culture, they had to fight or go under. Military resistance was the only thing they knew. But they did not prove to be impervious to the white man's guns as their witch-doctors had promised (the bullet did not turn harmlessly to water). In the circumstances, there really was no choice. One cannot imagine a situation in which they could have happily coexisted as equal partners with the Europeans. It can be safely assumed that ultimately they would have capitulated at the cultural level as has happened in virtually all situations where the west has cast its shadow.

For their enemies – the intruders – it was a familiar story. Another nation had been conquered. It had been a well-fought and worthwhile struggle against a half-respected but inferior foe. This was 'darkest Africa', so there was an avowed ideological dimension to this task of bringing the heathen to a knowledge of the true faith. But it is difficult to avoid the conclusion that in the complex of motives this took a secondary place to national pride, military glory, and economic aggrandizement.

10

THE ATHENIANS
The enemy as opponents of democracy

Any consideration of the Athenian state must be set in the overall context of classical Greek society. Prior to this, proto-Greek civilizations had flourished in Crete from *c*. 2000 to *c*. 1400 BC and on the Greek mainland from *c*. 1400 to *c*. 1200 BC. It is generally conceded that the two historically persistent features of Greek culture were language and religion, and it is now reasonably well established that in these two earlier societies a form of the Greek language was used, albeit 'disguised' by a quite different script, and that certain recognizable elements of Greek religion were also present. What brought these societies to an end is still uncertain, but from about 1200 BC or a little after – perhaps due to the incursions of foreign invaders – Greece declined into a 'Dark Ages' period which was characterized by lower levels of cultural and architectural achievement.

By the eighth century BC a proto-classical civilization had begun to emerge. It was centred on the mainland and the adjacent islands, and on the coastal strip of Turkey known as Ionia, and it was at this time that there began to develop that singular feature of Greek society, the polis or city-state. These were often located around some kind of defensible citadel or acropolis (literally, high place, as in Athens) from which the surrounding peoples could be efficiently administered. Within the poleis various forms of political organization were possible, and many of these states exported their particular brands of organization to the colonies that were established as far afield as Italy, Sicily, north Africa, and the Black Sea. Colonization had important results. It uncovered and exploited new and necessary sources of raw materials – Greece was particularly short of woods, metals, and grain – and established new markets for Greek exports, especially wine, oil, and pottery. The new-found wealth which flowed in from these overseas ventures brought about significant changes in Greek society. It introduced the austere landowning aristocracy to new luxuries, facilitated – perhaps even necessitated – the development of a money economy, and gave rise to a class of merchants and entrepreneurs which indirectly undermined the position of the traditional eupatridai (well-born ones). In Athens, particularly, it also led to a considerable influx of immigrants who played a significant role in these new economic developments.

The rise of city-state organization coincided with the decline of the monarchy as an institution in most of Greece. From about the middle of the eighth century BC, strong oligarchic government was the order of the day in most states. In some, it meant that traditional aristocratic families controlled the political machinery, sometimes – as in Corinth – for several generations. A number of states were ruled by a series of tyrannoi, popular leaders who had originally seized power unconstitutionally, and who now held it whether by common consent or by coercion. By the beginning of the sixth century BC, in Athens at least, there were the first faint stirrings of something approaching democracy when certain socio-economic reforms were initiated by a leading official (archon) named Solon. These were variously received, and it was only towards the end of that century – after an ambivalently regarded 'tyrannical' interlude – that more far-reaching democratic innovations came to be introduced.

In the early years of the fifth century BC, tensions arose between the Persians, the great power of their day, and the politically emergent Greek world. The Persians acted repressively towards the recalcitrant Greek cities of Ionia over which they exercised a kind of suzerainty; the Ionian Greeks then appealed to the mainland Greeks for support, and this brought the Persians into direct conflict with Athens. To the Persians, the Athenians were an upstart people who needed to be taught a lesson, and thus began an on-and-off struggle which did not end until the final conquest of Persia by Alexander the Great in the following century.

The Persians had risen to power under Cyrus (the Great) in the sixth century BC. Their domains eventually stretched from Asia Minor to Afghanistan. This expansionist policy inevitably brought them into contact – and finally conflict – with the small colonies of Asiatic Greeks. It fell to one of Cyrus' successors, Darius, to subdue the Greeks of Asia Minor and to initiate a punitive expedition to the Greek mainland to show these recalcitrant people who were the masters of the known world. According to Herodotus, writing some fifty years or so after the events in question, the Persian forces, comprising 600 galleys, subdued many of the Aegean islands and received submission from many of the mainland poleis and reduced others to slavery. Their main objective, the subjugation of Athens, seemed to be a relatively easy task. The Athenians made the critical decision of meeting the Persians where they landed, at Marathon, rather than wait for them to arrive at the city itself. They had a pitifully small force of about 9,000 men, and were joined by their recent allies, the Plataeans, who added another 1,000 men to their numbers. A plea for help had been sent urgently to Sparta who could have fielded perhaps the most formidable fighting force in Greece, but they temporized on religious grounds – they were celebrating a festival at the time – an excuse which was not lost on the Athenians. Indeed, it may have been a portent of things to come. The Persians had at least twice as large a force as the Greeks, but against all the odds were driven from the beaches with a loss of some 6,400 men as opposed to the death of only 192 Athenians (490 BC).

When the Persians returned ten years later, it was a different proposition. This time they intended to do things properly. They mustered a huge force, possibly around 200,000 men in addition to about 800 ships. Their new king, Xerxes, had a reputation for pious barbarity. Herodotus records that when the army mustered at the Hellespont prior to the crossing into Greece, a storm destroyed two bridges which had been constructed for the purpose. Xerxes had the engineers beheaded, and ordered the waters of the Hellespont to be given three hundred lashes for their unruly behaviour. Later, Xerxes is said to have sacrificed nine boys and girls – presumably further to ensure his success. Herodotus – the only real authority we have – may have overdone the cruelty in the same way as he almost certainly exaggerates the Persian numbers which he gives as 5 million. But then his account is written primarily as an epic of Greek versus barbarian.

Athens prepared much more thoroughly for this invasion. She was joined by a number of other poleis, although many, especially in eastern Greece which might expect to bear the brunt of the initial onslaught, remained neutral, and a few, including the influential Thebes, actually co-operated with the enemy. This time, however, the Greeks had the help of Sparta who led the land-based operations whilst Athens, who had the most powerful navy of all the states, dictated warfare at sea. This coalition, again despite the odds, defeated superior forces by a mixture of guile and outstanding courage and tenacity. But it was a success that bred dissension. The two Greek powers became increasingly aware of each other, and suspicion inevitably led to hostility.

These victories consolidated Athenian power, and reinforced its leading position in the Greek world. In a sense, they also served to validate a particular form of political and social organization as being superior to that of oriental-type despotisms such as Persia. Athenians developed a new self-confidence. And this, in turn, generated a greater sense of allegiance to the city and an increased desire to participate in its life and policies.

The war initiated a period of unprecedented cultural achievement which still has an indirect influence on the modern world. Many of its artistic, architectural, and political developments took place in a 'golden age' of less than a hundred years, and were spearheaded by a city that controlled an area about the size of a small English county. It still seems amazing to the modern observer that so much talent could have been confined to so small a space in such a short period of time. It is a matter of debate whether this can be directly attributed to the much vaunted freedom of its democratic forms which at times could be as frustrating as they were liberating. What *is* certain is that it gave Athenians the self-assurance to experiment and explore the possibilities of new ideas in art and politics.

The polis that developed was both more democratic and less democratic than anything we understand by the term. It was, in the strictest sense, a radical democracy – a people's system. The Assembly of the citizens was the final arbiter on all matters of state. True, there was a council of 500, the Boule, but even this was not elected; members were chosen by lot, and operated on a rotation basis. In fact, virtually all the officers of state, magistrates, jurymen, chairmen of boards (of which there were many), etc., were chosen this way. No training was required – much to the disgust of some Athenian intellectuals like Socrates who argued that politics was an activity that required training and expertise. The Athenians regarded all citizens as potentially capable; they would learn the 'trade' once in office. Aristotle commented later that the best judge of a meal is not the cook who prepares it but the guests who have to eat it.

The main exception in this system of allocating tasks by lot was the military. The strategoi (generals) – possibly on the assumption that war was too important to be left to part-time politicians – were elected to office on a periodic basis. But even they were ultimately answerable to the Assembly for their actions. This is highlighted by the well-known instance of the trial of six military commanders who were accused of abandoning some of the survivors of a naval battle at Arginusai (406 BC). Socrates was serving his one day as chairman of the council, and refused to allow a proposal that they be impeached. He was overruled by an irregular action of the Assembly, and all six were condemned and executed.

It was the task of the council to convene the Assembly, arrange its operations, and ensure that its decrees were carried out. It scrutinized the qualifications of officials, and the allocation and use of funds. The Assembly itself was open to all citizens, i.e. males from the age of 18, providing they had the statutory birth qualification of being children of Athenian parents. It met forty times a year, although this might be supplemented by special emergency meetings, especially during wartime. Curiously enough, although we know so much about the general structure of the system, we are not at all sure about certain aspects of its administration. For example, we are not sure how many people attended the Assembly, or what constituted a quorum. There is some

146

indirect evidence that it was 6,000; this was certainly the number required to effect an ostracism, the banishing of a citizen from Athens – usually for a specified period – for actual, or potentially, undesirable activities.

In all, there seem to have been about 700 officials of one kind or another employed to conduct the affairs of this relatively small state, with more boards and committees than seem necessary to get things done. In addition, there were 6,000 jurors – also chosen by lot – who sat on the various 'benches' (dicasteries) which specialized in civil and criminal cases. Perhaps the idea was to distribute accountability and reduce the opportunities for peculation, or possibly to inculcate the virtues of civic responsibility which were integral to the polis. Whatever the motives, it was patently not free from corruption and abuses of various kinds. Ultimately, its vain attempts to ensure the 'purity' of the system led, perhaps inevitably, to the recognition of sykophantai (public informers) and the subsequent persecution of 'undesirable' elements within the society.

There were also *un*democratic features of Athenian society which seem incongruous to the modern mind, notably the inequalities built into its social structure. The polis was run by the citizens; these were the adult males who comprised only about one-fifth of the total population. They alone had the franchise, and they alone could determine the policies of the state. Free women, i.e. women of Athenian birth, were essentially jural minors. They could not attend the Assembly, had no vote, and therefore had no direct influence on affairs of state. What we may broadly call middle-class women – of whom we know most – had their own quarters in the household; they had their domestic and child-rearing tasks to perform, and were not normally encouraged to seek mixed company. A woman was always technically under the authority of a kurios (literally, lord or master), i.e. a senior male, usually a father or husband, but exactly how this worked in practice, we are not quite sure. In most patriarchal societies there are all sorts of anomalies, and there is reasonably clear evidence that Athens was no exception.

More serious was the position of the genuinely unfree, the metics (resident aliens) and the slaves. Most of the metics were probably Greeks who had migrated, for one reason or another, from their native poleis. It is almost certainly true to say that metics were as well treated in Athens as anywhere else in Greece, and we know that many of them were engaged in trades and commerce of various kinds, and that a few of them had become quite prosperous. Their political rights were severely circumscribed, and they had to pay a special tax, but – and this was regarded as a privilege – they were allowed to participate, in prescribed ways, in the defence of the state.

The situation of the slaves was quite different. Most of them were probably not Greeks (certainly by the fourth century BC, Greeks had become increasingly reluctant to hold other Greeks as slaves), and – again probably – most of them were either the victims of war or of piracy. We do not know the exact slave population of Athens, but it may have comprised something in the region of two-fifths of the total population. Slaves were the property of their masters who were usually individuals, not the state. They had no political or economic rights, and in any legal action had to be represented by their owners. On the other hand, they did have certain religious rights, and were sometimes allowed to join eranoi (mutual support clubs) and even buy themselves out of slavery. In practice, so much depended on the form of slavery in question; this could range from domestic slavery – not unlike household servants – to slavery in mines and quarries where life was usually agonizing and mercifully brief. Normally, slaves did not serve with the military – after all, it might give them ideas – although sometimes they were given body-servant duties, and in cases of national emergency were pressed into service as rowers in the Athenian fleet.

In pre-classical times, the power of the army had been concentrated in the person of the king with his companions and retainers who were conveyed to the battlefield by horses and chariots. But by the late seventh century BC, a little prior to the classical period, things had begun to change. The cavalry, who represented the aristocratic strata, were still important, but they gradually assumed a more subordinate role, and precedence was given instead to heavily armed infantry (hoplites), and the ubiquitous lightly armed skirmishing troops and archers who were often drawn from the lower echelons of society. This development in Greek military organization probably reflects not so much military exigency as the growing democratization of Greek society. The emergence of the polis as the predominant form of political organization had necessitated the formation of citizen militia to ensure its defence, and this, in turn, had given increased status to those farmers, shopkeepers, artisans, etc., who comprised that militia. The equation was simple: if they shared in its defence, they must also share in its policy-making administration.

Hoplites normally provided their own accoutrements of war. These comprised lances, short swords, and small shields made of metal and leather. They were also equipped with body armour, made of bronze and leather, which covered the upper torso but did not adequately protect the loins. They wore elaborate metal helmets which completely masked the head and neck, and were often plumed to designate status or affiliation. They fought in tight formations, or phalanxes, several lines deep, and much depended on the thoroughness of their drills and manoeuvres. But well ordered as their techniques might be, the tactics were relatively unsophisticated. The intention was simply to thrust and stab until the enemy line broke, and then the rout would sometimes turn into a massacre. Given the limited weaponry at their disposal, there were few possible variations on this theme.

In Athens, training in the gymnasia was an essential element in the male educational programme. A premium was put on physical fitness, not least as a preparation for war. Military service was mainly the prerogative of citizens: indeed, anyone – say a metic – found impersonating a citizen was peremptorily sold into slavery. All male citizens, therefore, between the ages of 18 and 60 were liable for military call-up and consequently had to undergo a period of training. Initial (ephebic) training was from 18 to 20 during which time recruits were exempt from political duties and even legal prosecution. They were enrolled on a tribal basis, the annual recruitment being estimated at about 700. Thereafter until the age of 50, men could be mobilized for active service. After this, they were classified as veterans, and might be required to undertake less strenuous tasks such as guard duties or the manning of border or boundary fortifications. In peacetime, the bulk of the army was held in reserve, but to be at peace was an abnormal state of affairs. Between the battle of Marathon (490 BC) and the battle of Chaeronea (338 BC) in the time of Macedonian supremacy in Greece, Athens was at war more than two years in every three, and never had more than ten consecutive years of peace.

The Athenians, ostensibly in the interest of other Greeks as well, had formed a league of states, usually known as the Delian League. This comprised those poleis which were already subject to Athens, and those who joined for the express purpose of countering any further Persian incursions. To this end they contributed money and ships. But as time went on, Athens began to see itself as the commanding power in what was originally a type of federal organization. From being a first among equals, it began to assume the leading role in a hegemony. Indeed, people spoke of an Athenian empire, especially when it effectively confiscated league funds from the neutral island of Delos and housed them 'for safe-keeping' at the Athenian acropolis.

And this was not all. Athens began to interfere more and more in the affairs of other states outside its immediate orbit, although it should be stated – in fairness – that it was not uncommon for smaller states to call upon larger states for help when they found themselves embroiled in disputes. It was this situation that eventually brought Athens into conflict with another powerful polis, Corinth, which was already suffering as a result of Athens' growing economic supremacy. But Corinth was not entirely a free agent; it was a member of what amounted to a rival coalition of states, the Peloponnesian League, of which Sparta was the dominant force. Thus, not for the first time, the two leading powers in Greece found themselves in contention.

Who was really to blame for the outbreak of hostilities is still in dispute. Sparta and its allies voted for war because of Athens' purported treaty violations. But it could equally well be argued that the Athenians were spoiling for a fight that they knew was inevitable sooner or later, so they decided to force the issue.

At the opening of the Peloponnesian War in 431 BC against the Spartans and their allies, Athens had a regular army of perhaps 13,000 hoplites, 1,000 cavalry, who still bore themselves with a kind of aristocratic hauteur, and a territorial reserve comprising 1,400 epheboi and 2,500 veterans. These were supplemented by some 1,600 archers drawn from the thetes (lowest citizen) class, together with about 9,500 metics who might be employed as lightly armed troops and auxiliaries. The whole force was commanded by a supreme general (polemarchos) assisted by the other strategoi chosen by the Assembly. In this war, the Athenians took the view that they were ranged against the enemies of democracy, and they were joined by allies (subjects?) in the Delian League. Whether the allies were there because they were like-minded or because they were leaned on by a dominant partner to fulfil their treaty obligations is still a matter of conjecture.

Strong as the Athenian army was, it was still no match for the well-drilled ranks of the Spartans, so they avoided any direct confrontation where they could. Even when their territory was invaded and the crops and homesteads were destroyed, they still did not give battle, but instead encouraged those citizens in the outlying areas to bring their families and movable chattels into the city. This was a highly controversial policy, but siegecraft techniques were so rudimentary that strong city walls did afford a large measure of security and it is significant that in the entire thirty years of the war, the Spartans never made a direct assault on the city itself. This 'retreatist' expedient was made possible by the strength of the Athenian navy which was able to bring supplies of corn to the city to compensate for the losses in the countryside.

The Athenians and their allies constituted what was probably the strongest naval force in the ancient world. Besides the considerable contingents from the islands of Chios and Lesbos, the Athenians themselves had 300 to 400 triremes, 150-feet-long warships with three banks of oars necessitating about 170 rowers – usually poorer citizens or metics. They were commanded by trierarchoi who were nominated by the board of generals, and were often wealthy citizens who had contributed to the cost of the vessel in the first place. Triremes had only one mast, but normally travelled under sail until they engaged the enemy. Then the rowers took over. Again, the tactics were crude. Naval warfare consisted of ramming enemy ships, often to break their oars and/or securing them with grappling irons so that they could be boarded and their crews captured or slaughtered. In the Peloponnesian War there was no 'front' as such, so sometimes the navy was used to launch raids on enemy shores. These hit-and-run tactics could be very effective, especially when there was stalemate as was often the case.

The war was a very long-drawn-out affair with fortunes fluctuating on both sides. In its initial stages, Athens was devastated by a plague – perhaps indirectly as a result of the acute overcrowding in the city. She gradually recovered, and won several important victories despite the ravages of the plague which claimed so many of her people – including their war-leader, Perikles. She withstood the havoc the Spartan army wrought in the surrounding countryside in the first years of the war, and within four years she had captured Pylos, located in enemy territory, together with a number of important Spartiates who were used as bargaining counters (425 BC). It was at this point that some kind of settlement could have been made. Sparta sued for peace, but the offer was rejected on the advice of the extreme imperialists – especially the demagogue, Cleon, a leather-tanner by trade, who had become one of the most vociferous voices in the Athenian Assembly. Sparta, in her turn, recovered from this set-back and had some notable successes in northern Greece. It was now stalemate, and both sides resigned themselves to an armistice based on the status quo – the Peace of Nicias – in 421 BC. Predictably, the peace was marred by violations on both sides. These infringements and constant intriguing led to a resumption of hostilities in 418 BC, followed by further agreements, and then direct confrontation between Athens and Sparta again in 414 BC.

Until this time, the overall strategy of the Athenians had been to contain the enemy on land by a defensive policy of interrupted attrition whilst seizing the initiative at sea. For a while it proved quite successful. It eventually foundered for two reasons: first, because the Peloponnesian League also built up a formidable naval force under a gifted and unscrupulous leader, Lysander; and second, because the Athenians attempted a disastrous invasion of Sicily (415–413 BC) in which they lost some 200 triremes and about 10,000 irreplaceable hoplites, besides thousands of auxiliaries.

This became the turning-point in the war which had now effectively divided most of the Greek world. The situation became so critical for Athens that she even resorted to the abandonment of her radical democracy and instituted a form of oligarchy in 411 BC, but this lasted a mere eight months. Her fortunes went from bad to worse. The war dragged on but the reverses became so severe that by 404 BC the Spartans and their allies after a long siege forced the Athenians to surrender. The terms of the capitulation were not as humiliating as they might have been, and it is to the credit of the Spartans that they did not allow their allies, particularly the Thebans, to destroy Athens completely and have the inhabitants sold into slavery.

There was bad feeling on both sides. The war had hardly been an honourable one. Unspeakable atrocities and pointless killing of both soldiers and civilians had taken place. Athens was fortunate that the Spartans only insisted on the destruction of her walls, the surrender of all her remaining triremes except twelve, and what amounted to the right to determine her constitution.

The great days were now past. There was a revival – there usually is, but in this case Athens never recaptured her former glory. Greeks still respected her reputation, she was still revered – even by her enemies – as the state that saved Greece from Persian bondage. Her arts and sciences flourished, and she still produced high scholarship and keen political debate. Athens still had influence, but the *power* was no longer there.

We can see from this study that inter-poleis differences were sometimes resolved at a terrible cost. It seems to have all been part of the contest-morality that governed inter-state rivalry. It is, therefore, important to see what happened when a polis was either hammered or starved into submission. It must be borne in mind that, within the conventions of the ancient world, the vanquished became the property of the victors. There was no status, for instance, corresponding to the modern 'prisoner-of-war', and no specific term to designate such a person. There were really only four courses of action open to the victors: release the prisoners gratuitously – which was somewhat unusual; ransom them; enslave them or – more profitably – sell them into slavery; or as an ultimate expedient, execute them. Merciless treatment of the conquered was quite common in Greek warfare, and it was not unusual to kill the men – always a potential source of further trouble – and enslave, and possibly sell, the women and children, although male slaves usually fetched far more money. The Athenians carried out variants of these in a number of city-states that had either flouted their authority or had just happened to back the wrong side. And this was not always done at the whim of a local commander, but as the deliberate policy of the democratic Athenian Assembly. The fate of the city-state of Melos in 416 BC is a case in point.

Militarism in general and the treatment of the enemy in particular can often be related to the relevent ideology, but the nature and outworking of that relationship in Greek – and particularly Athenian – society is fascinatingly ambiguous. At the religious level, the Greeks give the impression of having been a very devout people. The temples, especially those that adorn the Athenian acropolis, are regarded as testimony of this. The sanctuaries and oracular centres such as Delphi and Eleusis, with their esoteric cults, and the popular shrines and household images all speak of the same mentality. There were rituals for all occasions, not least of all for war. Some commanders took their ritual specialists and soothsayers to war with them, sometimes with unfortunate consequences, as in the case of the Athenian general, Nicias, in Sicily, who refused to evacuate his troops from an impossible situation at Syracuse becaue the omens were not favourable. On some occasions, commanders might dedicate the property and even the persons of their enemies to the gods, and defeat was not unusually attributed to divine disfavour. But what did all this mean? The rituals seem to have had no *moral* force, and the complex corpus of mythology gives no hint of moral obligation. There is an eclecticism about Greek religious practices that generates the suspicion of superficiality. Certainly as far as Athens is concerned one is left wondering if the real preoccupation of the citizens was with the city itself and its distinctive ethos. Perhaps the ideology of Athenians was really Athenianism.

There was a kind of dualism in the Greek world which was reflected in the Athenian mentality. It was the unresolved dilemma between normative democratic idealism and substantive ambition. The main Athenian problem was not resource scarcity but position scarcity. She had her economic difficulties, it is true, but her primary concern – as the contemporary writer Thucydides makes clear – was that of national recognition and esteem. Athens and Sparta had mutually exclusive and mutually incompatible values, but they did have mutuality of ambition – both wanted to be the dominant power in the Greek firmament. They both feared and envied each other, and ostensibly each wanted to impose its own particular system on its neighbours. None of this had anything to do with religious ideology; indeed – if anything – religion had a consolidating effect on their divisions. The real problem was one of hegemonic status exacerbated by the conflict of irreconcilable political goals.

11

THE MAOISTS
The enemy as class antagonists

Any account of the military activities of the Chinese communists must include some discussion of the determinative nature of their revolutionary ideology and of their philosophy of war. The term 'ideology' can be used in two principal senses: as a body of ideas that serves as a guide and impulse to action, and – as in Marxist usage – as a systematic distortion, exaggeration, or simplification which political leaders use to further their own interests. In this sense, it is not so much an attempt to understand social realities, as a devious and manipulative use of rational and emotional symbols for political ends. As such it is condemned by Marxist writers as yet another tool of the dominant classes for the oppression of the masses. But as the social analyst, Karl Mannheim (1948), has pointed out, Marxism itself must be open to the same strictures. It too is an ideology which is employed in the interests of a particular group, and it too can be cynically propagated for covert purposes. And there is no better example of this than in the communist Far East.

Most political thinking begins with the assumption that men have a common human nature, and that despite their conflicts of private interest, they have fundamental common interests which enable them to achieve a political community. The political doctrine of communism, on the other hand, is based upon a theory of class struggle. In keeping with Marxist teaching, communists hold that men are shaped primarily by their class situation. Class interests are necessarily antagonistic, and therefore no common interests can ultimately bridge these divisions. The class struggle is not caused by human malice, but by social conditions, and while these classes exist the conflict between them is irreconcilable. Marx held that the very existence of the state was proof of this. The situation cannot therefore be ameliorated by controls or improvements – which, indeed, may be seen as mere sops to the suffering masses. It can only be remedied by radical structural change, and this can only be effectively brought about by revolution. While class inequalities exist, communists believe that the struggle must continue

154

until total victory. 'The liberation of the oppressed class is impossible . . . without violent revolution' (Lenin 1969: 10).

There appears to be a historical inevitability about this process which will eventually bring the classless society into being. Furthermore, it is the moral duty – one might almost add the sacred task – of 'believers' to do all that is possible to aid and abet this process, and bring the 'new society' to fruition. Lenin, in a speech given to the Russian Young Communist League in 1920, makes the position quite clear,

> We repudiate morality that is taken outside of human class con-
> cepts. We say that this is deception, a fraud which clogs the brains
> of the workers and peasants in the interests of the landlords and
> capitalists. We say that our morality is entirely subordinated to
> the interests of the class struggle of the proletariat.
>
> (Lenin 1969)

In all this, there is still some confusion as to the actual function of the proletariat. Although communists no longer expect the proletariat to comprise the majority on the day of liberation, the myth of the redeeming role of the proletariat still persists. And it is on this issue – or, more specifically, on what actually constitutes the proletariat – that there is an apparent division within the communist camp. Mao-Tse-Tung is often credited with shifting the revolutionary initiative from the urban (manufacturing) poor to the rural peasantry, although the documentary evidence makes it clear that this was in keeping with ideas put forward earlier by both Lenin and Stalin. Whichever position is adopted, the role of the proletariat is still something of a myth in so far as it is the Party, acting on behalf of the masses, who will actually instigate and implement revolutionary action. It is the Party who will act as the guardians of proletarian interests. They alone will monitor progress and control activities. The state as such may eventually 'wither away' – but it won't be yet. When the dictatorship of the proletariat will be realized is an interesting question; at what point the people themselves will take over is anyone's guess.

Meanwhile, it is all a protracted struggle against the enemies of socialism – both those inside and outside the system. The operational principles whereby this is to be achieved have been laid down in a number of classic statements on the strategy of revolutionary wars, pre-eminently by Lenin and Mao-Tse-Tung. They involve the necessary matching of feasible cost against minimal risk. At the internal level, the permanent revolution is a matter of neutralization – concentrating the pressure against the 'weakest link in the chain'. This necessarily involves the rejection of opportunism; the fight for social improvements is regarded as mere piecemeal social engineering. Only the complete and lasting transformation of society is worthwhile, but this may have to be achieved in successive stages. The objective is to raise the social consciousness of the masses so that revolutionary change alone will satisfy them, and then to neutralize the power of the dominant classes so that they can no longer continue to resist the forces of change. Only this combination can lead to a successful revolution. The fundamental issue is that of securing and maintaining political power; as Lenin himself put it, 'War is part of the whole [and] the whole is politics' (Lenin 1969).

At the external level, communist operations are often aimed at undermining the morale and comprehension of their political opponents. This may be done by disrupting their social and economic structures, by undermining their military capabilities, and even by creating the kind of pervasive disaffection which will induce their opponents to accept communist 'solutions'. But territorial expansion may not be the primary objective, as it can sometimes involve over-commitments which leave the revolutionary cause vulnerable to counter-revolutionary responses. It is often far more important to recognize that the *accumulation* and organization of power are the keys to further success. After all, there is such a thing as diminishing administrative returns.

Whenever non-violent means can be employed to undermine the 'enemy', the eventual use of violent means is made less risky. But the preliminary use of infiltration, subversion, and proselytization are usually not enough. The classic statements on the revolutionary struggle insist that real success cannot be achieved without violence, although it is admitted that this must never be an end in itself, and must not be used in all instances. Violence may sometimes be necessary in the preparatory phases of the revolutionary cycle which can take the form of guerrilla activity or local uprisings, although the seizure of power itself may be achieved by legal or quasi-legal means. However, once the regime is established, violence will almost certainly be used to quell any rebellious spirits and to liquidate the worst class enemies.

Communist doctrine, as proclaimed by the early Soviets and expanded by Mao-Tse-Tung, claims that its goal is world peace. But it is emphasized that this can only be brought about by the ultimate triumph of the 'forces of peace'. To attain this, domestic revolutions and international wars may be necessary. 'We are opposed to imperialist wars for the division of spoils among the capitalists, but we have always declared it to be absurd for the revolutionary proletariat to renounce revolutionary wars that may prove necessary in the interests of socialism' (Lenin 1969). There is here a variant of the old Catholic just and unjust wars distinction; in this case, the inherent justice of war is not only related to the cause but also to the focus of hostility – the class enemy. It's really a matter of who happens to fight whom. Wars fought in the interests of imperialism are necessarily unjust, but those fought

156

in the interests of the oppressed peoples are self-evidently just. The instigation of wars is therefore a 'peace-loving' act if it is done in the right cause. In Mao's words, 'the just war will lead to eventual peace' (quoted in Niemeyer 1966).

The Chinese communist revolution is a particularly interesting case in point. Not that their contribution to revolutionary doctrine was in any sense original – as is sometimes erroneously supposed – but because of the ways in which this doctrine was adapted in practice. Radical political change in China had its immediate roots in events in the late nineteenth century. At this time, the threat and the promise of modernization – already a growing feature of rival Japanese society – combined with the fear of western aggression and involvement had fomented a spirit of political and economic uncertainty which ultimately led to the revolution of 1911. This movement, which, at last, cast off the power of the old imperial dynasty and all its abuses, was essentially anti-Manchu rather than democratic in nature. Despite its good intentions, China's fortunes did not improve. Later on, the settlements after the First World War left China in an even more parlous condition. Japan refused to release the conquered German possessions, and threatened to make China a Japanese protectorate. Foreign gunboats patrolled China's rivers; trade was concentrated in treaty ports where foreigners had their concessions and enjoyed extra-territorial privileges, and foreign finance dominated much of the commercial activity. China wanted complete self-determination, but the western powers either would not, or could not, do much to help. So the Chinese looked elsewhere and found new friends among old neighbours – this time in the recently established Soviet Union.

Amidst this burgeoning nationalism, the country was still in ferment. Local warlords, often commanding armies several thousand strong, controlled vast tracts of land, and their ruthless depredations only meant further grief for the peasants. They were little more than bandit-chiefs who could survive only as long as they could feed their men and their families. The number of peasants who died at their hands is incalculable. The strongly walled city of Choctow was besieged for nearly three months and its 100,000 inhabitants starved. Another city in West Honan changed hands seventy-two times; people were often taken for ransom and tortured to make them reveal where they had hidden their valuables; if they hesitated they were sometimes cut in two at the waist as warning to others. The poverty was often so extreme that some people were said to have sold their children into prostitution simply in order to survive. The ongoing rivalries of these hordes of marauding brigands did little for the cause of Chinese unity and prosperity.

These warlords were mainly interested in gain. They exacted what they could from the peasants, and fought one another for richer shares in what little wealth there was. No principles were involved. There was no obvious conflict between liberty and tyranny, no particular political creed was at stake, no ideology in jeopardy – and no visible identifiable resolution of the essential problems. For many – perhaps most – it was incomprehensible confusion. There was a retreat of the rich from the countryside. All kinds of essential maintenance tasks were neglected, especially the huge irrigation and drainage works which fell into decay. Floods brought disaster; there was little relief from famine; and these merely exacerbated an ongoing situation in which there was dislocation of communications, a decline of inland trade, and general administrative chaos.

All this contributed to the breakdown of the old order of society. 'Military rule alienated both scholars and peasants; it defied every moral restraint and outraged every hope of improvement; it was the direct cause of the . . . Chinese Revolution' (Fitzgerald 1966: 53). A powerful national force was obviously needed to deal with a worsening situation; the country was ripe for a new and unifying form of nationalism.

In 1925, the national party, the Kuomintang, became the ready instrument in a new bid for power under its new leader, Chiang Kai-Shek, who wanted to unify the country under the Kuomintang banner and reinforce his own position as leader. Chiang emphasized Chinese nationalism and tried to capitalize on a mood that was antipathetic to foreign influences. To do this, he had first to reach an understanding with certain business interests in order to put his party on a sound economic footing. He then came to an accommodation with some of the warlords so as to maintain a free hand in his own territories. But he had one further problem – the Communists.

The Chinese Communist Party had been formed in 1921, and Communists had infiltrated the Kuomintang and now dominated the left wing of the Party. Chiang was astute enough to realize that there would have to be a showdown with them eventually, and he decided that this should be sooner rather than later. In 1927 his purge of the Communist elements was carried out with cold-blooded efficiency. He engineered a conflict situation with them and then ordered mass arrests throughout China. Sometimes they were duped into surrender, others gave in voluntarily. But they all met the same fate – only the method varied; some were beheaded, others were either shot or strangled. A few changed their allegiance – but their time was to come.

Mao-Tse-Tung, already the most prominent figure among the Chinese Communists, was incredulous. He could hardly believe that his erstwhile colleague could betray his friends and effect such a complete takeover of the Party apparatus. Instead of fleeing to the north or the Soviet Union as he was advised, Mao insisted on returning to Chang-

Sha to check the facts out for himself, only to find that the situation was worse than he supposed. He thought it might be possible to mobilize members of the Peasant Association, but this proved to be fruitless. The Party was demoralized. Certain key members of the Committee had gone underground, and the hunt was on for Mao himself. Within hours he and his wife were captured by Chiang's forces; Mao was beaten and imprisoned, but he hoped that his wife's pregnancy had saved her from a similar treatment. Fortunately his cell was not very secure and he was able to escape and run to the open land on the outskirts of the town. From there he watched impotently as his wife was tied weeping to the strangling-post in the field where he lay hidden from the executioners. Her murder was a traumatic experience he would never forget. Later on, he wrote:

I cut my hands on the cords of the strangling-post
But no blood spilled from my veins
Instead of blood I watched and saw the pity run out of me.
(Quoted in MacGregor-Hastie 1961: 90)

Until this time, the Chinese Communists had operated largely on directives from the Soviet Union, and Moscow did not believe that they were ready for revolution. It was because Moscow had not been optimistic about the Communists' chances that it had ordered them to surrender to the Kuomintang, to bide their time, and eventually undermine that organization from within. As it turned out, it was a recipe for disaster. When it was too late, the Russians and the Chinese realized that they had both been deceived. By the time Moscow had given the order to 'fight to the death in every street', a large proportion of the Party had already been liquidated. It was to be many years before the Chinese Communists could make their bid for power. Communist orthodoxy taught that a successful revolution required a particular association between workers and intellectuals, but for China this was not the correct formula. They had a different blueprint. The industrial proletariat was very small; 80 per cent of the population were peasants, so in China the revolution was to have a peasant base.

But this was all some way ahead. Before there could be any serious thought of challenging the national forces, considerable regrouping and retraining had to take place. Mao led some remnants into the mountains to get some respite from attack. In these retreats, the refugees set about organizing the peasants and setting up model co-operatives. Mao's hostility towards the landlords won him an enthusiastic following among the people, but it also aroused the disapproval – and perhaps suspicion – of the Central Committee of the Chinese Communist Party, which expelled him in 1929. He and his supporters were undeterred by this expulsion, and they continued to build up the nucleus of the future Red Army. Meanwhile, Chiang – largely ignoring the looming Japanese threat – conducted further offensives against Mao's forces, usually with very indifferent results. The Japanese, encouraged by this obvious failure of the Nationalist Army even to put down a peasant revolt, launched their campaign against Manchuria in 1931. It was to be the beginning of a prolonged and debilitating war which was to last another fourteen years.

Under increasing pressure from the Kuomintang, Mao and his supporters embarked upon the epic 'Long March' in 1934 which covered some 6,000 miles along the fringes of the Gobi desert and Tibet, and eventually led them to an area of north-western China, Shensi, where they could settle in comparative freedom, build up their forces, and perfect the techniques of guerrilla warfare. It was one of the most incredible feats of the twentieth century. They had few uniforms, an ill-assorted miscellany of weapons, and little by way of supplies. Some were already wounded; within two months of the beginning of the march, some 7,000 of these had died. Mao allowed little time for rest or recuperation, nor would he permit any serious deviation from the route. He had good intelligence from the peasant communities *en route*, and this enabled him to take necessary avoiding action where possible, but at times his undeviating determination gave his movements a certain predictability. This meant that in the early days the marchers left themselves open to concerted attacks from the Kuomintang – sometimes with disastrous consequences. At just one precarious river crossing in December 1934 they lost 13,000 men, and by the time they had covered only a third of their journey, their losses had risen to 20,000. They braved atrocious weather conditions, especially over the Great Snow Mountains bordering Tibet. Food shortages and lack of reasonable accommodation further reduced their numbers, and it is thought that of the original 100,000 or so that set out (estimates vary), of whom perhaps 20,000 were non-combatants, possibly fewer than 10,000 troops survived. Certainly by 1936, the core of the Red Army numbered only about 30,000. Demanding as the Long March had been, it reinforced the authority and determination of the Party, and became part of the mythology of the future Communist State.

Chiang only really gave half his attention to the Japanese; he was convinced that the true threat to his authority came from the Communists, but necessity finally dictated policy. By 1936, in the face of increased Japanese aggression, an uneasy alliance was formed between the newly developed Communist forces and the Nationalist Army, and this remained a nominal arrangement throughout the Second World War. The Japanese despaired of trying to woo Chiang away from this alliance, and in 1937 they extended their operations to the south and took over ports and other key centres of trade. The Nationalist Government, which was fast losing popularity, had to flee from its capital at Nanking and set up shop 400 miles away at Hankow. It was then ignominiously forced to retreat yet again, and spend the rest of the war at Chungking. By the beginning of 1939, the Japanese had occupied all of north China, the middle Tang-tse valley, and the coastline, so that most of the industrial areas and commercial enterprises were in their hands.

The Japanese actually made all the classic mistakes. Their advances into the interior of China extended their lines of communication, and left them exposed to increasingly dangerous guerrilla attacks. In the vastness of the country they were unable to bring the main Chinese armies to battle, so they remained a potential threat which the Japanese found difficult to assess. They hoped that their capture of Chinese cities would bring capitulation, but in allowing their troops to commit wanton atrocities on both civilians and prisoners of war, they generated hatred among the people and, at the same time, alienated foreign opinion.

In purely tactical terms these policies could not have served the Chinese better: they simply drove the population to a determined opposition to the invasion. The continued repression of the people also served the Communists well, whether it derived from Japanese repression or Kuomintang incompetence. It swelled their ranks. Even the Honan famine in 1942–3, one of the greatest tragedies of the war in which some 2,500,000 people died indirectly as a result of Kuomintang policies, could not fail to bring advantages for the Communist cause.

Meanwhile, Chiang took a leaf out of Mao's book. He decided to sit tight, defend what he had, occasionally snipe at his 'allies', and wait for Japanese imperialism to take on more than it could handle. It was a policy that took patience. He lost about half a million Kuomintang troops who went over to the Japanese and served as a 'puppet-army'. But it was also a policy that ultimately paid rich dividends – especially in aid from the west from 1942 onwards. Chiang was conserving his strength and saving his forces for the inevitable showdown with the Communists once Japan had been defeated.

After the Japanese surrender in 1945, there were token attempts to patch up the differences between the Kuomintang and the Communists. Each side promised partial demobilization, but the agreements were not conspicuous for their sincerity. It soon became clear that the Allies – especially the USA – were unable to enforce any kind of compromise, and the Americans compounded the situation by becoming, in effect, 'dishonest brokers' in the negotiations. Their wish to support the legitimate government and their fears of Communism combined to shift their attention from a negotiated settlement to a policy which favoured the Kuomintang. Chiang had over 4 million men under arms; his forces controlled the large cities and with them the economic life of the country. Mao had less than half this number, although he did enjoy the qualified support of the peasants and students whose demonstrations were ruthlessly suppressed.

At this point, then, the sides were certainly uneven. Chiang controlled most of China, especially many of the large urban areas. Business interests supported him partly because they feared that a Communist takeover would strangle economic enterprise, and partly because they were convinced that China now needed American aid, and this would only be forthcoming if they assumed the correct ideological stance. Mao, on the other hand, did have a great deal of support in the rural areas, and his forces were receiving some help from the Soviet Union though on nothing like the scale of their help to the Kuomintang during the war with Japan. Sometimes this came directly from the Soviet authorities, but in other instances it was indirect as with, say, the handover of captured Japanese ammunition dumps in Manchuria. This cost the Soviets nothing, yet these arms kept the Communists going all through their north-eastern campaigns against Chiang's forces.

Chiang had made up his mind that he was going to crush the Communists once and for all. He produced a *Manual on Bandit Suppression* which was really a battle-plan for an extermination campaign against Mao's forces. In the early engagements of 1946–7 he had considerable success, including the capture of the Communist capital at Yenan. But in 1948, Mao's forces in the north reversed the situation, and Yenan was retaken. By this time, the Chinese economy was at a very low ebb. Inflation was astronomical, protests and general industrial discontent were rife. Workshops and factories began to close, and in January 1948 the first of a series of strikes in the textile industry was organized in Shanghai by Communist sympathizers. Workers were gassed and shot, but this only brought out the crowds on to the streets, and the stoppages spread throughout the south.

Chiang's fortunes went from bad to worse. His troops were unsuccessful in taking the northern territories – particularly Manchuria – and then they found it increasingly difficult to maintain their strongholds in the south. Whole Kuomintang armies were either beaten or starved into submission. By the end of 1948 the march on Shanghai had begun, and by January 1949 Mao's armies had captured the old imperial capital of Peking. By now it became clear to the Americans that they had backed a loser. Under pressure from the USA, Chiang was advised to make a deal 'from strength', but these peace overtures were rejected out of hand. By October 1949 the civil war was over; Chiang fled to Formosa nursing the faint hope that one day he might return. Reorganization and retaliation were now about to begin.

The task facing the Communists was enormous. Commerce and industry in China were not highly developed. What there was had been very much under overseas control or had been largely dominated by foreign investment. Worse still, the lot of the Chinese peasant had never been enviable. Farming methods were antiquated and production levels were low. The plight of the peasant was exacerbated by the heavy rents for tenant-farmers, and by the intolerable rates of interest on loans. In the 1920s, in Kiangsi, for example, they had to surrender between 50 and 80 per cent of their produce to cover rent and interest charges. In good years there was perhaps enough left for peasants and soldiers; in bad years, there might be just enough for the soldiers. Under Communist control, much of this began to change quite rapidly.

To start with, the entire tax system which was riddled with sharp-practice and corruption was completely revised. Apparently some Kuomintang tax-collectors had been demanding taxes years in advance and lining their own pockets with the proceeds. The textile industry, which had almost fallen into decay, was revitalized only to produce that drab blue uniformity which one associates with the Chinese proletariat. Most urgent of all were the agricultural reforms which within a year of the takeover – so it is claimed – ensured that no one any longer went hungry.

The work of reconstruction was difficult. Natural resources had to be harnessed to the needs of the people, and labour power had to be mobilized in order to maximize the potential for redevelopment. All 'distractions' were actively discouraged, and in some cases actually proscribed. There was a show of 'intellectual liberty', but this permitted only a very narrow interpretation. Religion, for instance, the traditional consolation for the masses, was not actually outlawed but its practices were severely restricted, particularly in its Catholic forms. Or to take quite a different example, prostitution: this was abolished by decree; Shanghai, which once boasted some 45,000 prostitutes, became theoretically 'sin-free' under Communist rule.

The people could readily forgive the draconian measures of a regime that could ensure that everybody was fed. The new Central People's Republic set out to industrialize China in the shortest possible time, and bring her living standards into line with those of the industrialized nations of the western world. Instead of doing this with overseas capital, she intended to rely on vastly increased agricultural production and the export of minerals and manufactures to pay for the importation of capital goods and industrial material. The Big Brother – and somewhat distrusted – Soviet Union had done this in forty years; Mao's China aimed to do it in fifteen.

Land reform was the first essential. Landlords, who represented only 10 per cent of the population, owned about 70 per cent of the cultivated land; 'middle-range' peasants, representing about 20 per cent of the people, owned 20 per cent of it; and 70 per cent of the people – many of whom were landless labourers – owned the remaining 10 per cent. After the Agrarian Reform Law (1950), there was a massive redistribution of millions of acres of land among some 300 million peasants, and over 30 million tons of grain, which would formerly have been appropriated as rent by the landlords, went for the peasants' own use. Similar changes were made on the industrial front. The share of the private sector of gross industrial output fell from over 60 per cent in 1949 to 25 per cent in 1954.

By the end of the first Five-Year Plan in 1957, it is reported that total industrial and agricultural production had increased by an impressive 68 per cent. Despite all the ambitious claims, it is disputed whether the reforms were quite as effective or far-reaching as the propagandists would have us believe. Development was vitiated by inherent contradictions. Originally, the idea was of a redistribution of land to the peasants so that the nation could be self-supporting. It was then quickly realized that grain was needed for export. Even after a year of 'serious famine', in 1955, collectivization began in the interests of 'social industrialization'. The regime effectively gave with one hand and took away with the other in order to boost exports. The peasants had to eat less to facilitate 'the great leap forward'. Peasants' private plots were absorbed in a commune system because necessity dictated the virtual militarization of agriculture.

The system which accomplished these reforms was designated a 'people's democratic dictatorship', that is, an alliance between labour and the peasantry with the former – including the skilled artisans of manufacturing industry – in the leading role. This was actually something of a fiction as dictatorship was exercised by the Party itself through its cadres of officials with the consent – or, at least, the acquiescence – of labour and the peasants. Power was highly centralized and control was mediated through delegated agencies. This was facilitated even further when collectivization began, and large sections of the population were organized into productive units.

Landlords, capitalists, and 'reactionaries' were suppressed. In practice, this meant that either they were re-educated – university professors sent to work on the land, or reckless drivers publicly admonished in the street – or they might be unceremoniously eliminated. All this follows the well-tried early Soviet pattern. The Chinese Communists were neither heretical nor original in the field of doctrine and strategy although they were more innovative in practice. From the 1920s, Mao had ordered assaults on the 'bad gentry', and once the Agrarian Reform Law had been promulgated in 1950, the rural poor were encouraged to participate in the public terrorization and even liquidation of the old upper classes. Landlords who had been arrested were often openly humiliated, tortured, sent to labour camps, or simply killed. It was not unusual for student groups to be taken on 'tours' to villages where landowners were accused of exploiting the community, and deliberately invited to choose the appropriate punishment. In a quite typical instance, the wife of a proscribed landlord who had fled was made to strip and – despite her protestations and prayers – was stoned and beaten to death (Wittfogel 1966).

All this was not unlike the earlier revolutionary situation in Russia. Evidence suggests that the Tsarist police were positively restrained by Soviet Secret Police standards. During the Lenin government in 1918–19, it is estimated that the Cheka were carrying out a thousand executions a month of 'political enemies' alone. But the police mandate for suppression was much broader than this. The proscribed included 'all kinds of harmful insects', a term which covered such groups as teachers, nuns, priests, monks, and even trade-union officials. Whole sections of people were categorized as class enemies, and therefore fit only for imprisonment or annihilation. As Lenin put it,

> we are not carrying out a war against individuals. We are extermi-nating the bourgeoisie as a class. . . . The first question we ask is – to what class does he belong, what are his origins, upbringing, education or profession? These questions define the fate of the accused. This is the essence of the Red Terror.
>
> (Quoted in Johnson 1985: 71)

So much for revolutionary Communism and its enforced reforms. In Russia there had been the liquidation of the kulaks; in China, there were mass trials of counter-revolutionary elements. From the beginning, Mao had appealed to the anti-bourgeoisie attitudes of the peasantry. 'Land-lords' who owned more than 4½ acres came within his proscriptive 'legislation'. In the early days of the movement he had shown himself to be as ruthless as Chiang or any other warlord in purging the country of undesirables. By 1930, he had his own secret police, and this led to the execution of over 2,000 of his own men who were suspected of covertly belonging to the Anti-Bolshevik League. Unlike so many war-lords, Mao's forces were not, in general, allowed to rape and pillage, and they suppressed prostitution, gambling, and opium-poppy grow-ing. On the other hand, they ill-treated and murdered members of the middle classes, they burned churches and temples, and sometimes killed missionaries and priests.

The situation had been further exacerbated by the Japanese invasion, although Mao saw in this new opportunities to further his purposes. In 1937, he had told his generals that the Sino-Japanese conflict gave the Communists more opportunity for expansion – a policy which was carried out to the letter. As we have seen, even the Japanese atrocities – notably at Nanking where some 20,000 Chinese civilians were massacred – were grist for the Communists' ideological mill. They merely served to unite Mao's forces and increase the support of the masses in the interests of the cause.

When the inevitable showdown came between the Communists and the Kuomintang, it is still disputable whether it was really rooted in economic and class factors. In the areas where the Communists were stronger, most of the peasantry already owned most of the land they worked; indeed, it might even be argued that the vast majority of China's population were not *directly* involved in the struggle at all. Perhaps the essential issue was not one of landownership, but more a question of who could provide peace and stability to a nation ridden with strife and uncertainty.

It is doubtful whether Mao supposed that his success would be anything like as rapid or complete as it proved to be. It is also possible that it was altogether too successful from Moscow's point of view. For one thing, it is questionable whether Moscow wanted a revolution it could not control; potentially the Chinese success threatened its hegemony in the communist world. Furthermore, it was not quite according to the book, and might therefore set a dangerous precedent for other states. Insurrections and bush wars at Moscow's instigation were one thing, but the wholesale conversion of sundry transitional societies must surely one day result in a possible challenge to Soviet power.

The communist world has always been divided on the inevitability or otherwise of war. The Chinese, traditionally, have veered towards greater military extremism and have endorsed the idea and practice of violent revolution. Everything is centred on the cause. War can always be justified if it is in the interests of the appropriate class. Until recently, peaceful coexistence with capitalist states was seen as a surrender to the claims of imperialism, whereas it was the duty of good communists to assist in the liberation of colonial peoples. Such strictures extend pre-eminently to the class enemies within one's own ranks. So the Cultural Revolution of the 1960s was a way of cleansing the system of dissident elements, namely, those teachers, journalists, etc., who were insufficiently active in the interests of the cause. In fact, it is estimated that the Communist takeover led to the proscription of at least 2 million people, the majority of whom perished in the purges.

It was all part of a well-tried totalitarian pattern. China's problems were thought to be so vast and seemingly intractable that any kind of piecemeal engineering was considered to be hopelessly inadequate. Drastic measures were needed. Everyone wanted radical reform: Mao sought it, Chiang advocated it, and even the lesser warlords paid lip-service to it. This pursuit of incompatible utopian ideals brought death and destruction to China on an incalculable scale.

Mao's new society was only realizable through revolutionary war, and this had to be waged with political consciousness. This alone gives the correct incentives and generates the right morale because war is 'politics with blood'. Even a possible future nuclear war, with all its unimaginable wholesale destruction, can be justified on a utilitarian basis; eventually it would bring lasting peace for the majority of mankind – who would, hopefully, be Chinese.

Obviously, anything can be – and has been – validated in these terms. The extreme irony of the Chinese situation is that, with all the misery and devastation in recent history, it is still questionable whether anything like the visions of the early idealists have been realized. All this was ostensibly done for the good of the masses, and in the name of the proletariat. But if the Chinese experience teaches us anything, it is that ideology and expediency constitute a lethal combination. Religion may be the 'opium of the people', but revolution is certainly the hallucinogen of the radical intelligentsia.

12

EXCURSUS ON RACE, MASSACRE, AND GENOCIDE
The enemy as racial inferiors

It is now generally conceded that we cannot take a naïvely reductionist approach to race (Kuper *et al.* 1975): the subject can only be addressed intelligently if it is studied on a multi-perspectival basis. Thus it can be looked at in *moral* terms, with an emphasis on ethical judgements; in *biological* terms, stressing genetic factors; in *psychological* terms, concentrating on character formation; in *cultural/historical* terms, and in *sociological* terms with a focus on power/class relationships, etc. (Haralambos 1985). But it would be unwise to try to reduce the understanding of race to any one of these perspectives alone.

The term 'race' is not exactly easy to define, and the expression 'ethnic group' is not really very much better. A distinction that can be made is to reserve the term 'race' for those showing similar physical characteristics, and 'ethnicity' for those with similar cultural characteristics. Obviously, it is important to distinguish between that which is genetic and that which is socially learned, but it is doubtful whether the terminology is always correctly applied in practice. The term 'race' may have little or no scientific meaning, but it is still useful inasmuch as people attach meanings (real or assumed) to physical and cultural differences and this contributes to their social significance. Differences between people do exist, even if the criteria whereby they are assessed may not always be agreed. There may, of course, be broad historical reasons for making these distinctions. The old biblical divisions between Hamitic (Negroid), Semitic, and Caucusoid races, traditionally based on the sons of Noah, Ham, Shem, and Japheth, do not help us very much, but then they were made prior to the days of modern exploration. The now conventional extension of this simple schema to include Mongaloids and Australoids gives it a kind of general commonsense validity. But refinements of categorization beyond those demanded by one-time geographical isolation can turn the whole matter into a canonistic numbers game (e.g. Coon 1962).

The whole idea of race does have biological dimensions, but there are formidable difficulties in trying to account for genetic mutational changes, and in tracing the effects of selection in controlling differential rates of reproduction, fertility, and the survival of particular genetic combinations. It is reasonably certain that – in part – these must take place in response to environmental conditions which, in turn, affect differential migration and the 'mixing' of populations (Darlington 1969).

The 'concept' of race is bound up, too, with the problem of perception – how and why we perceive the differences we do. And this, in turn, is related to the unsolved questions surrounding historical development. Did 'true man' evolve in one localized area and become diffused throughout the globe? This is a theory which obviously encourages the essential 'brotherhood of man' view. Or did man evolve in many places at different times? This is a more popular view and tends to underpin the idea of race, especially as it also posits early conflict between different racial groups (Howell and Bourliere 1964). How else are we to account for the 'triumph' of certain physical types over others in these early communities? Surely this cannot be explained in terms of environmental conditions only (Howell 1971)?

What is undisputed is that early man, no matter what his origins, lived in relatively undifferentiated societies – if, indeed, 'societies' is the correct word. Gradually, skills were developed: the fashioning of crude artefacts, weapon-making and hunting techniques, and the institutionalization of co-operation and aggression in order to survive. In particular, there was the development of language which both unites and divides human society. Those who speak together, breed together. Mate selection is largely mediated by speech, as is also the sense of community. If people speak differently, act differently and – better still – look different, *ipso facto*, they *are* different. They are not one of *us*. It is not so much actual differences as perceived differences that matter; and not only seeing them differently, but *wanting* to see them differently.

The danger in looking at race in purely physical terms is that either it can lead to extreme forms of biological reductionism which ignore the cultural dimension, or it can veer towards some kind of environmental determinism which permits of too many historical exceptions (Gabel 1964). Indeed, any kind of heuristicism must be suspect. There is no one unquestionable 'key' to the understanding of race. Within their own unpredetermined limits, biological, historical, psychological, and socio-cultural factors all play their own complementary parts.

THE PROBLEM OF PREJUDICE

The phenomenon of racial prejudice illustrates the need for a comparative approach. In trying to understand prejudice as an attitude – as opposed to discrimination which is really a form of behaviour – it is often difficult to disentangle social factors from hypothesized psychological factors. Prejudice is influenced by the inculcation of beliefs and values, and these, in turn, are reinforced by observation, exposure, and example. The considerable overlapping of psychological and sociological perspectives in the study of prejudice is well illustrated by the somewhat dubious 'authoritarian personality' thesis (Adorno 1950). This maintains that there is a particular personality pattern which displays a marked tendency to prejudice. This is said to be evidenced by the fact that:

1 It has a *general* prejudiced nature, i.e. it is prejudiced against *different* kinds of racial groups, e.g. Jews *and* negroes.
2 It has marked ethnocentric values.
3 It favours strong, authoritarian leadership.
4 It is insecure, conformist, and often overbearing to 'inferiors'.
5 It tends to be anti-intellectual and anti-scientific.

The authoritarian personality thesis has inspired a great deal of research, but is open to criticism on the grounds that its methodology is weak, and its conclusions suspect. It largely ignores the fact that authoritarian personalities are found among both radicals and reactionaries (e.g. in the French Revolution), and tends to overlook the possibility that *both* authoritarianism and prejudice are to be found among those who lack exposure to alternative values. Though this last point would hardly be true of, say, Adolph Eichmann – a notorious principal of the Nazi extermination programme – who was steeped in Jewish lore and culture, and used this to considerable advantage in his dealings with Jewish groups, especially prior to the deportations of Hungarian Jews in 1944 (Weissberg 1956). The thesis also takes too little account of the possibilities for *learning* prejudice, especially where this is part of a concerted behaviour modification programme; this is well supported, for example, by research into the training of SS personnel (Dicks 1972). It is studies such as these which clearly demonstrate the complex nature of value-formation and the personality.

Evidence also suggests that prejudice can be notoriously inconsistent. Reasons which are given for, say, biased statements or hostile policies can often be shown to be contradictory. For instance, in Nazi Germany, the Jews were criticized for being too exclusive, and therefore inviting suspicion and – at the same time – as being too intrusive, especially in commercial affairs. They were seen to be both capitalistic money-makers *and* subversive communists (Grunberger 1964). Prejudice can thus be procrustean inasmuch as values tend to be rationalized to suit a particular argument despite the equivocal nature of the evidence.

There is, however, a cognitive dimension to all this. It is salutary to remind ourselves that although prejudiced attitudes may be *ir*rational, they are not always *non*-rational (Deaux and Wrightsman 1984). The onus of proof is largely on the critic to explain his attitudes and to give reasons for his actions. He may correctly adduce that certain local situations, such as all-night partying by West Indians, justify racial criticism, or that deviant norms such as the use of 'ganja' by Rastafarians are bound to provoke members of the host community. Without doubt, incongruent normative behaviour can be a problem, indeed a provocation in certain circumstances, and raises the question as to whether these customs involving religion, dietary rules, etc., should be maintained only at the private level by the ethnic communities themselves. And this is sometimes compounded by commercial practices which exacerbate tensions within and between those communities.

We must be wary of racial stereotyping and – at the same time – be cautious about stereotyping race relations which are so often characterized by ambivalence (Kovel 1970) and inexplicable anomalies (Piliavin *et al*. 1981). But the existence of random specificities can hardly add up to a justification for discriminatory behaviour to every member of a racial group. The existence of divergent rationalities can hardly excuse programmes of wholesale persecution.

THE MINORITY GROUP THESIS

The whole question of persecution is related to what has been termed the 'minority group' thesis (e.g. Zanden 1972). This takes as its starting point the assumption that attitude-formation, including prejudice, is inextricably associated with group-formation. The thesis maintains that a minority group is a formation which is singled out on the basis of physical and/or cultural characteristics for unequal treatment, and is therefore the object of collective discrimination and even persecution.

Broadly speaking, groups form in response to a sense of common identity and a recognition of common interests. They therefore tend to pursue common goals and, where hostility is evident, will normally unite in the face of common need. The general characteristics of the minority group are said to be:

1 that they suffer disadvantages at the hands of others, and this may involve unequal treatment and exploitation;
2 that their group characteristics may be clearly visible, e.g. language, colour, religion;

3 that they tend to develop a strong group identity perhaps because of the shared experience of suffering;
4 that they are *not* usually a voluntary group: members are born into the group and therefore it is virtually impossible for them to relinquish membership;
5 that they are normally endogamous – a situation which may be forced upon them by the dominant society.

Persuasive as this thesis is, it is subject to a number of serious qualifications:

1 The term 'minority group' is something of a misnomer because it cannot simply refer to those who are numerically inferior only. The minority may actually be the dominant elite as in, say, South Africa (1:5) or better still, ancient Sparta (1:25).
2 Group characteristics may not always be clearly evident, as with Jews who share a certain social 'language' but who have only very tenuous links with the religious culture of Judaism.
3 Group identity, implying brotherhood and unity, may be something of a myth, as with, say, the nationalist Jewish groups in Palestine during the 'troubles' of 1946–7, or the warring Palestinian factions in Lebanon today.
4 Group membership can be flexible, especially if it is not defined in terms of colour but in terms of language and religion. It is worth noting that the Nazis – the self-styled experts on race – made Jews wear yellow stars on their clothing for easier identification. It surely goes without saying that religious groups – historically some of the most persecuted people – are almost invariably voluntary groups.
5 Endogamy is admittedly the norm, but exogamy is by no means unknown even in slave–citizen situations.

The 'minority group' is all right as a model, but it breaks down in the face of actual circumstances. It is probably generally true to say that groups often form through natural affinity, and not as the result of discrimination or persecution. Furthermore, groups can be artificially created and perpetuated for political purposes. And it is when these purposes claim ideological justification that the fine line between racialism and racism is exposed.

If race is broadly defined as a biological subdivision of mankind which is characterized by common ancestry and – more debatably – by common physical features, then racialism may be defined as a recognition of these distinctions for social purposes. People have differentiated between themselves and others on some basis or other since time immemorial. As we have seen, the ancient Egyptians, at least since the

4th Dynasty (i.e. from *c*. 2700 BC) spoke of the Nubians on their south-ern borders as 'non-people' and the Greeks regarded non-Greeks – even the sophisticated Persians – as 'barbaroi', i.e. people who could not speak the Greek language (Snowden 1983). The list of those who have made similar distinctions is endless. Racism, on the other hand, is a relatively modern phenomenon. It can be defined as the irrational belief – though usually perceived as rational – that there are *intrinsic* qualities in racial groups which mark them as being inherently superior/inferior to others. Such beliefs are ideologically validated, and used as a basis for discrimination and even persecution. In short, racism is prejudice intellectualized as fact.

PATTERNS OF RACE AND ETHNIC RELATIONS

If we view the question of race and ethnic relations comparatively and historically we can see that there is a very wide spectrum of practices and possibilities. In broad terms, these include (Simpson and Yinger 1972):

1 *Assimilation* which may be either racial or cultural, or both. In practice, this often means that the culture of the dominant group is actually adopted – a kind of east meets west situation. If – as in some cases – assimilation is enforced, it simply aggravates matters by reinforcing a consciousness of differences between those concerned.

2 *Pluralism* where cultural diversity is either tolerated or positively encouraged. But there are two things to note here. First, plural-ism may not mean *de facto* equality for all concerned, and, second, pluralism may appear to be the best 'solution' in a particular social context simply because assimilation – in the fullest sense – is either impossible or actively resisted.

3 *Legal protection of minorities/unenfranchised* may be necessary to protect underprivileged or unassimilated groups where blatant or merely vestigial hostility exists.

4 *Population transfer* is an expedient which has been practised since early times as a way of reducing hostility between groups. It acts as a preventive measure against the possibility of armed insurrection by dispersing populations and dividing their poten-tial leadership. Historically, it has taken many forms, ranging from the population displacement activities of the ancient Assy-rians, to Nazi slave-labour practices (effectively a form of popu-lation dispersal), to the more recent Africanization policies re Asians (e.g. in Uganda) and the 'home lands' policies in South Africa.

5 *Subjugation* is practised where the dominant group continues with a policy of systematic repression because it has no intention of sharing power with others. These may or may not be thought of as inferiors – the real problem is that they are regarded as an ever-present threat. Needless to say, it was a particular feature of societies with large and potentially dangerous slave populations.

6 *Extermination* is obviously the most extreme 'solution' to the problem of the alien group. Extermination may be *accidental* in that it involves the inadvertent spread of infectious diseases as in colonial Polynesia where there was no natural immunity against such things as smallpox, measles, and even the common cold; or *incidental* as part of a larger policy of repression as in Spanish America; or cruelly *methodical*, in which case it may take the form of either massacre or genocide.

MASSACRE AND GENOCIDE

Leo Kuper defines genocide as 'a coordinated plan of different actions aiming at the destruction of the essential foundations of the life of national groups' (Kuper *et al.* 1975: 22). This is fine in general terms, but three qualifications need to be made about this statement: (1) Genocide does not always entail the immediate annihilation of these groups; it may be a long-term process. (2) It may not always involve national groups; cultural, racial, religious, and even class groups could qualify. (3) The plan may not always be co-ordinated; it may – at least, at first – just 'grow' by accident rather than by design, like a kind of lethal snowball, or it may be the 'rational' development of other persecutory practices as with the Nazis whose 'final solution' programme evolved from an unholy amalgam of pogroms against the Jews and the enforced euthanasia of selected mental patients.

Does massacre, as such, constitute genocide? This is an interesting theoretical question. Massacre, the mass killing of enemies – even captives – has always been a feature of certain kinds of warfare. It can be seen as part of the systematic depredations of the Assyrians (from the ninth to the late seventh century BC). They fought mainly for territory and tribute, and if they were thwarted or resisted they could be ruthless in the extreme (Saggs 1984). In the Old Testament, their armies are likened to a 'plague of locusts' which stripped the land bare. Their refinements included deportations, slavery, mutilations, torture, and death. Ashurnasirpal II (d. 859 BC) recalls,

[of] those who rebelled . . . I flayed all the chiefs and covered the pillar with their skin . . . some I walled up . . . some I impaled.

174

Many captives from among them I burned with fire . . . from some I cut off their noses, their ears and their fingers, of many I put out their eyes. I made one pillar of the living and another of heads.

(Carlton 1973)

And so it goes on in a dispassionate and self-satisfied way.

Similarly, the Mongols in the thirteenth century AD, as we have seen, pursued expansionist policies which entailed wholesale slaughter that was unparalleled in the pre-industrial world. What is the point of carnage on this unimaginable scale? Admittedly it inspired a sense of terror, and helped to cow the masses into a necessary subservience, but neither the Assyrians nor the Mongols had any unifying ideology. Their enemies were regarded as military dwarfs, as effete degenerates who deserved their subordination. It was largely slaughter for slaughter's sake – all in the interests of power and gain.

So is this genocide? And how does it relate to the question of race? By definition, extermination is a feature of genocide which is consciously pre-emptive in that it anticipates difficulties with the proscribed group, and attempts to circumvent these by a systematic and final 'solution' to the problem. Genocide differs from 'simple' massacre in so far as it is – probably invariably – ideologically motivated.

Three general reasons can be hypothesized for persecution as a precursor to genocide: political expediency, cultural incompatibility, and ideological intolerance. It should be noted, however, that these are not mutually exclusive; they can be related in subtle ways, e.g. one (say, ideological intolerance) may be used as a cover/justification for another (say, political expediency). They may be genuinely confused in the minds of the persecutors themselves, and any one of them may disguise other hidden (say, economic) factors which are crucial to the situation.

Political expediency

In all manner of societies it has been found expedient to subdue and exploit an underclass. This is particularly true of complex pre-industrial societies where the slaves, serfs, etc., were the machine-substitutes of the system. In the Roman latifundia (slave-estates), for example, they were regarded as an agrarian necessity, besides being useful for general domestic duties and constructional work. The Romans could, at times, be quite ruthless with those who questioned or resisted their right to rule, but wholesale slaughter was not normally an instrument of occupational policy. There were exceptions, of course, e.g. Caesar's treatment of the Germans and Gauls, but generally speaking the dominant groups in pre-industrial societies *utilized* their underclass. They did not exterminate it.

175

The true political expediency motive can – as we have noted – be seen to better effect in developed societies. The initial phase of the Russian Revolution under Lenin, and the later 'terror' of Stalin, may both be considered genocidal in form. Under Stalin, the purges, the show trials, the labour camps, enforced collectivization, etc., may have accounted for some 10 million people. And, on a much smaller scale, there were similar atrocities in the satellite territories with the Communist takeovers after the Second World War (Johnson 1983).

Cultural incompatibility

At the practical level, this is often very difficult to disentangle from political considerations. This can be seen particularly in situations where expansionism has involved the problem of what to do with the conquered. They can sometimes be assimilated, the Norman–Saxon solution, or they can be enslaved, or – failing this – they can be exterminated, the policy of the Ottoman Turks who, under Sultan Abdul Amid, massacred all the Christians in Trebizond in AD 1894. In this 'legitimate' expedient, conducted over a period, about 100,000 people suffered (Barber 1974).

Colonialism, too, with all its attendant evils and benefits, has sometimes exhibited a genocidal dimension. Much of the modern literature on colonialism tends to concentrate on the eighteenth and nineteenth centuries, especially Africa where coastal tribes conspired with European intruders to attack tribes in the interior, killing unwanted villagers and enslaving the able-bodied, and transporting them to the Americas (Elkins 1963). But one should not forget the depredations of earlier civilizations, especially the Spanish and the Portuguese in South America where rapacity and greed for gold were strongly bound up with a fervent desire to convert the heathen (Hagen 1974). Likewise it would be imprudent to ignore the many atrocities committed by Africans against Africans, as in Nigeria and Burundi in the 1960s, which may have involved the deaths of over a million people; or the African–Asian, Asian–Asian, and Indonesian conflicts which have too often been overlooked in western society.

Neo-colonialism, the sort of thing to be found recently in Meso-America and Afghanistan, is the focus of much current criticism and is often operationalized by the 'great powers' through co-operative neighbouring states. But in these situations, unlike those of some earlier forms of colonialism, coercion is used selectively; intimidation and economic sanctions are often found to be much more effective than outright persecution.

Ideological intolerance

This can take a wide variety of forms and can range from straightforward politico-cultural antagonism to irreconcilable religious conviction. It is also often paradoxically associated with both group-envy *and* misunderstanding and suspicion. Both were present, for instance, in Nazi attitudes to the Jews, and the whole situation was compounded by the Aryan superiority myth. Nazism saw itself as the agency that would purge the world of its most 'persistent [racial] impurities'. The eradication of Jewry came then to be seen as something of a providential mission. Interestingly, this idea was largely absent from other forms of facism. For example, Spain had a long tradition of anti-Semitism which stemmed, in the Middle Ages, from a particular brand of extremist Catholicism, but it was never genocidal in the tragic sense of the term. Another, more pertinent, example is Mussolini's Italy: although there were marked racist attitudes in some of the African colonies, concerted persecution of the Jews did not really begin until 1938 – and then possibly under German influence. Actual deportations of Jews from Italy – which were not even endorsed by many of the fascist hierarchy – did not take place until the German takeover in 1943. The ideological dynamic was certainly behind the entire 'final solution' programme of the Nazis (Hohne 1972).

As soon as the Nazis came to power in 1933, a series of legal enactments against the Jews came into force. These introduced every sort of discrimination: Jews were dismissed from their posts, forced to relinquish their property, deprived of citizenship, and forbidden to marry non-Jews. Many emigrated, but moves to get out of Germany became increasingly difficult, and those that remained were subjected to all kinds of physical and social abuse. But all this was merely a precursor to the systematic persecution that ensued after the German attack on Poland in 1939 and successful invasion of France in 1940, and the Balkans and large areas of Soviet Russia in the following year. Almost unbelievably, the Aryan Research Department of the Reich, the Ahnenarbe, which provided the philosophical and 'experimental' underpinning for that programme, cost more to run than the 'Manhattan Project' (the building of the first atomic bomb). So much for the insanity of irrational racial theory.

The outcome of these anti-Semitic sentiments – already clearly evident in Hitler's *Mein Kampf* – was to be seen in the carefully crafted 'total solution to the Jewish problem'. The sentiment became intellectualized as ideology, and this, in turn, was operationalized as a full-scale extermination industry in which it is estimated that some 150,000 people took part.

The policy became a programme, and its first phase began with the activities of the Einsatzgruppen, extermination squads of the SD/SS (the security forces) who followed the victorious Wehrmacht into the conquered territories and killed some half a million people, mainly by shooting. In many instances these were led not by brutalized thugs but by well-placed German intellectuals like the cultured economist, Otto Ohlendorf, who was eventually held responsible by the Allies for the murder of 90,000 people.

The second phase of the programme was more subtle and more systematized. It was accepted from the outset that the world might not understand, nor might many of the Germans themselves, so orders for its operations were largely verbal, or where written were usually couched in euphemistic terms; so wholesale slaughter was often expressed as 'transportation' and 'resettlement'. This actually involved the mass transportation and subsequent gassing of millions of Jews and others in custom-built camps. The victims were mainly the old and the very young; the fit and able were designated for other tasks – they could eventually be worked to death. Everything was highly routinized and – in the main – carried out with dispassionate efficiency. The operation was deemed urgent and vital, and – not least – justifiable. After all, Alfred Rosenberg, the high-priest of Nazi race theory, had argued that Europe would not be safe until the Germans had eradicated 'the last evil traces of Jewry' and a member of his staff had elaborated that 'the world would not gain rest until this fungus of decomposition is extirpated' (see Nova 1986). Hitler himself had likened Jews to 'tuberculosis bacilli' and others had followed his lead with references to 'vermin' and 'microbes'. The programme was therefore seen as a clinical necessity.

All this was the outworking of the Aryan superiority myth. The Nazis, according to Professor Karl Alexander von Müller, president of the German Academy of Sciences, were the leading protagonists in a 'community of destiny', the inaugurators of a 'New Order' in Europe. Other systems were old and discredited, and the war was really a titanic struggle against the forces of tradition and cultural intransigence. More and more intellectuals were recruited to support the ongoing crusade for the new Europe, a crusade based not on outmoded liberal concepts of democracy, but on nature, race, and geography. All responsible nations must therefore collude in the solution of the Jewish question. So German institutes and scholars fostered this 'Europeanization' of the Nazi mentality by helping their allies and collaborators to set up anti-Jewish institutes and organizations.

Ideologies are sets of beliefs which define and validate the policies and practices of particular systems. They may not be new or original; in fact, they may simply recall already existing ideas and sentiments, as with Nazi anti-Semitism (Greenleaf 1966). Certainly totalitarian ideol-

178

ogies may not involve the imposition of new realities. Rather they are the rediscovery and re-imposition of old realities. Ideologies, then, not only supply the necessary imperatives for action, they also provide the system with the requisite legitimations. It is important for a system to explain itself to itself and to the world at large in order to justify its actions, and to those individuals within its ranks who require psychological support.

Is the term 'genocide', therefore, used too loosely? It cannot, as we have seen, simply mean massacre, although – by definition – mass killing is necessarily involved. Genocide is relatively rare whereas massacre is – sadly – not that uncommon. Neither can genocide simply mean persecution, although this normally accompanies genocide. Strictly speaking, genocide means the killing of a tribe (Greek, *genos*), i.e. the extermination of some entire group. By extension this can imply the complete eradication of a political, cultural, or religious entity. The totality of intention is important. But what is crucial to any distinction between massacre and genocide is the ideological dimension. It is not so much the mode of implementation of the programme as the ideological imperatives which inform the system. Ideology involves belief, and belief is not just conditioned by the context in which it operates – important as this is. Belief matters. It is not just reactive (*contra* Wright Mills 1960), it is often proactive. It is not simply a dependent variable, an intellectualized response to political exigencies. In certain circumstances, it becomes the dynamic of the situation.

Persecution and genocide, whether of racial or religious groups or whatever, are not just the cynical exercise of cruelty by unconvinced sadists. They are often the coldly methodical application of terror by convinced ideologues. In the closing days of the Second World War, when the Wehrmacht desperately needed rolling stock to bring its beleaguered armies back for one last stand against the Allies, absolutely top priority was still being given to the transportation of yet more Jews to the death-camps. A very similar mentality can be seen in other impersonal extermination systems from the Inquisition to the French Revolution. Pointless as they all were, the ideology had to be realized. The genocidal impulse has its own strange rationality. There is little that is more perplexing – or more frightening – than the 'true believer' (Hoffer 1960).

Section IV

WAR AND THE PROBLEM OF VALUES

As we now draw together the main threads of our discussion, we can see that any examination of military values involves the question of values generally. To what extent is the enemy seen according to a set of predetermined values? Do particular encounters with the enemy condition the formulation of such values? There are instances where the values themselves seem to be *implicit* in particular military cultures as with, say, the ancient Assyrians who regarded war as a way of life and their opponents as so many exploitable sources of wealth. On the other hand, there are the situations where the values appear to be *imposed* by a feared dictator or highly regarded military leader, as was the case with Napoleon who came to believe increasingly in his own invincibility, and saw his enemies as military dwarfs (Nicholson 1985).

How, then, are values derived and how are they established? Are they to be regarded as somehow 'given' in the nature of things, or are they contrived for purposes of social harmony and cohesion? Here some analysis is needed; this is important to any serious consideration of war and its social implications. The term 'value' denotes shared cultural standards related to objects of need, attitude, or desire. Their scientific importance is not so much dependent upon their validity and 'correctness' as upon the fact that they are believed to be true and correct by those who hold them. For the *scientific* observer, values only have relevance if there is an observable relationship between the actions of subjects (individuals, groups, etc.) and the objects of their concern. Therefore, it is the *holding* of values and its social manifestations which is, arguably, of primary concern.

This begs the question as to whether there are such things as 'objective values' – values which are true for all time. It must be admitted that this has been given relatively little attention by social scientists. This is not because it is deemed unimportant, but simply because it is generally regarded as a problem which is ultimately insoluable. It is not, in some sense, a 'false' problem; it is just that it does not seem to permit any completely satisfactory answers. Although there are no certain criteria for assessing even the common values of society, no one seriously disputes that values are important; they lie at the very heart of social experience and social integration. The debate about values is not misconceived, but it is bound to be inconclusive. Nevertheless it is indispensable to our understanding of war and its justifications.

Values are inextricably bound up with perception. We 'see' things as we want to see them. This certainly applies to perceptions and misperceptions of the 'enemy'; and it is a short step from misperception to misunderstanding and misrepresentation. The enemy is very much an image in the mind. This image may conduce to any one of a number of already recognized stereotypes: a racial inferior, a class antagonist, etc. Complementarily, the image may result from a mosaic of impressions shaped by historical experience. Any image we may entertain of the enemy, or, for that matter, any image the enemy may entertain of us, must be influenced by a complex of factors – psychological and social – of which we are not always consciously aware. And, as we have seen, these images will reflect values which are expressed as beliefs/ideologies.

The underlying question here concerns the subordinate or superordinate status of values. Do values determine our actions, or are they merely the intellectualizations of the need for action? Or, in relation to war, do particular values precipitate conflict or are they simply used to justify it? Much will depend on particular situations, as our case studies have shown.

It will help to clarify matters if we break down the discussion into a number of supplementary 'problems' and see how these can be related to the question of war. The first and most tortuous of these is *the problem of origination*. This poses the key question about how values arise, and is concerned more with the forms and derivations of values than with their social manifestations. Are values innate? Is it the thinking person who establishes the standards of objectivity? Here the emphasis is switched from the object to the subject, from the thing to be known to the knowing subject. What is implied is that the individual is the ultimate source of values; the values themselves may be socially *conditioned* but not socially derived. The form the value takes is, therefore, not to be confused with the value itself. The implication here is that people know instinctively or intuitively what is right or wrong, good or bad.

This subjective certainty approach is open to all manner of objections. If we assume that all people are born with the *same* values, how can we account for moral and cultural differences? On the other hand, if we believe that everyone is born with an *individual* sense of what is right and wrong, how do we satisfactorily explain moral and cultural

181

similarities? Perhaps some elucidation of the problem is offered by the philosopher, Emmanuel Kant, who maintained that all men have an innate sense of 'ought', but this is socially conditioned in that men feel a sense of ought about *different* things (Ewing 1953). Social experience structures the nature of obligation. The *need* for values may, therefore, be innate, but exactly *which* values is left undetermined.

By contrast, there is the view that values are socially derived. This view probably has its greatest vogue among sociologists. Society, conceived in its most general sense, is seen as the ultimate – and obvious – source of human values. Indeed, it may be that it is part of the ideology of sociology that values originate in society itself. To some extent, this may be a salutary reaction against certain extreme forms of biological determinism, but it involves the type of thinking which is only resolved by an unsatisfactory social reductionism. In emphasizing the primacy of society, many sociologists maintain that categories of thought are not inherent in man's nature as such, but are directly related to the group structures of the particular societies to which men belong. Collective social life is the primary reality; it ultimately determines the modes of cognition and the principles by which reality is apprehended. Thus society ultimately determines all our values, and this, by definition, includes the whole realm of moral ideas (Durkheim 1968).

As a basis for moral values and moral authority, this kind of reasoning has a frustrating circularity. In what conditions is value-formation supposed to occur? And why does it take the forms it does? To say that society simply produces values in and of itself explains nothing – it merely restates the problem at one remove (Ginsberg 1956).

In looking at the argument that values and categories derive from social experience, we should also look at the argument which maintains that they derive from *differences* of social experience. This is represented pre-eminently by Karl Marx who maintained that men pursue fundamental goals which, in turn, necessitate the formation of social relationships. These are conditioned by the control of resources and the relations of production. On these assumptions, human conduct can be explained in terms of the logic of each situation which men face, and the problems which they are compelled to solve. This kind of instrumental rationality, therefore, purports to explain how the economic substructure of society has hegemonic functions in relation to the wider institutional complex, and how economic circumstances determine the intellectual and moral superstructure of society (Aron 1965).

Marx held that needs and values derive from those whose practical interests are capable of realization – the ruling class who are in a position to influence both social sentiments and the social order. Values, therefore, are an expression – even a contrivance – of the dominant class, and are promoted to enhance and reinforce the interests of privilege. The conscious manipulating and patterning of values, which may be a highly rational process, itself constitutes an ideology. Marx went even further. He insisted that the dominant class may actually hire intellectuals, artists, priests, and philosophers to advocate that its social view is *the* social view, and that its view of the truth is *the* truth. It is for this reason that Marx often relates ideology to false-consciousness, for when the non-dominant class sees its own situation in the terms which the dominant class has imposed, it may then *mis*perceive its situation, and still not be aware of the truth of its condition. So, for example, many were susceptible – especially between the world wars – to the plausible idea, perpetuated by some Marxists, that war is really just a product of unscrupulous, capitalistic armaments manufacturers. A view which is as simplistic as it is fallacious.

This whole approach poses a number of awkward problems. It is open to question whether there is any one-to-one relationship between the economic, social, and political circumstances of the individual or group, and the values which they espouse. It certainly cannot be established that moral and religious values are direct 'translations' of social experience. The forms which they take cannot be explained, they can only be described. Furthermore, if all social values merely reflect economic conditions, why are so many basic values fundamentally similar in widely divergent societies? This all raises what might be termed the 'hall-of-mirrors' problem. If all relations and the values which inform those relations are socio-economically derived, and social consciousness is simply a function of those relations, then so are all theoretical formulations which also express those relations. We are again involved in endless circularity.

An interesting variant of the social origins view which is particularly relevant here is the argument that social values derive from various social pressures and contingencies which, in their specific historical forms, have now become lost to memory. This leaves the values intact as given features of a society which are then accepted without serious questioning. They become part of the fabric of society, rather like subterranean forces producing changed or new topographical features in the landscape whilst themselves remaining incapable of specific identification (Elias 1977). It could be argued that this is really Freudianism at one remove. Instead of pushing back the origins of social values and practices to the unconscious, we are asked to substitute an analogous process of sociogenesis. This is just as unsatisfactory and equally unverifiable because it still does not answer the question of why such practices developed or why they came to be promoted as values.

Perhaps underlying this problem is the confusion in popular thinking between the value itself and the *form* the value takes in any particular society. We could take as an example the question of military honour. This is an esteemed value among all military personnel, but it takes many different forms. Sometimes these appear to be highly rationalized, but on other occasions they may seem to be non-rational. For instance, in traditional Japanese culture – and notably in the Second World War – there was an extremely interesting, tragic relationship between honour and self-destruction. For the 'falling cherry blossom' pilots of the Kamikazi, among whom demand was surprisingly exceeded by supply, suicide was an act of heroic desperation. For those of the sinking flagship *Admiral Yamamoto* in one of the last great naval engagements of the war, it was a way of expiating failure. For those too who vainly but courageously clung to the Pacific islands, death had to be preferable to dishonour, and only a tiny proportion were taken alive. This may help us to understand why the Japanese treated Allied prisoners so atrociously; they had nothing but contempt for those who had surrendered.

Not everyone, of course, sees honour in these death-or-glory terms; most cultures have not followed the Japanese pattern – certainly not at the institutional level. Values may, therefore, only be relative in the sense that they take different forms in different cultures. The ultimate *goals* of moral action may be much the same everywhere.

A more extreme – but less popular – view is that values are based on 'revelation'. This implies that values emanate from some extra-mundane source. This tends to be dismissed almost out of hand by most social scientists, (1) because by its very nature it cannot be substantiated, and (2) because it involves metaphysical assumptions about which the social sciences, *per se*, are unable to make valid judgements. Statements about the ultimate verities of human existence stand outside their province. The notion of supra-personal values connotes the religious dimension which there is an all-too-ready tendency to dismiss without due consideration. In the social sciences, explicit beliefs have often been taken as symbolic expressions of something else: social consensus or national unity or whatever. Beliefs in external referents – in *actual* supramundane beings – have often been something of an embarrassment simply because such possibilities are outside their normal terms of reference (Parsons 1971). Nevertheless, naturalistic explanations of religious ideas and values have been shown to be consistently unsatisfactory.

This supra-personal 'solution' implies belief in the objective status of values regardless of their subjective apprehension and appropriation. Belief, therefore, in the independent nature of values as opposed to the recognition of certain *value-forms* severely circumscribes the possibility of value relativism – the view that values are relative to particular cultures. The first difficulty here is that where everything is believed to be relative, to cultures, people, situations, or whatever, nothing can be *known* to be relative unless there is a fixed point of reference (Kolb 1957). The view that *all* values are relative, like the argument that *every*thing is socially determined, can be self-stultifying. It is really a variant of the idea that either everything is 'true' or that nothing can be known to be 'true' – including the *statement* that nothing can be known to be true (Hospers 1961). The whole argument, therefore, becomes infinitely regressive. The second difficulty is in the confusion between ends and means. A more analytical approach to the problem suggests that it is the means that are relative, not the ends of human action. So, for instance, the search for status could take the form of competitive games among the Greeks, but head-hunting among the Dyaks.

A further problem is that of the *prioritization of values*. This may be calculated on the basis of whether or not they are held to be socially useful, or the extent to which they are regarded as socially workable. Underlying all such systems of values is some implicit notion of rationality. This may assume that the values themselves, or at least some of them, are rationally chosen, or it may be a complementary assumption that the values are essentially non-rational but that the means whereby they are pursued are rationally chosen. This can be illustrated in terms of war and aggression. It cannot always be discerned – let alone *explained* – why men have recourse to war. But having once decided on war as the possible solution to their problems, they prosecute the war as effectively and efficiently as they can. The 'means' of human action are readily understood, but the 'ends' may involve the pursuit of some amorphous ideas such as national honour or the vindication of a religious ideal. In a strictly technical sense, such goals are not 'rational', but may simply be regarded as worthwhile, *in themselves*, and therefore not in need of any further justification.

Values, then, are concerned with the 'grounds of meaning', i.e. the basic perspectives from which groups and societies organize their lives. They are orientations towards the problems of life; indeed, they are the vehicles whereby men invest their activities with clarity and purpose. But the question still remains as to whether they choose – perhaps even contrive – certain values for practical purposes, or whether the values themselves dictate the actions that are taken. How any particular action can be attributed to any particular value is probably beyond scientific demonstration; the connection may be psychologically persuasive, but cannot be logically deducible from the value itself (Parsons 1966).

The problems of origination and prioritization admit no satisfactory solutions. The arguments are illuminating and often provide the basis for further discussions, but there is no indication that this can be done with any sense of finality. Therefore, the only practical course of action is simply to accept values as part of the human condition and as necessary components of the social process. In effect, it seems much like the response that people make to the most fundamental issue of all – the matter of human existence. Most people spend few of their waking moments ruminating about the imponderables of life and its possible meanings – they simply live it. The issues are resolved pragmatically; people usually do what works.

This should, however, be qualified in at least one important respect. In certain sets of circumstances, people will often cling tenaciously to certain values even though they seem to be denied by experience. For instance, when people in many traditional societies were defeated in battle, they did not abandon the gods who had let them down, but rather believed that the gods had abandoned *them* because of some real or imagined infringement of the ritual law. In 332 BC when Alexander conquered Tyre and in his pent-up anger and exasperation had 2,000 men crucified and 30,000 women and children sold in slavery, the Tyrian priests could only chain the idols of their gods to the altar lest they desert them. Such is the potency of deeply held ideological conviction.

Whether to adopt or *adapt* values raises another issue, namely, *the problem of rationalization* – a term sceptically defined as giving good reasons for bad actions. This, in turn, raises questions about expediency and justification in relation to values and is particularly pertinent to any discussion of war and aggression. To highlight the problem, we might take the matter of *patriotism* which – in the form of loyalty – appears to be a universally held value. It enshrines the virtues of courage and duty and carries with it the implicit notion of a willingness to die for one's country and one's friends. But one difficulty – among many – is to decide who *are* one's friends. This presented few problems in tribal societies where people were usually only too well aware that their 'friends' were those to whom they were closely connected by ties of kinship. And kinship relations were often coterminous with spatial relations, so they were often the people in the same village or, possibly, neighbouring villages. Complementarily, those against whom one was called out to fight might also be well known, perhaps even personally. They would be traditional enemies, and it is most likely that the occasion for war would be appreciated by all members of the tribes or groups concerned; it would be a 'cause' in which all could share. But the idea of patriotism becomes far more worrying when we extend it from simple societies to state-type societies.

For example, in medieval England a yeoman would be called by his local lord, who, in turn, would be rallying men for the baron who would take his orders from the king. Feudalism was essentially a system of social control, so the baron had certain obligatory commitments in return for the king's patronage. The grievance which occasioned any particular war might well be something to do with the king's claim to lands in France. This would obviously mean little to the yeoman, who might never have heard of Aquitaine or Brittany, or wherever it was that the king claimed as his possession. He would simply be told that the French were the enemies of the king, and therefore *his* enemies too. But he would not *feel* this to be true until the battle was actually joined, and it became a choice between their lives and his.

The entire issue becomes much more complicated with modern states. For the Englishman, for instance, the traditional enemy keeps changing. Until the last century it was France – with certain marginal additions. Then it became Germany and now it is possibly the Russians and the Chinese, both of whom were our allies in the last world war. It is highly doubtful if many Englishman feel any enmity towards any particular Russian or Chinese. But they are reliably informed that these people are not to be trusted, and that they may even be bent on their destruction. This is not to say that such fears are entirely groundless, although there is always the suspicion that distrust and hostility may be manufactured or, at least, exaggerated by those whose particular interests are threatened. And patriotism may be invoked to support their interests. Such seemingly natural responses as loyalty and disloyalty can – in a variety of situations – crystallize into values such as patriotism which, if violated, can carry quasi-legal implications of treason. It hardly needs to be stressed that if there is a Third World War, it will probably bring such instant and incredible destruction that there will be little opportunity for patriotism and heroics. This is not to decry such values, but merely to question their practicality in certain possible circumstances.

One can also see rationalization even more obviously at work in the case of religious belief. We have examined the relationship between religion – particularly institutionalized religion – and war and found that it is a fascinating study in incongruity and ambiguity. It takes many forms, ranging from *post facto* religious 'explanations' to the positive instigation of aggression in the name of religious necessity. This probably applies to most religious systems, and particularly the 'high' religions which are totalizing in their demands for commitment and propagation. Certainly the history of Christianity is tainted in this respect. As we have seen, it is exemplified in the Crusades against the Islamic Saracens in the Middle Ages, and in the later depredations of the Spanish Catholics in parts of South and Meso-America, not to mention the sorry saga of Christians against Christians – all ostensibly in the interests of some particular doctrinal position or sectarian line. And none of this is unusual; similar situations can be found in Islam and Judaism. The foregoing discussion has shown us that war can always be justified by suitable exegetical manipulations or satisfied by

187

ecclesiastical fiat. But whether religious systems have always been the initiating agencies, or whether religion has simply been 'used' to justify policies and practices that were determined elsewhere, is still open to dispute – and investigation.

Lastly, we come to the *problem of legitimation* which is inextricably bound up with the question of ideology. This takes us back to the beginning of our discussion. We began by considering the fundamental issue of the relationship between belief and action. We asked in what ways does belief – intellectualized as ideology – affect social behaviour and, more specifically, military activity? And we have found that although it is impossible finally to demonstrate any direct correspondence between any specific ideological belief and any particular social form or pattern of behaviour, it can be shown that the association – if not conclusive – can certainly be persuasive.

We have noted, too, that ideologies are forms of belief-system which explain and justify a preferred social order or situation. This may already exist or simply be proposed, in which case the ideology may constitute a believed strategy for its attainment. This may then generate an emotional appeal which, in turn, may call for some kind of moral commitment. This can be seen particularly in relation to the establishment of totalitarian regimes where these infused ideals help members to interpret – or reinterpret – their past, explain their present, and anticipate their future.

Sometimes ideologies seem to be self-sufficient and self-explanatory, yet sometimes they are self-contradictory and internally inconsistent. How, for example, could classical Athens purport to represent the democratic ideal, yet try to enforce that ideal among its allies by subversion and even repression? How could she claim to lead Greece against Persian imperialism when she was in the process of carving out her own Empire by similar means? Ideologies involve beliefs in 'true' principles which are not usually open to negotiation. In their religious forms, they are frequently inflexible and absolutist, and their strong inspirational orientations may have little time for logical proofs other than those enshrined in traditional – and perhaps unquestioned – codifications. Ideologies can undergo development, especially when pragmatism demands some modification of doctrine in the light of changed circumstances. But normally ideologies are typically resistant to change. So, to cite classical society once again, the Athenians – contrary to custom – were prepared to use their slaves as warriors in the direst extremities of the Peloponnesian War, but once the emergency was over, they resorted to traditional norms and their slaves were returned to their slave-type activities.

As belief-systems, ideologies sometimes claim to discern what is or ought to be. They do not simply exist to legitimate practice. Bizarre as they can often be, they are hardly the 'flights from reality' that some writers have maintained (Arendt 1958). Rather, they are often attempts to discover or rediscover an old, or 'true', or 'original' reality; an atavistic retracing of history to recapture certain believed natural principles of equality or superiority, or whatever, as is so often true with modern totalitarian ideologies. For instance, we know that the Nazis generated extreme anti-Semitic feeling in Germany in the 1930s and 1940s, but we also know that these sentiments were already present in the nineteenth century. So a counter claim could be made that the Nazi ideology merely sanctified and encouraged existing ideas about the Jews in Germany, and helped to give them legitimate expression. In such cases, normal tests of reality may actually be inappropriate; all that can be studied are the factual assertions, the reliability of the promises and predictions, and their feasibility in given historical situations. Ultimately, one can never apply logical tests of their truth or falsity.

In a sense, ideology is to politics and religion what poetry is to music and literature. As poetry is the music of words, so ideology is the harmonization of rhetoric. It is a particular fusion of aims and capacities in that it reconciles human aspiration with human frailty. In the last analysis, its formulation and popularization may not be amenable to rational explanation.

But having said all this, it would be a mistake to dismiss ideologies as errant nonsense, or to claim – as some theorists do – that they are mere contrivances which aid the dominant classes in their repression of the masses. This conspiracy, or interest, view of history does not take into account the many other ways in which ideology functions, or how it enables a society to explain itself to itself (Carlton 1977). Similarly, it would be unwise to see ideologies simply as substitutes for scientific facts or as ideas that derive from discrepancies in our understanding of those facts. Yet they can often operate in this way, as with racist ideologies, where there is sometimes a confusion or distortion concerning biological facts and the cultural ideas associated with those facts. On the other hand, ideologies may play an inspirational role in circumstances where science has no final answer, as in the case of religious belief.

The very idea of society presupposes social control, and this is inseparably linked with ideology. Why do members of society conform and continue to co-operate in the maintenance of any system? Presumably because people subscribe to the given structures of society either out of expediency or from a sense of moral commitment. Expediency can involve the threat or actual use of coercion which may take physical, moral, or even symbolic forms. Agencies such as the army and the police operate for control purposes, but these agencies are obviously not the only ways whereby control can be achieved.

Social control requires legitimation, and a belief in the legitimacy of the social order is inculcated and cultivated in a variety of ways. If members of a society are to fulfil their obligations, it follows that 'there must be available a morally acceptable explanation of the society's particular system of institutional arrangements, including its social disparities' (Nottingham 1964: 42). An ideology, then, adds a special – perhaps convenient – rationality to social arrangements. Ideology is, of course, implicit in *all* systems; capitalism with its market economy is just as much underpinned by its respective ideology as communism. Systems simply vary in their degree of conviction and commitment. Ideology may provide a *total* explanation of those arrangements as in, say, extreme Islamic systems, or, where it cannot supply all the necessary legitimations, it may simply play a reinforcing role as it does in more pluralistic systems.

An ideology's credibility rests upon its ability to demonstrate workable solutions to those that believe. But even for the adherent, it may not just be a matter of economic gain or political advantage; the ideology may serve much wider purposes by satisfying questions concerning the moral order and the meaning of things. These help men to cope with the uncertainties and ambiguities of life. They provide rules, specific goals, and theories of rights and obligations which enable adherents to evaluate, too, the conduct and beliefs of others. They are therefore guides to collective action and judgement. It follows that aggressive acts based upon believed ideological imperatives cannot simply be dismissed as rationalizations. Thus, the 'jihad', or holy war, of Islam is taken as a cause to which all 'right-thinking' Muslims should be committed. It is not simply an artifice or a contrivance to justify political ambition. Of course, it can be this *too* – motives are always mixed; so much would depend upon the complexion of the particular Islamic group or sect involved. Given these assumptions, the west would do well to take the ideological dimension seriously; indeed, it could hardly do otherwise with the persisting powder-keg situation in the Middle East.

Ideologies, then, have a number of social functions. They are of incalculable worth to authoritarian regimes, partly because they tend to anaesthetize the intellectual and doubting processes, and partly because even where individuals demur at the margins, the ideology will usually ensure that they will conform and comply according to socially approved cues. But social order cannot rest exclusively – or even primarily – upon force; 'even the tyrant must sleep'. The ideology is usually something that the majority accepts, and the degree of consent may depend very largely on the extent to which the ruling hierarchy believes its own doctrines, and, of course, on the ways in which it presents and justifies its case.

Ideologies can be classified in a number of ways. One of the most useful is the well-established distinction between conservative and revolutionary ideologies. The conservative ideology is virtually self-explanatory; it is concerned with that which supports the interests and values of existing social arrangements – whatever these happen to be. It might well be associated, or even identified, with a religious belief-system of a society, in which case it will uphold the structural arrangements of that society whilst also legitimating its traditions. So we find in the Old Testament that when the Israelite war-leader, Joshua, led the tribes into the Promised Land (Canaan–Palestine), he was able to declare that his wholesale destruction of certain cities, e.g. Ai and Jericho, was a ritual necessity. These cities were herem (accursed), according to Israelite belief. This meant that every living thing had to be put to death, the towns and their movables were burnt, and the metal objects removed and dedicated to Yahweh (Joshua 6. 18–24). This, of course, was a practice that was not peculiar to the Israelites or to the Old Testament. For instance, we find from extra-biblical sources that Mesha, King of Moab in the ninth century BC, boasted that he had massacred the entire Israelite population of Nebo in honour of his god Ashar-Kemosh.

These are really yet further examples of the 'holy war' which in other forms is still with us. All these acts are invested with divine sanction and authority, and are therefore regarded by the participants as legitimate and without need of further justification. This was evident in both sides in the Crusades. The Crusader knight and the Islamic Saracens were equally convinced of the rightness of their cause, and both were prepared to pursue their religious convictions to their ultimate conclusion. There were, of course, other interests at stake – economic gain, political advantage, and the more amorphous virtue of warrior status – yet there is little doubt that the primary imperatives were religious. But whether motives can justify method is another issue. Much of the reasoning behind these campaigns may be regarded as 'honourable', but the ways in which the objectives were realized is open to question. Does the conviction that your enemy is an infidel and unbeliever justify his physical extermination?

A quite different case is presented by the Aztecs. Here the motivation can be construed as virtually unadulterated. It is true that these people were following in a tradition which had been well established in Meso-American society for at least a thousand years before their time. But it is rare to find war so inextricably bound up with the 'need' for sacrifice. The assumption that all ideas and practices are generated by socio-economic needs must be called into question by the Aztec experience. The 'needs' argument does not explain the cosmology itself, nor why this extensive bloodletting should in any way be connected with the survival of the universe. Admittedly, the Aztecs were a politically aggressive people who were bent on becoming the dominant power in the Mexican hinterland. Their short and productive history makes that amply clear. But there is no reason to suppose that what they saw as their cosmic mission was only a convenient religious rationalization to disguise their obvious territorial ambitions. It is difficult to avoid the conclusion that here we have a reasonably unambiguous instance of ideology as an independent variable.

Whilst some of the societies we have examined were obviously informed by religious imperatives, others were seen to be more problematic. The ideologies here are secular in tone, and are not so easy to categorize. The Mongols were clearly motivated – like so many expansionist societies – by territorial ambition and were quite ruthless in the pursuit of their aim. They were also the most unashamedly rapacious of all the societies we have examined. Their consuming passion was conquest for conquest's sake; the will to conquer became an ideology in itself. As with other nomadic peoples, the cheapness of their equipment and their superior mobility made them virtually invincible. Subject populations probably preferred the exactions of unifiers such as, say, the Romans, to the devastation and pillage wrought by predatory tribesmen; at least such exactions were predictable – they knew where they were. The Romans, on the other hand, were expansionists in quite a different mould. They came to see their continued success in their early wars as evidence not only of a right to conquer but also of a right to rule. Their control of the Mediterranean world and beyond for the best part of six hundred years was interpreted as a mission to bring a particular form of civilization to others. In the later empire period – partly out of conviction and partly out of expediency – more and more non-Romans were allowed to join the club. The policy of domination gave way to unification; and nationalism was extended to imperialism.

Whereas conservative ideologies are directed towards the preservation of the social status quo, revolutionary ideologies – by definition – are more concerned with the possible disruption of the current social order. This is the case with most modern 'freedom' movements throughout the world, though it is often difficult to know if the ideological imperative concerned is basically Marxism or nationalism. This is exemplified by movements as different (or similar?) as the Khmer Rouge in Cambodia and the US-backed Contras in Nicaragua. In the Marxist-inspired movements in particular, the ideology in question is avowedly secular, but curiously religious in tone. It is fervently held and applied with evangelical zeal to the detriment of its opponents. As with so many ideologically motivated systems, extremes meet. It is then not unusual for a revolution to devour its own children.

An interesting variant is the reactionary ideology. These can derive from either conservative or revolutionary forms because they usually support the restoration of certain revitalized versions of the system. Mahdism, for example, would be a case in point. The Shiah Muslims have believed since the ninth century that in Allah's good time the 'well-directed one' would again lead Islam to worldwide victory. The true Mahdi would destroy the wicked and convert all mankind to the true faith. A number of supposed Mahdis have appeared in Muslim history, most notably Mohammed Ahmed (d.1885), the leader of a temporarily successful revolt in the Sudan in the late nineteenth century. The intention was both political, in that it was directed against British rule, and religious, in that it was an attempt to purify the current social order by the extermination of the infidels. Although it failed – as indeed it had to, considering the respective resources of the contenders – it had considerable success in mobilizing the Arab world in what it saw as a just cause. Mahdism is, of course, still extant in somewhat modified forms. It is a very potent force, and is particularly attractive to the more extremist elements in the Muslim world who want to call believers back to the pristine truths of Islam.

Interiorizing this entire discussion has been the implied distinction between religious and secular ideologies. Indeed, the term 'ideology' is often used interchangeably with that of religion. This is merely a matter of convenience; technically, they are not necessarily the same thing. Arguably, all religion is ideology, but not all ideology is religion. Both are concerned with belief-systems, but whereas ideology can be defined inclusively to encompass such things as Nazism and nationalism, the term 'religion' should be definitionally linked to the supernatural. However, we have found that whether war is motivated by religion, nationalism, economic necessity, or sheer rapacity, it seems to make little difference to the actual *conduct* of war. Where religious imperatives are evident, they undoubtedly add an extra dimension to the problems of instigation and justification. Men can be just as unfeeling and indiscriminately cruel no matter what the ideology. Bravery too does not seem to depend very much on belief; people from all cultures display courage. On the other hand, what may be broadly called nobility in war may have some relationship to belief.

Whatever form the ideology takes, what ultimately matters is specificity of control, and the evocation of an obedient response. So our interest is not only in the nature of ideology, but also in the manner in which it is implemented. Ideology is a 'tidy' weapon. It can be the most potent – and certainly the least expensive – means of persuasion and justification in all political affairs. War, by contrast, is untidy. It is, of course, often necessary, but it is almost always expensive and grossly inefficient, the product, ultimately, of man's irrationalism. It is rather a pity that the two so often go together. They make a formidable combination.

So we end with the problem with which we began, still asking the question: is aggression inherent in the human makeup, and if it is, what can be done about it? Is man really the 'master of his fate' and the 'captain of his destiny', or is he at the mercy of the dark forces which may be part of his very nature? Is recourse to violence simply a primitive phase which future man will eventually outgrow? Man is a paradoxical creature; he seems to need enemies to hate, *and* comrades to share the risks of dealing with them.

Certainly the history of civilization to date does not leave much room for optimism. Nor, of course, do current trends. The industrialization of war may have largely erased old ideas of soldiering, but the age-old attitudes to enemies, and the preparedness to use force, still generate a frightening instability in the modern world. Indeed, there has been a quantum leap in the possibilities for mass destruction *at a distance* since the advent of the bomber. In one sense, this makes warfare even more horrific: to kill dispassionately an enemy you cannot see and certainly do not know adds a dimension of calculated insensitivity to the whole enterprise (Wright Mills 1960).

War is now a growth industry. It is estimated that at the present time something in the order of one-tenth of all the world's resources are being used in preparation for war. Indeed, it might be argued that with those resources growing smaller, there will be a reversion to type as men scramble for the limited remains. Half the world is still hungry, and tomorrow – and each day – there will be another 200,000 more mouths to feed. There is still illiteracy and ignorance, and – above all – unnecessary premature death through lack of education and health care (McGraw 1983). With so much eradicable need and with so many natural enemies, it seems incomprehensible that men should add to their number by the wholesale carnage of war.

The capacity for violence certainly seems to be endemic to mankind. War seems to be 'macroparasitic' – a disease of the species (W. McNeill 1983). Macroparasites – as opposed to bacterial microparasites – are those which specialize in violence and survive by taking from others. Fortunately disease-experienced populations are more resistant to infections than others. But no one is immune.

Of course, in all kinds of circumstances, war has its advantages. In ancient Greece it certainly contributed to the development of democratic structures. City-state warfare required the formation of citizen armies, and this meant that war was no longer the privilege of an aristocratic elite. Similarly, in Rome patricians made increasing concessions to the plebeians who were needed to defend its borders as its empire

194

expanded. But there is a very real sense in which these advantages were mere by-products of an otherwise questionable activity.

The socio-economic arguments that we have considered for the incidence of war obviously have some cogency, but are they sufficient as all-embracing explanations? As we have seen, war is not waged for any one reason. Not only do the reasons vary with different societies but also with the *same* societies at different times. Undoubtedly, economic factors play a critical part in the waging of war, but they certainly do not 'explain' every war, or why societies with their economic wants satiated will still pursue expansionist policies to their eventual economic disadvantage, as was the case with imperial Rome. In many societies socio-political status rather than economic need has been the key problem. It has not been so much a matter of possession scarcity as position scarcity, as Thucydides made clear in relation to Athenian–Spartan conflict in the fifth century BC. Racial issues, too, have sometimes been prominent, though history shows that it has usually been power relations rather than race relations that have been the critical factors as in, say, the conquests of the Americas which also had marked ideological overtones.

It is perhaps here that war and aggression should be separated. Socio-economic factors undoubtedly condition the forms that aggression takes – particularly as war – but they do not account for the aggression *itself*. Furthermore, it is difficult to explain in purely social terms what we might call the autotelic nature of much warlike activity – the apparent enjoyment of war for its own sake; nor do socio-economic factors account for the pathological ferocity which often accompanies the actual execution of war. This can be vaguely ascribed to cultural norms and these, in turn, to faulty socialization which is often cited as the real 'cause' of human violence. But this is, in fact, no explanation at all. Socialization, as such, does not account for the values implicit in war, only for the *perpetuation* of those values. Socialization is not an explanation, it is merely the *description of a process*; it does not – and cannot – account for the values *themselves*.

It seems impossible, therefore, to accept that aggression is simply the result of faulty learning, and war no more than a cultural invention. These popular views are hardly supported by even a superficial reading of history. Perhaps people believe this because they *want* to believe it. It seems to accord with that optimistic view of human nature which regards the individual as unsullied until he is corrupted by the contaminating influence of society. There is a kind of monumental insanity about mankind which is not helped by persistent claims that the problem is all a matter of inadequate socialization or unequal distribution. This insistence that man is somehow better than his performance is a myth without any real evidential foundation (Davies 1944). If man is not naturally aggressive, that is to say if aggression is alien to his 'real' nature, why does he continue to solve his problems by war? One suspects that this is a view which has been well-meaningly perpetuated by those who wish to see man as victim of the past, of society, of the system, or whatever. Contrary to accepted sociological 'truth', the reverse may be the case. Things may only change, not when society changes, but when man comes to terms with his own remediable nature, and takes an intelligent purchase on his own future.

BIBLIOGRAPHY

GENERAL

Althusser, L. (1969) *For Marx*, Harmondsworth, Middx: Alan Lane.

Althusser, L. (1976) *Essays in Self-criticism*, London: New Left Books.

Andreski, S. (1968) *Military Organisation and Society*, London: Routledge & Kegan Paul.

Apter, D., ed. (1964) *Ideology and Discontent*, New York: Free Press.

Arendt, A. (1958) *The Origins of Totalitarianism*, New York: Meridian.

Aron, R. (1965) *Main Currents in Sociological Thought*, Harmondsworth, Middx: Penguin, 109–80.

Bloom, S. (1957) *The Peasant Caesar*, Commentary.

Bylinsky, G. (1976) *New Clues to the Causes of Violence, Readings in Psychology*, Connecticut: Dushkin.

Carlton, E. (1977) *Ideology and Social Order*, London: Routledge & Kegan Paul.

Christenson, R. M. (1972) *Ideologies and Modern Politics*, London: Nelson.

Claster, J., ed. (1967) *Athenian Democracy*, New York: Holt, Rinehart & Winston.

Davies, D. R. (1944) *Down Peacock's Feathers*, London: Centenary Press.

Davies, N. (1973) *The Aztecs*, New York: Macmillan.

Durkheim, E. (1968) *The Elementary Forms of the Religious Life*, London: Allen & Unwin.

Durkheim, E. (1970) *Suicide*, London: Routledge & Kegan Paul.

Elias, N. (1977) *The Civilizing Process*, Oxford: Basil Blackwell.

Ewing, A. C. (1953) *Ethics*, London: English University Press, 54ff.

Fest, J. (1972) *The Face of the Third Reich*, Harmondsworth, Middx: Penguin.

Fromm, E. (1976) 'On human aggression', in Adelbert Reif, *Readings in Sociology, 1975–76*, Connecticut: Dushkin.

Garlan, Y. (1975) *War in the Ancient World*, London: Chatto & Windus.

Gibbon, E. (1979) *The Decline and Fall of the Roman Empire*, London: Bison Books.

Ginsberg, M. (1956) *On the Diversity of Morals*, London: Heinemann, Chapter XIV.

Gorer, G. (1938) *Himalayan Village*, London: Michael Joseph.

Gould, J. (1964) 'Ideology', in J. Gould and W. Kolb, eds, *Dictionary of the Social Sciences*, London: Tavistock, 315–17.

Gramsci, A. (1971) *Prison Notebooks*, ed. Hoare and Nowell Smith, London: Lawrence & Wishart.

Greig, I. (1973) *Subversion*, London: Stacey.

Hall, S. (1977) *On Ideology*, London: Hutchinson, 12.

BIBLIOGRAPHY

Hilberg, R. (1967) *The Destruction of the European Jews*, London: Quadrangle.
Hobbes, T. (1963) *Leviathan*, introduced by J. Plamenatz, London: Fontana.
Hospers, J. (1961) *Human Conduct*, New York: Harcourt Brace & World.
Howard, M. (1976) *War in European History*, Oxford: Oxford University Press.
Kirk, G. 1973) *Myth*, Cambridge: Cambridge University Press.
Kolb, W. (1957) 'Values, positivism, and the functional theory of religion: the growth of a moral dilemma', in M. J. Yinger, ed., *Religion, Society and the Individual*, London: Macmillan, Chapter 38, 599–608.
LaPiere, Richard (1954) *A Theory of Social Control*, New York: McGraw-Hill.
Lipset, S. (1976) 'Social structure and social change', in P. Blau, ed., *Approaches to the Study of Social Structure*, Wells, Somerset: Open Books, Chapter 11, 172–209.
Lorenz, K. (1966) *On Aggression*, London: Methuen.
Lorrain, J. (1979) *The Concept of Ideology*, London: Hutchinson.
Lukacs, G. (1971) *History and Class Consciousness*, London: Merlin.
McGraw, E. (1983) *Population Today*, London: Kaye & Ward.
Mack, R. and Snyder, R. (1970) 'The analysis of social conflict', in A. Etzioni and M. Wenglinsky, *War and its Prevention*, New York: Harper & Row, Part 4, 162–214.
McNeill, W. (1983) *The Pursuit of Power*, Oxford: Blackwell.
Mannheim, K. (1948) *Ideology and Utopia*, London: Routledge & Kegan Paul.
Marx, K. and Engels, F. (1965) *The German Ideology*, Foreign Languages Publishing House.
Milgram, S. (1970) 'Behavioural study of obedience', in A. Etzioni and W. Wenglinsky, *War and its Prevention*, New York: Harper & Row, Part 5, 245–59.
Montgomery, B. L. (1972) *A Concise History of Warfare*, London: Collins.
Mosca, G. (1939) *The Ruling Class*, New York: McGraw-Hill.
Nicholson, N. (1985) *Napoleon: 1812*, London: Weidenfeld & Nicolson.
Nottingham, E. (1964) *Religion and Society*, New York: Random House.
Pareto, V. (1935) *The Mind and Society*, New York: Harcourt, Brace.
Parsons, T. (1954) *The Role of Ideas in Social Action in Essays in Sociological Theory*, Glencoe.
Parsons, T. (1966) *Societies: Evolutionary and Comparative Perspectives*, Englewood Cliffs, NJ: Prentice-Hall.
Parsons, T. (1971) 'Belief, unbelief and disbelief', in Roco Caporale and Antonio Grimelli, *The Culture of Unbelief*, California: University of California Press.
Piliavin, J. *et al.* (1981) *Emergency Intervention*, London: Academic Press.
Plamenatz, J. (1971) *Ideologies*, London: Macmillan.
Polantzas, N. (1975) *Political Power and Social Classes*, London: New Left Books.
Robertson, I. (1977) *Sociology*, New York: Worth.
Schneider, D. (1976) *Classical Theories of Social Change*, Morristown, NJ: General Learning Press.
Schumpeter, J. (1965) 'Is the history of economics a history of ideologies?', in D. Braybrooke, *Philosophical Problems of the Social Sciences*, London, Macmillan, 109–12.
Spiro, M. (1966) 'Religion: problems of definition and explanation', in M. Banton, ed., *Anthropological Approaches to the Study of Religion*, London: Tavistock.
Stark, W. (1958) *The Sociology of Knowledge*, London: Routledge & Kegan Paul.
Sutton, Francis, ed. (1956) *The American Business Creed*, Cambridge, Mass.: Harvard University Press.
Time magazine (1981) 23 March.

198

Vagts, A. (1959) *A History of Militarism*, New York: Free Press.
Walzer, M. (1977) *Just and Unjust Wars*, Harmondsworth, Middx: Penguin.
Weiss, J. (1967) *The Fascist Tradition*, New York: Harper & Row.

CASE STUDIES

Adorno, T. *et al.* (1950) *The Authoritarian Personality*, New York: Norton.
Aldred, C. (1956) *The Egyptians*, Chicago: University of Chicago Press.
Aldred, C. (1972) *Akhenaten*, Tunbridge Wells, Kent: Abacus.
Andrewes, A. (1976) *The Greek Tyrants*, London: Hutchinson.
Barber, N. (1974) *Lords of the Golden Horn*, London: Macmillan.
Barber, R. (1974) *The Knights and Chivalry*, London: Cardinal.
Barrow, R. (1963) *The Romans*, Harmondsworth, Middx: Penguin.
Becker, P. (1966) *Rule of Fear*, London: Panther.
Bengtson, H., ed. (1969) *The Greeks and the Persians*, London: Weidenfeld & Nicolson.
Bloch, M. (1965) *Feudal Society*, London: Routledge & Kegan Paul.
Boak, W. and Sinnigen, W. (1965) *A History of Rome to A.D. 565*, New York: Collier-Macmillan.
Bowra, C. (1971) *Periclean Athens*, Harmondsworth, Middx: Penguin.
Brandon, S. (1969) *Religion in Ancient History*, London: Allen & Unwin.
Breasted, J. (1906–7) *Ancient Records of Egypt*, vol. 2, Chicago: University of Chicago Press.
Bridge, A. (1980) *The Crusades*, London: Granada.
Burland, C. (1976) *Peoples of the Sun*, London: Weidenfeld & Nicolson.
Burn, A. R. (1976) *The Pelican History of Greece*, Harmondsworth, Middx: Pelican.
Bury, J. and Meiggs, R. (1978) *A History of Greece*, London: Macmillan.
Caesar (1951) *The Conquest of Gaul*, trans. S. A. Handford, Harmondsworth, Middx: Penguin.
Caesar (1967) *The Civil War*, trans. Jane Gardner, Harmondsworth, Middx: Penguin.
Carlton, E. (1973) *Patterns of Belief*, vol. II, London: Allen & Unwin.
Carlton, E. (1977) *Ideology and Social Order*, London: Routledge & Kegan Paul.
Carpenter, Rhys (1973) *Beyond the Pillars of Hercules*, London: Tandem.
Chambers, J. (1979) *The Devil's Horsemen*, London: Weidenfeld & Nicolson.
Cohen, D. (1970) *Conquerors on Horseback*, New York: Doubleday.
Collier, J. (1956) *Indians of the Americas*, New York: Mentor.
Coon, C. (1962) *The History of Man*, Harmondsworth, Middx: Penguin.
Cornfeld, Gaalyahu *et al.* (1964) *Pictorial Biblical Encyclopaedia*, London: Macmillan.
Covensky, M. (1966) *The Ancient Near Eastern Tradition*, New York: Harper & Row.
Crawford, M. (1978) *The Roman Republic*, London: Fontana.
Darlington, C. (1969) *The Evolution of Man*, London: Allen & Unwin.
David, A. R. (1982) *The Ancient Egyptians*, London: Routledge & Kegan Paul.
Davidson, B. (1974) *Africa in History*, London: Paladin.
Davies, J. (1978) *Democracy, and Classical Greece*, London: Fontana.
Dawson, R. (1972) *Imperial China*, London: Hutchinson.
Dawson, R. (1975) *The Legacy of China*, Oxford: Oxford University Press.
Deaux, K. and Wrightsman, L. (1984) *Social Psychology in the 80's*, Monterey, Calif.: Brooks/Cole.
Dicks, H. (1972) *Licensed Mass Murder*, London: Chatto/Heinemann.

Driver, H., ed. (1964) *The Americas on the Eve of Discovery*, New York: Prentice-Hall.
Ehrenberg, V. (1968) *From Solon to Socrates*, London: Methuen.
Elkins, S. (1963) *Slavery*, New York: Grosset.
Fagan, Brian (1984) *The Aztecs*, Oxford: Freeman.
Fine, J. (1983) *The Ancient Greeks*, Cambridge, Mass.: The Belknap Press of Harvard University Press.
Finley, M. I. (1968) *Ancient Sicily*, London: Chatto & Windus.
Finley, M. I. (1971) *The Ancient Greeks*, Harmondsworth, Middx: Penguin.
Fitzgerald, C. (1966) *The Birth of Communist China*, London: Pelican.
Fitzhardinge, L. (1980) *The Spartans*, London: Thames & Hudson.
Fohrer, Georg (1973) *History of Israelite Religion*, London: SPCK.
Forrest, W. (1971) *A History of Sparta*, London: Hutchinson.
Fryer, J. (1975) *The Great Wall of China*, Sevenoaks, Kent: New English Library.
Gabel, C., ed. (1964) *Man Before History*, New York: Prentice-Hall.
Ganshof, F. (1952) *Feudalism*, London: Longman.
Gardiner, A. (1961) *Egypt of the Pharaohs*, Oxford: Oxford University Press.
Gillingham, J. (1978) *Richard the Lionheart*, London: Weidenfeld & Nicolson.
Gonen, Rivka (1975) *Weapons of the Ancient World*, London: Cassell.
Grant, M. (1969) *Julius Caesar*, London: Panther.
Greenleaf, W. (1966) *Oakeshott's Philosophical Politics*, London: Longman.
Grunberger, R. (1964) *Germany 1918–1945*, New York: Harper & Row.
Hagen, V. von (1961) *The Aztec: Man and Tribe*, New York: Mentor.
Hagen, V. von (1974) *The Golden Man*, Lexington, Mass.: Heath.
Haralambos, M., ed. (1985) *New Directions in Sociology*, Ormskirk, Lancashire: Causeway.
Harden, D. (1971) *The Phoenicians*, Harmondsworth, Middx: Penguin.
Harris, M. (1978) *Cannibals and Kings*, London: Collins.
Harvey, J. (1967) *The Plantagenets*, London: Fontana.
Herm, G. (1975) *The Phoenicians*, London: Futura.
Herrman, Siegfried (1975) *A History of Israel in Old Testament Times*, London: SCM.
Herzog, C. and Gichon, M. (1978) *Battles of the Bible*, London: Weidenfeld & Nicolson.
Hoffer, E. (1960) *The True Believer*, New York: Mentor.
Hohne, H. (1972) *The Order of the Death's Head*, London: Pan.
Howell, F. (1971) *Early Man*, New York: Time-Life.
Howell, F. and Bourliere, F., eds (1964) *African Ecology and Human Evolution*, London: Methuen.
Hoyle, Fred and Hoyle, Geoffrey (1971) *The Molecule Man*, New York: Harper & Row.
Hudson, G. (1971) *Fifty Years of Communism*, Harmondsworth, Middx: Pelican.
Humble, Richard (1980) *Warfare in the Ancient World*, London: Guild.
Innes, H. (1969) *The Conquistadores*, London: Collins.
Jeffrey, L. (1976) *Archaic Greece*, London: Benn.
Johnson, Paul (1985) *A History of the Modern World*, London: Weidenfeld & Nicolson.
Keaveney, A. (1982) *Sulla: the Last Republican*, Beckenham, Kent: Croom Helm.
Keller, Werner (1980) *The Bible as History, Revised*, London: Hodder & Stoughton.
Kitchen, Kenneth (1977) *The Bible in its World*, Exeter, Devon: Paternoster.
Kovel, J. (1970) *White Racism*, New York: Pantheon.
Kuper, L. *et al.* (1975) *Race, Science and Society*, London: Allen & Unwin.

Lenin, V. I. (1969) *Selected Works*, London: Lawrence & Wishart.

Lenski, G. (1976) 'Social structure in evolutionary perspective', in P. Blau, ed., *Approaches to the Study of Social Structure*, Wells, Somerset: Open Books, Chapter 8, 135–53.

MacGregor-Hastie, R. (1961) *The Red Barbarians*, London: Pan.

Mayer, H. (1972) *The Crusades*, Oxford: Oxford University Press.

Mitchell, H. (1952) *Sparta*, Cambridge: Cambridge University Press.

Morris, D. (1967) *The Washing of Spears*, London: Sphere.

Murray, Margaret (1963) *The Splendour that was Egypt*, London: Sidgwick & Jackson.

Niemeyer, G., ed. (1966) *Outline of Communism*, London: Ampersand.

Nova, Fritz (1986) *Alfred Rosenberg*, New York: Hippocrene.

Oliver, R., ed. (1968) *The Dawn of African History*, Oxford: Oxford University Press.

Oliver, R. and Fage, J. (1966) *A Short History of Africa*, Harmondsworth, Middx: Penguin.

Oliver R. and Oliver C. (1965) *Africa in the Days of Exploration*, New Jersey: Spectrum.

Parsons, T. (1966) *Societies: Evolutionary and Comparative Perspectives*, Englewood Cliffs, NJ: Prentice-Hall.

Payne, Robert (1962) *The Roman Triumph*, London: Pan.

Phillips, E. (1969) *The Mongols*, London: Thames & Hudson.

Picard, G. and Picard, C. (1968) *The Life and Death of Carthage*, London: Sidgwick & Jackson.

Polybius (1981) *The Rise of the Roman Empire*, trans. Ian Scott-Kilvert, Harmondsworth, Middx: Penguin.

Powell, A. (1988) *Athens and Sparta*, London: Routledge.

Purcell, Victor (1970) *The Rise of Modern China*, Historical Association.

Ritter, E. (1967) *Shaka, Zulu*, London: Panther.

Roberts, B. (1977) *The Zulu Kings*, London: Sphere.

Roberts, J. (1984) *The City of Sokrates*, London: Routledge & Kegan Paul.

Rodzinski, W. (1984) *The Walled Kingdom*, London: Flamingo.

Runciman, J. (1968) *A History of the Crusades*, Cambridge: Cambridge University Press.

Saggs, H. (1984) *The Might that was Assyria*, London: Sidgwick & Jackson.

Saunders, J. (1971) *A History of the Mongol Conquests*, Barnes & Noble.

Scullard, H. (1963) *From the Gracchi to Nero*, London: Methuen.

Simpson, G. and Yinger, M. (1972) *Racial and Cultural Minorities: an Analysis of Prejudice and Discrimination*, New York: Harper & Row.

Smart, Ninian (1974) *Mao*, London: Fontana.

Snowden, Frank (1983) *Before Colour Prejudice*, Cambridge, Mass.: Harvard University Press.

Soustelle, J. (1961) *Daily Life of the Aztecs*, Stanford, Calif.: Stanford University Press.

Southern, R. (1959) *The Making of the Middle Ages*, London: Arrow.

Southern, R. (1970) *Western Society and the Church in the Middle Ages*, Harmondsworth, Middx: Penguin.

Steindorff, G. and Seele, K. (1957) *When Egypt Ruled the East*, Chicago: University of Chicago Press.

Thompson, L. (1972) *African Societies in Southern Africa*, London: Heinemann.

Thucydides (1972) *The Peloponnesian War*, trans. Rex Warner, Harmondsworth, Middx: Penguin.

Vaillant, G. (1965) *Aztecs of Mexico*, Harmondsworth, Middx: Penguin.

Vaux, Roland de (1973) *Ancient Israel*, London: Longman.

Warmington, B. (1964) *Carthage*, Harmondsworth, Middx: Pelican.

Warry, John (1980) *Warfare in the Classical World*, London: Salamander.

Weber, Max (1930) *The Protestant Ethic and the Spirit of Capitalism*, New York: Scribner.

Weissberg, A. (1956) *Advocate for the Dead*, London: Deutsch.

White, L. (1962) *Medieval Technology and Social Change*, Oxford: Oxford University Press.

Wilson, J. (1956) *The Culture of Ancient Egypt*, Chicago: University of Chicago Press.

Wittfogel, Karl (1966) 'The peasants', in G. Niemeyer, *Outline of Communism*, London: Ampersand.

Wright Mills, C. (1960) *The Causes of World War III*, New York: Ballantine.

Xenophon (1949) *The Persian Expedition*, trans. Rex Warner, Harmondsworth, Middx: Penguin.

Zanden, J. (1972) *American Minority Relations: the Sociology of Racial and Ethnic Groups*, Oxford: Ronald.

INDEX

Abelard, Peter 97
Abu Simbel 35
Aduatuci 78
Africa 36, 132, 136, 137–40, 143, 172, 173
aggression institutionalization of 169, 194, 195; nature of 3–17; *see also* war
Ahab 89, 90
Alexander the Great 9, 53, 59, 144, 186
Althusser, L. 24–5, 31
Amalek/Amalekites 92
Amaziah 93
Amenhophis IV (Akhenaten) 37–8
Amenhotep II 41–2
Amenhohep III 39
Anatolia *see* Turkey
Andreski, S. 9
Antony, Mark 79
Appian 80
Arapesh (of New Guinea) 2
Archer and Garner 4
Argos (Argolid) 46
Aristophanes 51
Aristotle 59–60
Arveni 78
Assyrians 3, 8, 30, 54, 59, 82, 85, 88, 89, 91, 92, 93, 94, 173, 174–5, 180
Athens (Athenians) 10, 14–15, 30, 45, 46, 47, 48, 49, 51, 53, 54–5, 56, 59, 63, 143ff., 188, 194
atrocities (and sacrifices) 32, 41, 43, 52–3, 55, 62, 64, 66, 72–3, 75–6, 78, 91–2, 102–3, 105–6, 108, 115, 116, 119ff., 136, 137, 138–9, 140–1, 145, 152, 157, 158, 161, 162, 166, 174, 176, 177–9, 191
Augustine 3
Augustus 68, 71, 79
Aztecs 16, 32–3, 119ff., 191–2

Babylon (Babylonia) 36, 59, 82–3, 91, 93, 94
Baghdad 117
Bantu 132, 137
Batu 116–17
Berkowitz, L. 4, 12
Bernard of Clairvaux 104, 105, 108
Boers (Dutch in South Africa) 132, 134, 135, 136, 137, 140, 141–2
British, settlers in South Africa 132, 136, 137, 140, 141–2
Bushmen 132, 137
Byblos 36
Byzantium 68

Caesar, J. 6, 68, 70, 74, 76–9, 175
Canaan/Canaanites 57, 81–3, 88, 89, 90, 91, 92; *see also* Israel
Carthaginians (Carthage) 29, 30, 57ff., 68, 71, 72, 79
Catania 63
Cetshwayo 141
Chiang-Kai-Shek 158, 160–2
China 110–18, 156ff.
Chinese Communists *see* Maoism

Christianity (Christian Church) 31, 32, 96–100, 103–8, 187
Cicero 70
Cleon 151
Cleopatra 79
Constantine 104
Corinth 46, 53, 149
Corsica 66
Crassus 76, 77
Crete (Cretans) 42, 45, 46, 82, 143
crime statistics 7–8
Crusaders (Crusades) 20, 32, 95ff., 187, 191
Cyprus 36, 42
Cyrus the Great 144

Dallas 7
Dani 2, 17
Darius 59, 144
David 82, 89, 91, 93
Delian League 10, 149–50
de Vaux, R. 94
Dingane 140
Diodorus 62
Dionysus 63–4
Dorians 46
Durkheim, E. 14
Dyaks 185

Egypt (Egyptians) 9, 10, 14, 16, 24, 30, 34ff., 59, 78, 82, 85, 87, 88, 89, 91, 125, 172–3
enemy, perception of ix, 29–32, 40, 43, 54–6, 58, 60, 62, 88, 92–4, 100, 102, 103, 105, 108, 111, 115, 117, 126–31, 142, 150, 166, 181, 186, 194
Ethiopia 36
Etruscans 59, 67, 71
Exodus see Israel

feudalism 95–7, 111, 187
Freud, S. 4, 6
Fromm, E. 12
Fynn, Henry Francis 133, 139

Gaul(s) 6, 71, 72, 77, 78
Genghis (Chingis) Khan 111, 114, 117
genocide see atrocities

Gibbon, E. 14
Gideon 81, 91
gladiators (games) 75
Goliath 88
Gramsci, A. 23–4
Greeks (in general) 6, 8, 10, 14–15, 24, 27, 42, 45ff., 58, 59, 60, 61, 63–4, 65, 67, 68, 72, 79, 82, 83, 91, 143ff., 173, 185, 194

Hadrian 68
Hamilcar 61
Hamilco 62, 64
Hammurabi 87
Hannibal 61, 62–3, 66
Hebrews see Israel
helots see slavery
Helvetii 77
Henry II 101
Heracles 49
Herihor 40
Herodotus 34, 35, 61, 144–5
Himera 61–2
Hitler, Adolf 177, 178
Hittites 42
Hobbes, T. 3, 39
Homer (Iliad and Odyssey) 46, 58
Homosexuality see sexual mores
Hottentots 132, 137
Huitzilopochtli 119, 120, 124–5, 129

ideology ix, x, 9, 18ff., 29, 31–2, 37, 38, 42–3, 49, 62, 64–5, 79, 81, 85, 87–8, 91, 92–4, 95, 96–100, 103–8, 120, 123–31, 152–3, 154, 166–7, 172–3, 175, 177–9, 180ff.
Ionia see Turkey
Islam 16, 20, 94, 103, 104, 117, 118, 187, 190, 191, 193; see also Muslims
Israel (Israelites) 32, 35, 36, 81ff., 105–7, 191
Italy 8, 72, 74, 75, 143, 177

Japan (Japanese) 157, 160–2, 165–6, 184
Jerusalem see Israel
Jews 75, 91, 104, 105, 170–1, 172, 177–9, 189

Jivaro 2
Jonathan 82
Joshua 92, 191
Judah *see* Israel

Kadesh 42
Kant, E. 3, 182
Khafre 34
Khmer Rouge 31, 192
Khublai Khan 117
Khufu 34, 35
knights *see* Crusaders
Kung Bushmen (of the Kalahari) 2
Kuomintang 158, 160–2, 163, 166
Kuper, Leo 174

Laconia *see* Sparta
Lebanon 29, 35, 36, 57, 172
Lenin 155, 156, 165, 176
Leonidas 51
Lepchas (of Sikkim) 2
Levy, R. 11
Libya 39, 43
Lorenz, K. 5
Lorrain, J. 28
Lukacs, G. 23
Lycurgos 47
Lysander 53, 151

Machiavelli 3
Mahdi (Mahdism) 193
Mannheim, K. 22–3, 154
Mao-Tse-Tung (Maoism) 29, 31, 154ff.
Marathon 144
Marius 68, 72–3, 74, 75
Martel, Charles 96
Marx, K. 21–2, 31, 154, 182–3
Marxism 13, 21–5, 27, 31, 131, 154, 192
massacre *see* atrocities
Mau-Mau 21
Maya 16, 119
Melos 46, 152
Menkaure 34
Menninger, W. 4
Mentuhotep 35
Mesha 191
Meshwesh *see* Libyans

Mesopotamia 34, 38, 83, 84, 86, 87, 90, 116; *see also* Assyrians; Babylon
Messenia 46, 47, 55
Miami 7
Milgram, S. 11
militarism 3, 9, 31, 32, 43, 49ff., 54, 61, 111, 124, 128, 130–1, 133, 152, 184, 192
military organization and tactics 39–42, 51–3, 59, 60–1, 62–3, 68, 71–4, 88–92, 100–3, 110, 111–14, 128–30, 133, 135–6, 138, 148–9
Mithridates 73
Mongols 30, 31, 54, 110ff., 175, 192
Mont 43
Montezuma 121
Montgomery, Field Marshal 6
Mosca, G. 13
Moses *see* Israel
Mpande 140–1
Murray, M. 42
Muslims 9, 29, 96, 101, 104, 107, 117, 190, 193
Mycenae (Mycenean) 42, 46

Napoleon 180
Nazis 6, 19, 29, 31, 170–1, 172, 173, 174, 177–9, 189, 193
Ndebele (Matabele) 132, 138
Nervii 78
Nguni 132, 140
Nicaragua 192
Nicias 153
Norman Conquest 95, 176
Northern Ireland 12
Nubia (Sudan) 10, 36, 39

Ogdai 116
Ohlendorf, Otto 23, 178
Olmecs 119

Palestine *see* Israel
Palestinians 172
Pareto, V. 22
Parsons, T. 19, 25, 34
Parthians 78
Payne, R. 76, 80
Peloponnese *see* Sparta

Peloponnesian War 53–5, 150–2, 188
Pentateuch *see* Israel
Perikles 151
Persians 31, 52–3, 54, 55, 59, 61, 82, 116, 144–5, 173, 188
Peter the Hermit 9
Philistines 42, 82, 88, 91, 92
Phoenicians 29, 57, 63, 82
Plamenatz, J. 20
Plataea 52–3, 144
Plato 45, 50
Plutarch 50, 57
Polantzas, N. 25
Polybius 65
Pompeius (Pompey) 68, 74, 75, 76, 77, 78
Popes 97, 98, 100, 103, 116–17
Prescott, J. 4
Ptah 16
Pueblos 29
Punic Wars 65–6, 68
pygmies (of the Ituri forest) 2

Quetzalcoatl 124, 130

race 7–8, 9, 32, 168ff., 189
Rameses II (the Great) 16, 35, 42, 82
Rameses III 16, 38
religion *see* ideology
Richard I 106
Romans 6, 25, 30, 31, 55, 57, 59, 60, 63, 65–6, 67ff., 83, 94, 104, 175, 192, 194, 195
Rosenberg, Alfred 178

Sabines 71
Saladin 106
Salamis 52, 61
Samnites 71
Samson 81
Samuel 91
Saracens *see* Islam; Muslims
Sardinia 39, 42, 58, 66
Saul 82, 91, 92
Scipio Africanus 66
Scythia (Scythians) 90
Sea Peoples 16, 42
Sennacherib 89

sex (and sexual mores) 50–1
Shaka 133, 135, 136, 138–9
Sicily 8, 42, 58, 61, 62, 64, 65, 70, 71, 143, 151
Sidon 57
slavery (and serfdom) 41, 48, 55, 71, 75, 84, 85, 93, 111, 114, 121, 122–3, 124, 126, 147–8, 152, 175, 176
Smenkhakare 37
socialization 49–51, 123–4, 128, 133, 135–6, 195
Socrates 47, 146
Solomon 82, 89, 91, 93
Soviets (Soviet Union) 156, 157, 159, 162, 163, 165
Spain 58, 61, 62, 67, 68, 75, 77, 104, 177
Spanish Conquistadores 16, 30, 119, 120, 121, 124, 129–30, 187
Spartacus 75–6
Spartans 3, 30–1, 45ff., 145, 149–51, 172, 194
Spencer, H. 5
Stalin 155, 176
Suevi 78
Sulla 68, 69, 72–3, 74, 75, 76, 77
Swazi *see* Nguni
Syria 42, 82, 117
Syracuse 62, 63–4, 66, 153

Tahiti 11
Tenochtitlan (Mexico City) *see* Aztecs
Tezcatlipoca 127
Thebes (Egypt) 35
Thebes (Greece) 51, 53, 54, 55, 145, 152
Thermopylae 51, 52
Thucydides 30, 46, 48, 153, 194
Tlaloc 120, 124, 127
Toltecs 16, 119
Trajan 68
Troy 42, 46
Turkey (Turks) 8, 36, 42, 89, 100, 103, 105, 106, 116, 143, 176
Tutankhamun 37
Tyre 57, 58–9, 185

Uganda 173

Vagts, A. 3
values *see* ideology
Veneti 78
Vercingetorix 78
Vietnam 30

Waffen SS 17
Walzer, M. 10
war (and warfare) ix, x, 1ff., 52–3, 55, 62, 63, 65, 70, 71, 73, 74, 75, 78–9, 82, 90, 98, 111–17, 136–7, 138, 140–2, 144–5, 150–2, 155–6, 160–1, 162, 166–7; as a biological necessity 3–8; as a cultural product 11–14; as an economic expedient 8–10; and

ideology (religion) 9, 15–17, 18ff., 29, 31–2, 41ff., 53ff., 62, 64–5, 91–4, 100–8, 124, 128–31, 152–3, 154, 180ff.; and moral decline 14–15
Weber, M. 31
women 51, 147

Xenophon 8, 45, 51, 53
Xerxes 145
Xhosa *see* Nguni
Xipe 127

Yahweh *see* Israel

Zama, battle of 66
Zulu 17, 30, 45, 132ff.